CRASH COURSE *in* Family History

THIRD EDITION

**An Easy Step-by-Step Illustrated Guidebook
and Comprehensive Resource Book**

The Easiest Way to Trace Your Own
Family Roots and Stories

Paul Larsen

Larsen, Paul.
   Crash course in family history : an easy step-by-step illustrated guidebook and comprehensive resource book : the easiest way to trace your own family roots and stories / Paul Larsen. -- 3rd ed.

      p. : ill. (chiefly col.) ; cm.

   First two editions published as: Crash course in family history for Latter-day Saints : a step-by-step LDS guidebook to temple and family history work using the new, easy way ; 3rd edition heavily revised and expanded.
   Includes bibliographical references and index.
   ISBN: 978-0-9742695-4-2

1. Genealogy. 2. Genealogy--Handbooks, manuals, etc. I. Title. II. Title: Crash course in family history for Latter-day Saints.

CS16 .L37 2009
929/.1   2009902367

Published by
Fresh Mountain Air Publishing, LLC
P.O. Box 1758, St George, UT 84771-1758

Everything you need to make your genealogy easy.™

To comment, or communicate with the author,
e-mail paul@easyfamilyhistory.com

Bulk Purchases / International Sales
To inquire about or arrange bulk purchase discounts for sales promotions, premiums, fund-raisers, or information on translations or book distributors outside the U.S.A., please contact the publisher at the above e-mail or mailing address.

ISBN 978-0-9742695-4-2
Library of Congress Catalog Card No. 2009902367

Printed in Hong Kong

Contents

To Peggy,

my sweetheart

and soulmate

for all eternity.

Preface

About this Third Edition

You are about to embark on a fascinating journey that will take you back into history and forward into the eternities. Never has there been a more exciting time to trace your roots and connect with your ancestors. Computers, technology, and the Internet have dramatically affected how we do family history today. Technology and the Internet have continued to change rapidly over the last 6-8 years and continues even at a faster rate today, hence the need to keep abreast of new, exciting web sites, resources, tools, and technology.

We received many positive and rewarding responses from people about both the first edition (published August 2003) and the second edition (published July 2005) of this book. This third edition is a completely rewritten, updated version to help keep you abreast of the dynamic changes and progress in tracing your family roots and stories.

My desire is to help keep you up-to-date on new information and strategies to make it easier, as well  as empower you with the thousands of new and exciting resources available to help you. So in addition to this updated edition, we have developed a new companion website, *EasyFamilyHistory.com*, to help keep you informed and provide free, convenient hotlinks to all the web sites provided herein. This new Web site helps provide: *Everything you need to make your genealogy easier.*™

This step-by-step, illustrated guidebook is also a  comprehensive resource book on family history. However, it is not a beginner's guide on using software or the computer. I anticipated that you already know a few things about computers and software. My intention is to try and make things simple and understandable for you. I want to help make the process of learning how to plant your family tree, nurture it, watch it grow, and receive blessings for your family as easy as possible using today's technology.

How This Book Came To Be

Have you ever had a moment where you were given a thought or an idea that could change your life? You know, one of those moments where you were prompted by an unseen but real force to do something that you never really thought about doing before.

I've hesitated in telling my story before now because it is so close to my heart, but I wish to do so now. My wife and I were out on a date one evening. We ended up at a bookstore just browsing and enjoying the evening together when I heard a voice come into my mind. Most Christians believe that God answers prayers, and that the Holy Spirit can guide your life. Having experienced promptings by the Holy Spirit numerous times previously in my life providing personal guidance, I recognized the prompting.

Promptings are soft whisperings that are real, not imagined thoughts, impressions, or feelings from the Holy Spirit or guardian Angels to guide you in a certain direction, or warn you of

Some people differentiate between the terms *genealogy* and *family history;* genealogy meaning an account of kinship, and family history meaning the addition of details about lives and historical context.

danger, and they are usually right to the point. I know the difference between wishful thinking or pre-conceived thoughts and the voice of the Spirit communicating to my mind and heart and giving me impressions or ideas.

The still soft voice of the Spirit whispered to me: "You have the ability to write a book about family history, and there will be nothing like it in the marketplace." The voice said further, "A good title for the book is: *A Crash Course in Family History.*"

I just about fell on the floor in the middle of the store because this was such a foreign thought, such a surprise to me. I had absolutely no inclination or thought whatsoever about doing any such thing. I was very busy with a new business I had recently started. I was essentially overwhelmed with the business, and struggling to make it grow and become successful, struggling to make a living. How could I even consider doing such a time-consuming thing as writing a book at this time? I had written and published several short books on a different subject previously so I understood somewhat the commitment to write a major book.

Then I started thinking to myself. Well, I have created lessons to teach family history classes. I reasoned, these lessons could become the basis for such a book, and there currently is no up-to-date book in the marketplace on how to do family history using today's technology. I was quite aware of family history books and other resources then available in the marketplace and came to the conclusion that there was not sufficient information nor resources then available to offer simple yet

comprehensive assistance. I felt a great need and desire for people everywhere to easily learn how to do family history. This thought process required only a few seconds.

I believe that we should always try to do as we are prompted by the Holy Spirit because it's always for our—or others—good or safety. I've learned by experience that our life will always be better if we follow the promptings of the Holy Spirit no matter what. So and I made an on-the-spot decision that would have life-changing effects. Standing in the middle of the bookstore, I responded to the prompting I received, "OK I'll do it! I'll write a book on family history. I'll make it easy to follow, a simple step-by-step approach, and done in my own style with lots of colorful illustrations." I don't know if I responded out loud or just in my mind.

As we left the store, I told my wife that I'm going to write a book on family history. Knowing our situation, she was extremely surprised to hear me say that. I told her that I had received a prompting to write the book and she was satisfied with that. She knew that I could do anything I set out to do and she supported my decision wholeheartedly.

As we were driving home, I was going over in my mind how I could reorganize my time to be able to accomplish such a seemingly overwhelming feat. At least it seemed pretty overwhelming to me at that time in my life. I decided that I would arise

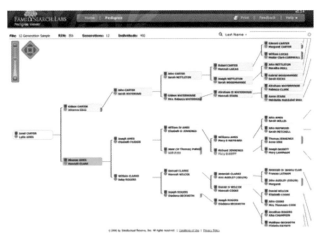

early each morning around 3-4 a.m. when my mind was fresh to try and fit it into my busy schedule. I would write until 8 or 9 a.m. and then go to my day job. So that's what I did nearly every day for about a year.

It was an *amazing* experience and blessing to write the book. It was such a refreshing time; with no sounds or distractions and nobody around at that early hour, I was able to focus with a totally open mind. I was able to make a connection with Heaven. It was magic. I received inspiration from Heaven in researching and writing. It was like light or electricity coming into my mind and then flowing down my arms into my fingers on the keyboard. I thought, wow this is efficient, inspiration flowing directly from above into a computer word processor. What could be better?

The words and thoughts just came into my mind and I could type as fast as they came to me. It was a wonderful, thrilling, life-changing experience! It took me about a year to write the first edition of this book even though it had taken many months the previous year to create the lessons.

I readily confess that I learned a lot about family history from this experience that I didn't know before, and about how we can best connect to our ancestors today. And I was *absolutely astounded* at many of the new technological tools and resources that are available to us to trace our family roots and stories.

I believe that the Lord is *anxious* for us to learn *how* to do this rewarding work, and that He has given His hand in the development of new technology to make it easier and more convenient for us to connect with our forebears. He has given us new exciting tools in order

for you and me to be able to connect with our ancestors. There is indeed a revolutionary wave of interest in family history in the entire world today.

Objectives of This Book

My main objectives for writing this book are to:

1. Describe and illustrate the new, easy, simplified process of how to do family history in an interesting step-by-step method that can be understood and followed by everyone; and provide a comprehensive, content-rich resource book of Web resources and insights about everything pertaining to family history.

2. Help people readily identify and link their ancestors, and work together as they identify names, and reduce duplication of the work.

3. Broaden the number of people connecting with their ancestors, and gain insight and strength by learning how they met life's challenges.

I hope that this new edition and companion web site are valuable resources and guides to assist you in planting your family tree, connecting to your ancestors, discovering your family heritage, stories and photos, and blessing the lives of your family in the process.

Paul Larsen
Author and Publisher

Family history is enjoying a worldwide revolutionary wave.

Introduction

Our Unique Opportunity

Using today's technology – the Internet, exciting, new computer tools, and new, readily available, rapidly-expanding databases of records from all over the world – genealogy and family history work is possible with ease and in record-breaking time. No people in history have ever had the opportunity to connect with their beloved ancestors, learn about their lives and challenges, and grow to appreciate our heritage as easily and readily as we do today.

J. Richard Clarke
© by Intellectual Reserve, Inc.

The Most Beautiful Family Tree

"Through family history we discover the most beautiful tree in the forest of creation – our family tree. Its numerous roots reach back through history, and its branches extend throughout eternity. Family history is the expansive expression of eternal love. It is born of selflessness. It provides opportunity to secure the family unit forever." (J. Richard Clarke, *Ensign,* May 1989, 60)

Suggested Activities

1. Begin to feel a "connection" to those who have gone before you.
2. Plant a seed in your heart for loving your ancestors that can sprout, and that you can nourish so it can grow and get root and bring forth fruit for you and your family for many generations.
3. Read, ponder and experiment upon the suggestions in this book; be persistent and patient.
4. Discuss ways your family can honor your ancestors.
5. Plan a special evening with your family to tell stories and enact a skit based upon your ancestors life.

Family History Insights - 1

Bruce C. Hafen
© by Intellectual Reserve, Inc.

A Bond that Ties Generations Together

"There really can be a bond and a sense of belonging that ties together generations. ... This bond gives us a sense of identity and purpose. Our ties with the eternal world suddenly become very real, sharpening our life's focus and lifting our expectations. ... We can discover within ourselves a reservoir of patience and endurance that we never will find without the deep commitment that grows from a sense of real belonging. Exerting such immovable loyalty to another person teaches us how to love – indeed, how to be more like the Savior. Our sense of belonging to one another... foreshadows our belonging in the eternal family of God. Our willingness to discipline our individual desires enough to honor [our] loved ones prepares us to belong to Him who is our Father." Bruce C. Hafen, *Liahona,* June 1998, 16

Alex Haley

Link to Our Past

"In every conceivable manner, the family is our link to our past, and the bridge to our future." Alex Haley

George Washington
by Rembrandt Peale

Prayer About Eternal Life

George Washington (1732-1799), the Father of our country, prayed regularly and earnestly. Here's one of his recorded prayers about being reunited with his family and friends after death:

"Daily frame me more into the likeness of thy son Jesus Christ, that living in thy fear, and dying in thy favor, I may in thy appointed time attain the resurrection of the just unto eternal life bless my family, friends & kindred unite us all in praising & glorifying thee in all our works begun, continued, and ended, when we shall come to make our last account before thee blessed saviour, who hath taught us thus to pray, our Father, & c." W. Herbert Burk, *Washington's Prayers,* 1907

Abraham Lincoln

Man Was Made for Immortality

"Surely God would not have created such a being as man, with an ability to grasp the infinite, to exist only for a day! No, no, man was made for immortality." Abraham Lincoln, *The Collected Works of Abraham Lincoln* edited by Roy P. Basler, Volume I, "Address Before the Young Men's Lyceum, of Springfield, Illinois (January 27, 1838), Rutgers University Press, New Brunswick, New Jersey, 1953, p. 109.

Shakti Gawain

Guided by Intuition

"...we need to be willing to let our intuition guide us, and then be willing to follow that guidance directly and fearlessly." Shakti Gawain, author

William Wordsworth

We Come From God, Who is Our Home

"Our birth is but a sleep and a forgetting: The Soul that rises with us, our life's Star, Hath had elsewhere its setting, And cometh from afar: Not in entire forgetfulness, And not in utter nakedness, But trailing clouds of glory do we come From God, who is our home." William Wordsworth (1770-1850), English Poet and Author.

The Greatest Blessings

Gordon B. Hinckley
© by Intellectual Reserve, Inc.

"God is the designer of the family. He intended that the greatest of happiness, the most satisfying aspects of life, the deepest joys should come in our associations together and our concerns one for another as fathers and mothers and children". Gordon B. Hinckley, *Ensign,* May 1991, 74

Why Family History?

Unaware to some, *a quiet power* is sweeping the earth as millions of people worldwide are discovering new meaning in their lives. They are doing this by simply connecting with their extended family and loved ones – whether it's a real life reunion or making a new connection with ancestors. Just the prospect of discovering one's family roots and heritage, and possibly reuniting with missing loved ones from long ago is absolutely *thrilling.* For many, it's a rewarding, deep-seated driving force. Family history is about families. And it's changing how some people see life, and helping them gain a sense of identify and purpose in life.

People all over the world, of all faiths, creeds and races, are inspired to search for their family roots and stories. Thus, they are increasingly enabled to more fully appreciate and value their precious and unique heritage, and rightfully honor their forefathers who have gone before them.

As generations pass, people and their lives may be forgotten, but researching your heritage gives you the opportunity to discover who your ancestors really are. And helps bring your family together. As you do this, your knowledge of your forebears will increase, you will gain strength by learning how your ancestors met life's challenges, you will gain a sense of identify and purpose in life, you will feel a sense of belonging that ties generations together, and your family will grow closer.

Connecting the Generations

I think that most people on earth believe, or want to believe, that life does not end at death, and that marriage and the family will continue beyond the grave. I believe that the family is central to the Creator's plan for the eternal destiny of His children and that we can be united with our family and loved ones in the hereafter.

Families can be forever. And tracing your family roots and stories helps establish a sense of belonging that bonds generations together. This bond gives you a sense of identity and purpose in life.

Sullivan Ballou

"Till We Meet No More to Part"

Many people have an unshakeable faith that families can be reunited after death. One such person was Major Sullivan Ballou who wrote one of history's most beautiful and moving love letters to his wife Sarah during the American Civil War.

Sullivan Ballou had overcome his family's poverty to start a promising career as a lawyer in Providence, Rhode Island. Sullivan and Sarah hoped that they could build a better life than they had known growing up for their two sons, Edgar and Willie. In addition to being a successful lawyer, Sullivan also served twice as the Speaker of the Rhode Island House of Representatives.

At the age of thirty-two, being a strong opponent of slavery and devoted supporter of President Abraham Lincoln, Sullivan felt the need to serve the Union, leaving what would have been a very promising political career to enlist in the 2nd Rhode Island Volunteers in the spring of 1861.

On July 14, 1861, Major Ballou was stationed at Camp Clark, near Washington, D.C., while awaiting orders that led him to Manassas, Virginia. When he heard they were leaving, and that in the very near future they were to do battle with the Confederate Army, and not knowing if he would ever get another opportunity, he sat down and wrote a poignant letter to Sarah. A week later on 21st July, 1861, Major Sullivan Ballou was critically injured when a cannon ball shattered his leg and killed his horse during an attack by the Confederate Army at Bull Run, along with four thousand other Americans. He died July 29, 1861, eight days after the Battle of First Bull Run, Manassas, Virginia.

Though Sullivan had many noteworthy achievements to his credit, it was this letter to his wife for which he will always be remembered. His words professed his eternal love for Sarah, his unwavering belief in his cause, his heartfelt desire for the happiness of his sons, and his faith that they would be reunited after death. It is a truly moving and beautifully written piece which to this day, serves as a glowing testimonial to the love of a Father for his family. *Yankee* magazine published an article on the letter in which they stated "... his words of undying love brought millions to tears". His letter is on the next page.

When Sullivan died, his wife was age 24. She later

moved to New Jersey to live out her life with her son, William, and never re-married. She died at age 80 in 1917. Sullivan and Sarah Ballou are buried next to each other at Swan Point Cemetery in Providence, RI. There are no known living descendants.

Passages from The Holy Bible About Family and being Reunited

"The Spirit itself beareth witness with our spirit, that we are the children of God."

(Romans 8:16, *King James Version*)

The spirit shall return unto God who gave it. (Ecclesiastes 12:7, *King James Version*)

God has...planted eternity in the human heart. (Ecclesiastes 3:11, *New Living Translation*, Wheaton, IL: Tyndale House Publishers, 1996)

This world is fading away, along with everything it craves. But if you do the will of God, you will live forever. (1 John 2:17, *New Living Translation*, Wheaton, IL: Tyndale House Publishers, 1996)

"And I will give unto thee the keys of the kingdom of heaven: and whatsoever thou shalt bind on earth shall be bound in heaven..." (Matthew 16:19, *King James Version*)

"Neither is the man without the woman...in the Lord. (1 Corinthians 11:11, *King James Version*)

"What therefore God hath joined together, let not man put asunder." (Mark 10:9, *King James Version*)

Reverend Billy Graham

The Soul of Man is Eternal

The Reverend Billy Graham delivered a message entitled *What Happens When You Die?* published in *Decision* magazine in June 2003. He was referring to the April 2003 death of NBC journalist David Bloom who died in Iraq of a blood clot.

In the article, he stated that it's not possible *"that a Creator would...allow His highest creation...to become extinct at death."* He went on to say that while our body is temporary, our spirit or soul is eternal and will live forever. You can read the full article at http://billygraham.com/ourMinistries/decisionMagazine. Billy Graham, "The Reality of Eternity," Decision magazine, June 2003, Charlotte, N.C., BGEA

Major Sullivan's Letter to His Wife Sarah

July 14th, 1861
Washington D.C.

My dear Sarah:

The indications are very strong that we shall move in a few days -- perhaps tomorrow. Lest I should not be able to write you again, I feel impelled to write lines that may fall under your eye when I shall be no more. ...

I have no misgivings about, or lack of confidence in, the cause in which I am engaged, and my courage does not halt or falter. ... I am willing -- perfectly willing -- to lay down all my joys in this life, to help maintain this Government....

Sarah, my love for you is deathless, it seems to bind me to you with mighty cables that nothing but Omnipotence could break; and yet my love of Country comes over me like a strong wind and bears me irresistibly on with all these chains to the battlefield.

The memories of the blissful moments I have spent with you come creeping over me, and I feel most gratified to God and to you that I have enjoyed them so long. And hard it is for me to give them up and burn to ashes the hopes of future years, when God willing, we might still have lived and loved together and seen our sons grow up to honorable manhood around us. I have, I know, but few and small claims upon Divine Providence, but something whispers to me -- perhaps it is the wafted prayer of my little Edgar -- that I shall return to my loved ones unharmed. If I do not, my dear Sarah, never forget how much I love you, and when my last breath escapes me on the battlefield, it will whisper your name.

Forgive my many faults, and the many pains I have caused you. How thoughtless and foolish I have oftentimes been! How gladly would I wash out with my tears every little spot upon your happiness, and struggle with all the misfortune of this world, to shield you and my children from harm. But I cannot. I must watch you from the spirit land and hover near you, while you buffet the storms with your precious little freight, and wait with sad patience till we meet to part no more.

But, O Sarah! If the dead can come back to this earth and flit unseen around those they loved, I shall always be near you; in the garish day and in the darkest night ...always, always; and if there be a soft breeze upon your cheek, it shall be my breath; or the cool air fans your throbbing temple, it shall be my spirit passing by.

Sarah, do not mourn me dead; think I am gone and wait for thee, for we shall meet again.

As for my little boys, they will grow as I have done, and never know a father's love and care. ... Sarah, I have unlimited confidence in your maternal care and your development of their characters. ... O Sarah, I wait for you there! Come to me, and lead thither my children.

                    Sullivan

(The Book of Love: Writers and Their Love Letters, by Cathy N. Davidson, Pocket Books, 1992; Brown University Alumni Quarterly (Nov. 1990): 38-42; Geoffrey C. Ward, The Civil War: An Illustrated History, New York: Alfred A. Knopf, 1990, 82-83.)

Turn Your Heart to Your Fathers

In the Bible Old Testament, the prophet Malachi offers a prophecy (or divine prediction) that the prophet Elijah would turn the hearts of the Fathers (our ancestors) to the children, and the hearts of the children (all of us as descendants) to our Fathers:

> *"Behold, I will send you Elijah the prophet before the coming of the great and dreadful day of the Lord: And he shall turn the heart of the fathers to the children, and the heart of the children to the fathers, lest I come and smite the earth with a curse."* (Malachi 4:5-6)

I believe that Almighty God has a wonderful plan to unite all of His children of all generations of time. His ingenious plan is to *bind the hearts together* of all those who have ever lived upon the earth − but who are yet alive in the after life − with the hearts of all of us who are alive today or will yet live upon the earth. The hearts of all of those who currently abide in the spirit world or afterlife are bound to us, their children, and they are looking for us to connect with them. Therefore they are helping us − even pushing us in the right direction − to find them and turn our hearts to them. As Bruce Hafen said, *"There really can be a bond and a sense of belonging that ties together generations."* (See the *Insights* page for the full quote.)

People all over the world, of all faiths, creeds and races, are inspired to search for their family roots and turn their heart to their Fathers. This is a quiet but deep-seated driving force that is changing how some people see life, and helping them gain a sense of identify and purpose in life.

Our ancestors were pilgrims and pioneers who lived in a time when they had to endure tremendous physical hardships, and spend much of their time just trying to survive. We live in a time when God's hand has helped provide new technology−a new easy, convenient way to trace and connect to our ancestors−and when vast resources of worldwide records and tech tools are available to assist us. With these tools, we are like partners with God in achieving His purposes for all of His children.

Old Testament Prophet by Ted Henninger

Who is the Prophet Elijah? and Why is it Important?

The story of Elijah is recorded in the Old Testament (1 Kings. 17-2; Kings. 2; 2 Chronicles 21:12-15), and reference is made to him in the New Testament (Matthew 16:14; 17:3; 27:47-49; Mark 6:14-15; 9:4; 15:35-36; Luke 4:25-26; 9:30; James 5:17).

He was a great prophet who performed mighty miracles. His recorded words are few but forceful, and his deeds are explicit evidences of his strength of will, force of character, and personal courage. He was an example of solid faith in the Lord. With his ministry are associated such colorful events as calling down fire from heaven, sealing the heavens with no rain for 3 1/2 years, and raising a boy from the dead. His life closed dramatically... "there appeared a chariot of fire...and Elijah went up by a whirlwind into heaven," (2 Kings. 2:11-12).

In the meridian of time, many people mistook Jesus for Elijah returned (Matthew 16:14). Today, the promise of Elijah is still remembered by the

Jewish people every year at Passover. A special place is still reserved for him at the dinner table as an invited guest, with a cup of wine. At a prescribed time during the meal, the door is opened for him to enter.

Elijah's mission then, in part, is to stimulate research for ancestors – to prompt all of us to trace our own family roots, discover our ancestor's stories, connect with their lives – and enable families throughout time to be linked together. He accomplishes this by helping turn our hearts to our Fathers. But God expects us to do this work ourselves in partnership with Him. This, then, is part of God's ingenious plan to unite all of His children. And we play an important part in His overall plan. Our part is simply to be touched by the *'Spirit of Elijah'* and turn our hearts to our Fathers. Our part encompasses tracing our own family roots, and connecting with the lives of our ancestors. And God will help you to accomplish this work.

Without Elijah

Jeffrey R. Holland said that without Elijah's mission to turn our hearts to our Fathers, "no family ties would exist in the eternities, and indeed the family of man would [be] left in eternity with neither root [ancestors] nor branch [descendants]." Jeffrey R.

Jeffrey R. Holland
© by Intellectual Reserve, Inc.

Holland, *Christ and the New Covenant,* 297-98

What Should We be Doing?

I believe that our family history opportunities may be threefold:

■ ***Develop a Desire to Turn Our Heart to Our Fathers.*** As we search out our ancestors, we grow to care more about those who have passed on, and feel a personal desire to connect with them. It all begins with a simple desire in our heart to love our ancestors. We should allow a thirst, a hunger, even a yearning for this marvelous blessing to take root in our hearts.

■ ***Determine What to Do.*** All of us can do something to search for our roots. It's not wise or necessary to attempt to do everything at once, but each of us can do something. Just what and how much we do depends on our own personal circumstances and abilities, and what our family may have already accomplished. We can, among other things:

- Complete family records as far as we can go
- Computerize our family history information and share with others
- Keep a personal journal and prepare personal and family histories, and
- Participate in family organizations.

■ ***Continue to Be Involved.*** We can be involved in some aspects of family history work throughout our lives. These are not necessarily activities we pursue for a brief time or put off until retirement.

Begin with a desire in your heart to love your ancestors. Plant a seed in your heart that can

sprout and grow and bring forth good fruit for you for many generations. Learning and writing about your ancestors can help you better understand them and yourself. Family history work not only helps unite family members for eternity, it also strengthens bonds between living family members.

Loving Your Ancestors

No previous experience is required to begin planting your family tree today. You don't have to become an expert, but you can and need to be an expert in loving your ancestors. Connecting with your ancestors, learning more about their lives, and honoring them is an expression of your love for them.

A Family Activity

Because family history is done *for* families, it is best done most efficiently *by* families. The blessings of tracing your family roots increase when families work together to identify your ancestors. Family members usually have information to share, or they may be willing to help you look for information. If you do not have immediate family members who are able and willing to assist you, then perhaps friends and extended family members can help.

The Importance of the Internet

One of my objectives for writing this book is to help portray the new, easy process and the sophisticated tools to help us. The Internet is one of these vital tools to help you connect with your ancestors.

The Internet has become the best and easiest way to publish and access vast resources of information available today for family history. The Internet is an excellent tool to get started searching for your family roots. One of the most amazing things about using the Internet is the ability to network with others. For example, *RootsWeb.com* hosts over 161,000 family history message boards devoted to surnames and other genealogy-related topics.

If you can't find what you're looking for, head to *Cyndi's List.com* which offers more than 265,000 links in over 180 categories. *See Chapters 6 and 7 for a directory of the Best of the Internet Family History Web Sites.*

People also talk about the vast amount of information on the *Web.* The Web is a bunch of searchable "pages" of information containing text, pictures, audio and video clips, animations, and *links* to other Web pages connected to each other around the world. And it's big! In 1998 there were about 26 million pages, and by 2000 it had reached the one billion mark. Today the Web has recently hit a new milestone: 1 trillion (as in 1,000,000,000,000) unique URLs (Web addresses), which can be compared to a map made up of one trillion intersections.

Essentially all of the Web sites described herein are free to access, however, I've added a **$$$** symbol to each Web site listing or software that you need to pay a fee or a subscription to access a substantial part of the content.

Sharing Family History

The Internet also provides a simple and inexpensive way for you to publish your family history, thus adding to a rapidly expanding pool of shared family history information. The best way to share your family history information with others is by using the Internet. *(See Chapter 10 for details on Sharing Your Family History.)* By sharing your information, you can help others in their research, and reduce the duplication of effort.

> The whole work of finding your family roots has grown exceedingly.

We are blessed with computers and the Internet to help us communicate easily with people around the world. E-mail makes the sharing of family data almost instantaneous. By sending out your information, you will reap a rich harvest. As you trace your own family roots and connect with the lives of your ancestors, you help weld eternal family links, and draw yourself and your family closer together.

Family History is Booming

In the early 1800s there were no organizations dedicated to gathering records of the dead. Beginning in 1837, England and Wales began mandatory recording of births, deaths, and marriages for everyone in their countries. Many countries around the world thereafter started recording more information in their census records. For example, Great Britain's censuses began recording names and ages of individuals in 1841, and the United States added names of family members in 1850 (previously only heads of household were named). In 1844 the New England Historic Genealogical Society was organized in Boston. Today, there are thousands of family history societies around the world.

In addition, many people were prompted to publish their family histories. The results have been dramatic. Between 1450 and 1836, fewer than 200 family histories were published. Between 1837 and 1935, almost 2,000 more were published. Today more than 2,000 family histories are published each week. Genealogy and family history has become immensely popular worldwide. If you search for the term *genealogy* on the Web, you get over 81 million hits on Google.com, 160 million on Yahoo.com, and 40 million on Live.com.

Popularity in America

A recent survey showed that 73% of the U.S. population was interested in or actively researching their family history.* This means that approximately 162 million adults in the U.S. are interested in or tracing their roots. Compare that to the voter turnout for the 2008 American presidential election was 131.2 million, the highest in at least 40 years. (* This survey was done in 2005 by Market Strategies, Inc. for Ancestry.com.)

Digging for Your Roots

"My fondest hope is that "Roots" may start black, white, brown, red, yellow people digging back for their own roots. Man, that would make me feel 90 feet tall."
Alex Haley

Alex Haley

Alex Haley, American biographer, scriptwriter, author (1921-1992). In 1965 Alex Haley stumbled upon the names of his maternal great-grandparents, when he was going through post-Civil War records in National Archives in Washington, D.C. He spent years tracing his own family back to a single African man, Kunta Kinte, who was captured

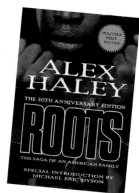

in Gambia and taken to America as a slave around 1767. That discovery led to Haley's epic book *Roots*, published in 1976 to wide acclaim. The next year the television miniseries *Roots* ran for a week on network TV and became a national phenomenon. *Roots* won a Pulitzer Prize and the National Book Award, and Haley is often credited with inspiring interest in family history. www.kintehaley.org

Do Your Ancestors Want to Be Found?

As you search for your family roots and stories, it's possible that you may make fortunate discoveries of significant information that you were not even looking for. This is called *serendipity or intuition* – the process of accidentally or coincidentally making meaningful family history discoveries while looking for entirely something else.

Most people that do family history have a healthy respect for serendipity and feel that the search for their family roots is often guided in mysterious, unexplainable, miraculous, coincidental ways. They usually have a similar story of an unlikely discovery falling into their lap, like a gift, which leaves them with a feeling of awe, as if their ancestors are helping with the search. It's almost as if your ancestors are standing behind you pushing you in the right direction.

This prodding may come in the form of inspiration, intuition, a dream, a thought that enters your mind, or *just being in the right place at the right time.* But it's a little help from above that can lead you to information you may never find otherwise.

Your ancestors are alive in the after life and want to be found as much as we want to find them. Clearly, as we do this work there is unseen but definitive help from those who have passed on before us.

Examples of Serendipity

- Running into a previously unknown cousin at a far-away cemetery, even though neither person had been there before *as if the meeting had been planned.*

- Effortlessly discovering an ancestor's grave that you shouldn't have easily found.

- Family photos and heirlooms that are reunited with their families under unexplainable circumstances.

- Mysterious discoveries of books that seemingly magically open to exactly the right page for long sought-after information.

- Having a book fall off the shelf and land on the floor to the page containing information you want.

- Several unacquainted people showing up at a library in a city where none of them live, on the same day, at the same time *each seeking the same common ancestor.*

Ancestors Will Meet You Halfway

"We do indeed honor our ancestors when we search for them, and it seems, they return the favor. ... When one makes the effort to learn about the lives of ancestors, they will often meet you halfway." Megan Smolenyak, *In Search of Our Ancestors,* 2000, Adams Media Corp.

Looking for a Needle

"Serendipity is looking in a haystack for a needle and discovering a farmer's daughter." "Serendipity, the art of making an unsought finding." Pek van Andel

Jules Henri Poincaré

Intuition Discoveries

"It is through science that we prove, but through intuition that we discover." Jules Henri Poincaré (1854-1912)

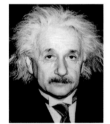

Albert Einstein

Valuable Intuition

"The only really valuable thing is intuition." Albert Einstein

Intuition and Inspiration

"I believe in intuition and inspiration; at times I feel certain I am right while not knowing the reason." Albert Einstein

Mark Twain

Instinct is Worth More

"For all the talk you hear about knowledge being such a wonderful thing, instinct is worth forty of it for real unerringness." Mark Twain (1835-1910)

Searching With an Open Heart

"I was amazed to find success in genealogy often comes from intuition, searching not with just the mind, but also an open heart, enjoying warm feelings with the deceased." George W. Fisk, author

RIchard Buckiminster Fuller

Cosmic Fishing

"I call intuition cosmic fishing. You feel a nibble, then you've got to hook the fish." Richard Buckminster Fuller (1895-1983), inventor

Help From the Other Side

Inspirational Stories

Our forbears are indeed alive and well in the hereafter world. And they are anxious for us to connect with them. Here are some inspirational stories that will warm your heart and illustrate the help provided from the other side of the veil of death in tracing your family roots. Also check out these books and Web sites for more stories.

Megan Smolenyak's Books -

www.honoringourancestors.com

You can enjoy many inspirational stories in Megan Smolenyak's books of how people have experienced amazing incidents in the search for their roots. She was struck by the number of stories about random acts of kindness, coincidence, intuition, and serendipity. She found herself inundated with stories of distant cousins "coincidentally" meeting while visiting the cemetery of their ancestors, and she learned of family photos, papers, and Bibles that were reunited with their original families under circumstances that boggle the mind.

Hank Jones

Hank Jones' Books -

www.hankjones.com

Henry (Hank) Z. Jones, Jr. has written two books concerning the positive influence of coincidence

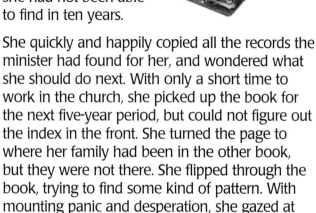

and serendipity in family history research. Over a hundred respected researchers discuss their experiences in light of synchronicity, intuition, and genetic memory. *Psychic Roots: Serendipity & Intuition in Genealogy* and *More Psychic Roots* contains a collection of stories and experiences contributed by people the world over. As the author concludes: *"I do believe that our ancestors have no wish to be forgotten: they want to be found."*

Genealogy Today.com -

http://genealogytoday.com/family/stories/serendipity.html

Joanne Rabun relates stories about people being led to certain information in some mystical way.

Ancestors at My Fingertips

Kathleen had spiritual promptings at various times throughout her life. She sensed her Swedish ancestors were there, somewhere, waiting for her. She had searched for information for many years without success, but decided to try again. Before long she had the opportunity to go to Sweden, and found herself in the village church of her ancestors.

She followed the old, white-haired Swedish minister down a narrow flight of stairs into a small room where rows of brown leather-covered volumes lined the shelves from floor to ceiling. She told the minister her grandmother's birth date. He pulled a book from the shelf, opened it, and pointed to an entry. It was her grandmother's birth record. With excitement she watched as he pulled other books from the shelves showing the records of her grandmothers and great-grandpar-

ents families. In five minutes, she had in front of her information that she had not been able to find in ten years.

She quickly and happily copied all the records the minister had found for her, and wondered what she should do next. With only a short time to work in the church, she picked up the book for the next five-year period, but could not figure out the index in the front. She turned the page to where her family had been in the other book, but they were not there. She flipped through the book, trying to find some kind of pattern. With mounting panic and desperation, she gazed at the books lining the shelves. At her fingertips were the records she had been wanting for so long, but she didn't know how to use them! Each book was too thick to go through page by page.

She opened the book again and flipped a few pages. What could she do? She simply sat there, numb with disappointment. Gradually, she became aware of the book that she had just opened. The names on the page looked familiar. Despair gave way to joy as she recognized the names of her great-great-grandparents. There were 417 pages in the book, but completely at random, she had opened it to the one page that had the records of her family. *Ensign,* July 1995, 39

The Face Beyond the Veil

G.G. Vandagriff wanted to learn more about her great-grandmother. She had all the "data" about the dates and places, but wanted to really know her. She felt drawn to her in a way she couldn't explain, and the desire to know her grandmother consumed her. In a bold move, she knelt and prayed one night that she might become familiar with her in an intimate way. She wanted to know what she looked like, what her personality was, what her feelings were by following her husband to seven frontier settlements.

She knew that she was praying for a miracle, but the next morning she received a phone call that shocked her. The phone call was from her unknown third cousin, Joyce, also a descendent of her grandmother. Her cousin had obtained her phone number by coincidence and stated that she was the granddaughter of the favorite grand-daughter of their grandmother and that she had her pictures, her quilts, and story upon story about her.

Within 36 hours of her prayer, she sat looking at her grandmother's face for the first time, and in the months that followed, she got to know her "face-to-face" through the veil. She now measures her character against her grandmothers, hoping that when they meet, that she will be worthy of her extraordinary heritage. www.meridian magazine.com/turninghearts/020919faceveil.html

One-Chance-in-a-Million

Cathy Corcoran was searching for information on her grandfather. She knew his birth date, but when faced with the daunting task of going through eleven thousand babies born in Boston in 1876 in someone's old handwriting, she was troubled. She randomly opened a dusty book and idly flipped to page 525. The name practically leaped off the page. What are the odds that she would open a book to that page and see that record? A million to one? It was amazing. It was a miracle. Read this story in Megan Smolenyak's book, *In Search of Our Ancestors,* p. 7-9.

My Ancestor Helped Me

Cheryl Bean went to the courthouse to view court records on her ancestor only to discover that the records had been misplaced during a recent move. After digging through book after book for some time in a huge basement room, she bowed her head in prayer, and then walked to the most remote row of books. She picked up the last volume on the shelf, but the title didn't look promising. She opened it anyway and discovered that the apparently mislabeled book had been used to record early territorial court hearings. She tried not to get her hopes up too high, but after some frantic page turning, there was the information she was seeking. She got an overwhelming feeling that she wasn't alone, and prayed silently again to be led to any additional information about her ancestor. She found herself drawn to another row where she plucked out a book at random and found additional information. After that experience, she was convinced that she was not alone in the work of searching for her ancestors. Read this story in Megan Smolenyak's book, *In Search of Our Ancestors,* p. 10-11

Their Families Finally Found Each Other with Help from the Other Side

Athena's Mother was suffering from terminal cancer, and she was near death. But her Mother said that she didn't want to go until she could find her family. Athena told her Mother that she would be with them soon, so why not send her back the information and she would see what she could do to help. Her father immigrated to the United States from Greece in 1915, and had changed his name, but they had never met any of his family, nor did they know any information about them, including their names.

Soon after her Mother passed away, Athena had some interesting things happen. In searching on the internet, she found a name that she thought was her father's true surname, but had never been able to verify it for sure. She wrote a letter and before long received a reply that his father was her grandfather's brother, and that they were living in Canada. Soon after that, she received a phone call from another man who told her that his wife was her mother's first cousin and they had emigrated from Greece to Canada and also been looking for them for many years. She came on the phone and cried and cried. She told her how they had come to Salt Lake many times trying to locate them, but they were never able to find them, due to the name change.

Not only were they able to associate with living members of the family as well as learn about ancestors for the first time, but from the information she received, she went to the Family History Library and found over 100 names of relatives. When they had their very first family reunion, the love between them was immediate and it felt as though they had always been in their lives and there was an immediate bonding. They realized that their families had been looking for one another for 85 years.

It seems there are times when family members can be more help to us in finding our roots from the other side of the veil. http://deseretbook.com

The Book Fell Open to the Right Place

Sherlene Hall Bartholome writes: "While living in New York...I had randomly chosen a book from among many about Ohio history. While thumbing through it, I remarked...that I sure would like to find the marriage of a certain couple from that state. No sooner did I name them than this book fell open to a page that had an entire paragraph about them, as their names practically jumped off the page to catch my attention! As the back of my neck went electric, and my eyes teared, I forgot any sense of reserve and demanded of the startled men: what names did I just mention to you? Look at this page – can you believe? Just look at this! This book fell right open to their names! Why, here's their marriage date! Do you know how long I've been looking for this? I tell you, there really are angels guiding this work! They inspected the open page, acknowledged that I spoke those same names before I opened it, and seemed to be almost as excited and caught up in the moment as I." www.ldsmag.com/turninghearts/021122bookfell.html

I Hope You Remember Me

David Heyen awoke one morning with a strong feeling that he had left something undone in his

family history and that *now* was the time to do it. The impression was so strong that he decided he should visit Rockport, Missouri, the place his father's family had lived. He hadn't visited there since he was young and was apprehensive about seeing long-lost family members, but the urgency he felt was strong so he decided to go anyway. His fears were soon put to rest as his relatives welcomed him with open arms. He became more and more astonished as piece after piece of his family's history fell into place. Family lines he had abandoned because of lack of information suddenly began to produce generous information. He found old photographs of grandparents four and five generations back whose information he had previously given up all hope of ever finding.

In reviewing the original documents his great-grandmother had given him, he happened upon a poem written in 1830 by John Brown, his fourth great-grandfather. It read, in part:

> *My Christian friends, both old and young, I hope, in Christ, you'll all be strong. I hope you'll all remember me, If no more my face you'll see. And in trust, in prayers, I crave That we shall meet beyond the grave. Oh glorious day, Oh blessed hope. My heart leaps forward at the thought! When in that happy land we'll meet. We'll no more take the parting hand, But with our holy blessed Lord, We'll shout and sing with one accord.*

His eyes filled with tears as he felt impressed that these words from 1830 were written for him. He felt that his family members on the other side of the veil of death were determined not to be forgotten and were urging him to discover who they were. He knew that someday he would have the chance to meet them in that joyous reunion John Brown wrote of so very long ago. By following the prompting he received, he found that a way was opened to him in his search, and now he knew we are never really finished with discovering our family roots and stories. *Ensign,* Mar. 2002, 70

Sheer Dumb Luck?

Beth Uyehara found her great grandfathers grave and decorated it with flowers. The next morning at the courthouse, while looking through deed indexes, she accidentally grabbed a book from the wrong shelf, and opened an index from the 1920s – decades after her family had left the area. Before noticing her mistake, she found two quit-claim deeds signed by her great grandfather's descendants and their spouses, showing their relationships and other valuable information. It was a bonanza of information. Was this just luck? In another city, while searching immigration and naturalization records for another great grandfather, she found his file and inside was not only his final certificate of citizenship, but also his personal copy of the Declaration of Intention. He must have left it behind at his swearing-in as a citizen. Since he died just twelve days after becoming a citizen, he had never returned to pick it up and there it sat for 120 years. As she and the clerk examined the file together, they discovered that the clerk's ancestor had been the character witness for Beth's ancestor when he applied for citizenship, so they had obviously been friends. Was their chance meeting just coincidence? Read this story in Megan Smolenyak's book, *In Search of Our Ancestors,* p. 3-5.

Quotations About Help From the Other Side

Boyd Packer
© by Intellectual Reserve, Inc.

Those Beyond the Veil

"It is a veil, not a wall, that separates us from the spirit world. ... Veils can become thin, even parted. We are not left to do this work alone. They who have preceded us...and our forebears there, on occasion, are very close to us. ... Those who go beyond the veil yet live and minister here." Boyd Packer, *Ensign,* May 1987, 22

The Light Will Move Ahead of Us

"We have not yet moved to the edge of the light. We have not used all of the resources yet available to us. I am confident that as we move to the edge of the light, like the cloud that led the Israelites, or like the star that led the wise men, the light will move ahead of us and we can do this work." Boyd Packer, Seminar, April 1, 1977

John Taylor
© by Intellectual Reserve, Inc.

Forming an Alliance

"We are forming an alliance, a union, a connection, with those that are behind the veil, and they are forming a union and connection with us; and while we are living here, we are preparing to live hereafter, and laying a foundation for this."
John Taylor, *Journal of Discourses,* 11:12/11/1864

Spencer Kimball
© by Intellectual Reserve, Inc.

What Do Your Ancestors Think?

"The spirit world is filled with the spirits of men who are waiting for you and me to get busy. ... We wonder about our progenitors—grandparents, great-grandparents, great-great-grandparents, etc. What do they think of you and me? We are their offspring. ... We have a grave responsibility that we cannot avoid, and may stand in jeopardy if we fail to do this important work." Spencer Kimball, *Ensign,* January 1977, 3, 5

Ezra Taft Benson
© by Intellectual Reserve, Inc.

Our Love Perpetuated Into the Eternities

"The spirit world is not far away. ... Sometimes the veil between this life and the life beyond becomes very thin. This I know! Our loved ones who have passed on are not far from us. Because Jesus lives, the love and family association we cherish on this side of the veil may be perpetuated into the eternities."
Ezra Taft Benson, *Tambuli,* Apr. 1994, 3.

Robert Millet

Our Ancestors Are Deeply Interested

Robert Millet told about Joseph F. Smith's remarkable address in 1916. "He spoke about the nearness of the world of spirits, and of the interest and concern the spirits have for us and our labors. He stressed that those who labored so diligently in their mortal estate...would not be denied the privilege of "looking down upon the results of their own labors" from their post-mortal estate. He said, "they are as deeply interested in our welfare today, if not with greater capacity, with far more interest behind the veil, than they were in the flesh. ... Sometimes the Lord expands our vision from this point of view and this side of the veil, that we feel and seem to realize that we can look beyond the thin veil which separates us from that other sphere. ... And so it is that [this] work...goes forward on both sides of the veil." Robert L. Millet, "Beyond the Veil" *Tambuli,* June 1986, 31

Free Beginners Tutorials and Lessons

You can find FREE beginner lessons, references and tutorials about how to do family history and tips on research on the Internet. A few of which are:

FamilySearch.org - www.familysearch.org
Get Started in the *Start Your Family History* box.

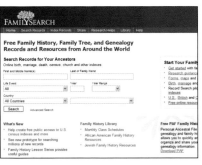

They briefly explain six basic steps to do research. In addition, there are many 'How To' articles under the *Research Helps* tab. There are also lessons and navigation tips for their free software program PAF (Personal Ancestral File) at www.familysearch.org/paf; click on *PAF Lessons* in the left hand column for 7 lessons.

Genealogy.com - www.genealogy.com >
Learning Center > Free Genealogy Classes

There are many different lessons under the following categories:

- Getting Started
- Getting Organized
- Developing your Research Skills

DearMYRTLE - www.dearmyrtle.com
Lessons

There are dozens of excellent lessons under the following categories:

Beginning Genealogy Lessons
Finally Get Organized
Kid's Genealogy
Step By Step
Using LDS Family History Centers
Writing Your Personal History

Here's some Things You Can Do Today to Get Started

10 Things You Can Do Today to Get Started

1. **Plant a seed in your heart** for a desire to connect to your ancestors; nourish the seed so it can grow; learn about the sacrifices they made to make your life better, prepare to receive help from your ancestors. (Pages 6-7, 10-16)

2. **Take a free online "How To" lesson** (or tutorial). (Page 16)

3. **Subscribe to** a free e-newsletter or magazine; register for a free blog. (Pages 18-21)

4. **Review and purchase** a family history software program and get acquainted with the basics. (Chapter 3)

5. **Write down everything you know** about your ancestors; contact your family's "keeper of the flame" (your family's historian), and ask him/her to share their information. (Page 29)

6. **Search existing online family tree Web sites** and published family histories for information on your ancestor. (Page 45)

7. **Scan your precious photos** and documents to a digital format to protect them and be able to easily share with others. (Page 186)

8. **Begin to write your family history;** gather your family stories; record the life stories of your parents/grandparents before its too late; record your own story while you can still remember; interview a relative; get grandkids involved to help establish a bond between generations. (Page 197)

9. **Collaborate with others** to add branches to your family tree using a social networking Web site; connect with your family, swap stories, and share photos, recipes and information. (Page 79, 212)

10. **Hold a family reunion;** organize your family; reach out to your extended family members; start a family blog or online photo album; volunteer to help index public records at home. (Page 219-221)

Ancestry.com - www.ancestry.com
Learning Center

They offer videos by experts and a Quick-Step Guide providing all the key components for beginning your family history. Their learning center helps you reach into the past and make meaningful connections with your forbears.

Center for Family History and Genealogy -
http://familyhistory.byu.edu

Click on *Online Lessons* in the right column for 8 (LDS-oriented) lessons. They also offer guidance in the deciphering of manuscripts and other old documents that were printed in old typefaces or written in old handwriting styles. Languages covered here include English, German, Dutch, Italian, French, Spanish, and Portuguese.

RootsWeb Guides -
http://rwguide.rootsweb.ancestry.com

RootsWeb Guides to Tracing Family Trees contain illustrated articles and valuable tips written by professional genealogists about: where to begin, types of records with links, and ethnic groups.

Free e-Newsletters Online

Newsletters contain news and announcements about family history. Here are the most notable newsletters currently. Most subscriptions are free and others are offered at a nominal fee.

Eastman's Online Genealogy Newsletter -
www.eogn.com **Free** or $$$

A popular, daily newsletter summary of events, tips, reviews, and topics of interest from genealogist, Dick Eastman, available in a *free* Standard Edition and a Plus Edition for $19.95/year.

Ancestry Weekly Journal -
www.ancestry.com/learn **Free**

Tips, news and updates. Subscribe free at www.ancestry.com; click on *Learning Center,* then click on *Ancestry Weekly Journal.* Also found at the blog site of Juliana Smith entitled **24/7 Family History Circle** located at http://blogs.ancestry.com/circle/?page_id=2.

Everton's Newsline -
www.everton.com/newsline **Free**

Offers a free monthly newsletter called *The Newsline* which provides tips and helpful information.

RootsWeb Review - www.rootsweb.com **Free**

This free monthly e-zine provides news about RootsWeb.com, its new databases, mailing lists, home pages, and websites. It also includes stories and research tips from its readers around the globe.

The Genealogy Newsletter -
www.genealogynewsletter.com

Provides free monthly newsletter that is useful, interesting, and current.

Topix.net - www.topix.net/hobbies/genealogy
Free

News on genealogy continually updated from thousands of sources around the net.

Global Gazette -
http://globalgenealogy.com/globalgazette/index.htm   **Free**

Canada's online family history magazine with helpful tips on researching family history. Includes "how-to" articles and genealogy news as well as general genealogy information.

Genealogy Today.com News Center -
http://news.genealogytoday.com   **Free**

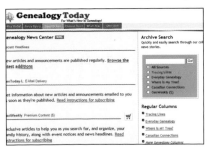

Articles and news releases from various resources both at Genealogy Today and around the Web.

Genealogical Magazines
The Latest Info for Tracing Your Family Tree

Family Tree Magazine -
www.familytreemagazine.com $$$

One of the leading how-to publications for those who want to discover, preserve and celebrate their roots. It covers all areas of potential interest to family history enthusiasts, reaching beyond strict genealogy research to include ethnic heritage, family reunions, memoirs, oral history, scrapbooking, historical travel and other ways that families connect with their pasts. Provides engaging, easy-to-understand instruction that empowers you to take the next steps in the quest for your past–with a beginner-friendly approach that makes genealogy a hobby anyone can do. $24.00/year

Everton's Genealogical Helper -
www.everton.com $$$

This bi-monthly magazine has long been regarded as the most read genealogy magazine in the U.S. It is the largest magazine with more than 170 pages in every issue packed with new information to help you find your ancestors. A complete online version of the magazine is now available complete with all of the hotlinks to the hundreds of website addresses found therein. *Hard Copy Edition* $25.00/year (includes access to the Online Edition), *Online Edition* $12.00/year.

Ancestry -
www.ancestrymagazine.com $$$

A recently revamped bi-monthly magazine published by Network Generations which features captivating contributions from leading industry experts. It provides readers of every skill set with the

best and most efficient ways to discover the stories of the lives of their ancestors. It's designed to show us how to bridge the gap between our own lives and the lives of our ancestors by offering tips, advice, the latest news and techniques and help us discover the fascinating world of family history. $17.95/year

Internet Genealogy -
http://internet-genealogy.com $$$

A bi-monthly magazine from the publishers of *Family Chronicle* and *History Magazine*. It deals primarily with doing genealogy research using the resources of the Internet. The rate at which new databases are coming online is staggering and many of these new records are linked to the original images, making them effectively original sources. $25/year

Digital Genealogist.com -
www.digitalgenealogist.com $$$

An electronic magazine (sent via e-mail as a PDF) published six times a year that focuses on the use of technology in genealogy and all its various applications. It brings the latest news and techniques for combining genealogy and technology. $20.00/year

Family Chronicle Magazine -
www.familychronicle.com $$$

Bi-monthly magazine especially written for family researchers by people who share their interest in genealogy and family history. This "how-to" genealogy magazine has gained a reputation for solid editorial, presented in a highly attractive, all-color format. $25.00/year

Forum - www.fgs.org $$$

The Federation of Genealogical Societies (FGS), consisting of more than 550 member societies and over 500,000 individual genealogists, publishes this quarterly magazine providing current information essential to the informed genealogist. $18.00 (non-member)/year

GenealogyInTime.com -
www.genealogyintime.com

Build your family tree online; search for your ancestors in 655 million family trees, census, birth, marriages, death and military records; and chat with others – send messages to other members to discover a shared family history for free from the UK's largest family history community.

Good Old Days -
www.goodolddaysonline.com $$$

A bi-monthly magazine that remembers the best of times. Feature stories and photos of the good old days of 1900 through 1949 are all contributed by readers. $19.97/year

History Magazine -
www.history-magazine.com $$$

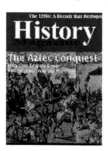

Covers social history, in particular the lives and times of ordinary people. How our ancestors lived and how their worlds changed; opens a window on the past, providing compelling stories about how our world became the place it is today. $22.00/year

Reminisce - www.reminisce.com $$$

A nostalgia magazine that brings back the good times, written by its readers from around the country and published bi-monthly. Advertising-free with real-life stories and family album photos — recalling times from the Roaring Twenties to the Fabulous Fifties. $14.98/year

Reunions Magazine - www.reunionsmag.com $$$

The only publication written for all types of reunion planners — family, class, military and others. This is a comprehensive source of tips, ideas, advice and resources to help you plan your reunion. You'll find articles about resources like facilities, suppliers, tools, equipment, games, activities and services to enhance your reunion. Some of the best reunion solutions are in the stories reunion planners share; published 5x per year. $9.99/year

Blogs

Free-style, Interactive Web Sites with News and Commentary on Family History

A blog (or web log) is a website consisting of entries appearing in reverse chronological order with the most recent entry appearing first. Blogs typically include comments, photos, and web links. You may want to consider creating your own family blog because it's a great way to connect with your extended family and others who share your interests. *See Chapter 10 for information on creating your own family blog.*

Ancestry Insider - http://ancestryinsider.blogspot.com

The unofficial blog of two big genealogy websites: Ancestry.com and FamilySearch.org.

Dear MYRTLE.com - http://blog.dearmyrtle.com

Pat Richley's website is a fun, helpful family history site with a regular blog column of free news and tips.

24/7 Family History Circle - http://blogs.ancestry.com/circle

A destination for anyone with an interest in family history. Long-time Ancestry.com newsletter editor, Juliana Smith, writes for the blog, which includes articles from family history columnists, as well as the occasional guest columnist. The *Ancestry Weekly Journal* is posted weekly on this blog, along with some unique content. You'll find helpful tips, how-to articles, research stories, etc.

Genealogy Insider - http://blog.familytreemagazine.com/insider

Diane Haddad's genealogy blog at FamilyTree Magazine.

Genealogy Blog - www.genealogyblog.com

Leland Meitzler's popular genealogy blog.

The Genealogue -
http://genealogue.blogspot.com

Genealogical notes, notions, and meanderings.

The Chart Chick -
www.thechartchick.blogspot.com

The brainchild of Janet Hovorka, Development Director at Generation Maps – a genealogy chart printing service. Content includes research and general genealogy how-to's, information on involving your family, genealogy charting ideas, genealogy industry insights and news, and other musings.

Think Genealogy - www.thinkgenealogy.com

A popular blog by Mark Tucker about genealogy, software, ideas, and innovation.

Genealogy Roots -
http://genealogyroots.googlepages.com

A newsletter and blog to help find online genealogy databases, records and resources. Major topics include death indexes, military, census, and immigration records. It is usually distributed about 1-3 times a month.

Randy's Musings - www.geneamusings.com

Genealogy research tips, genealogy news items, genealogy humor, and some family history stories.

RootDig.com - www.rootdig.com

Michael John Neill's genealogy blog website with news and information.

Olive Tree -
http://olivetreegenealogy.blogspot.com

Updates and news about Olive Tree Genealogy and other websites free genealogy records. Helping you find your family tree and ancestry.

What is a PodCast?

Genealogy News, Views and Interviews at Your Leisure

PodCasts are downloadable radio or TV-style shows that you can listen to or watch on your computer or MP3 player anytime you want. If you're not familiar with podcasting, you're missing a great source of information and inspiration. Podcasts have grown tremendously in popularity in the last few years with over 41,000 shows available online. You're in control to fast forward, rewind, stop, and start at your convenience. You don't need an iPod to listen, but with the companion software *iTunes* (www.apple.com/itunes) you can set up an account, listen, and organize any podcasts for free on your computer. Then you can download a podcast to your personal music device or burn onto a CD to listen to in your car if you wish. Anyway, it's a great way to keep up with the latest genealogy news or Web sites, or to pick up new techniques, tips and research skills. Learn more about PodCasts at http://video.about.com/ipod/itunes_podcasts-mov.htm. You don't have to subscribe to podcasts if you don't want, just visit the Web site of your favorite podcast whenever you wish to see what's new.

DearMyrtle Podcasts -
http://podcasts.dearmyrtle.com

Catch DearMyrtle's interesting *Family History Hour* podcasts at this site with hotlinks to the mentioned Web sites online.

GenealogyGuys.com -
www.genealogyguys.com

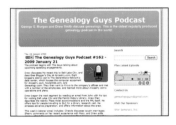

George Morgan and Drew Smith discuss genealogy news, new technology, and provide tips to help you with your research.

GenealogyGems.tv -
http://genealogygems.tv

Host Lisa Cooke shares research strategies and inspiration to help you get the most out of your family history research time. New podcasts are about 25 minutes long, and generally published on a weekly basis.

Books, Forms, Supplies, Marketplace

The Genealogy Shelf.com -
www.thegenealogyshelf.com

An excellent online and mobile genealogy store with over 100 different publishers of popular family history and genealogy books, CDs, software, supplies, and maps.

Heritage Quest.com -
www.heritagequestonline.com

Heritage Quest is a large comprehensive genealogical data provider in the United States and a leading purveyor of data, products, supplies and equipment to consumers and institutions with over 250,000 titles. The company is dedicated to producing high-use data, landmark publications, general reference books and timely, informative periodicals for genealogy enthusiasts. Available free by using your local library card, and at some Family History Centers.

Genealogy Charts and Forms -
http://genealogy.about.com/cs/freecharts

Free downloadable family tree charts, pedigree charts research logs and other free forms to help you in your genealogy research and keep your family tree organized.

Global Genealogy.com www.globalgenealogy.com

Shop online for family history supplies, maps, forms, software, books, etc.

Genealogical.com - www.genealogical.com

A publisher and distributor of 2000 genealogy books, CDs, and supplies.

Generation Maps.com -
www.generationmaps.com $$$

An easy to use, very affordable, genealogy chart design and printing service. They offer personalized working charts, beautiful decorative charts, custom heirloom charts, and a printing service for charts you've created. Now you don't have to fill in a chart yourself – just send your genealogy computer file and/or your digital photos, tell them how you want it to look, and it arrives on your doorstep for a very reasonable price. They can help you get your research out where you can see it and surround your family with a sense of their heritage. It's also a wonderful, easy way to explain to your family members the research that has been accomplished.

Alibris.com - www.alibris.com > *genealogy*

Alibris connects people who love books, music and movies to thousands of independent sellers around the world. Their proprietary technology and advanced logistics allow them to offer over 40 million used, new and hard-to-find books to consumers, libraries and retailers.

Heritage Books.com -
www.heritagebooks.com

Has over 12,000 genealogy books, maps and CDs.

Picton Press.com - www.pictonpress.com

Specializes in publishing genealogical and historical manuscripts.

Ancestry Store.com -
www.theancestrystore.com

Family history and genealogy books, software, photos, and maps.

Family History Store -
www.thefamilyhistorystore.com

An international online retailer of a growing line of genealogy and history related products & gifts since 2003.

RootsBooks.com - www.rootsbooks.com
and www.rootsbooks.co.uk

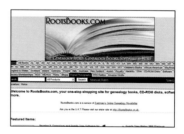

A one-stop online genealogy bookstore for books, computers, software and more.

Use Wisdom and Order in Your Quest

Dallin H. Oaks
© by Intellectual Reserve, Inc.

Dallin Oaks wrote an article regarding using wisdom and order in your quest to finding your family history. He said that there is much each of us can do toward finding our roots, and each person can contribute according to your individual circumstances and abilities. He gave these general guidelines:

- **First:** Our efforts should be to accomplish finding our family roots and stories, increase our knowledge and better understand our ancestors, strengthen bonds between family members, and gain a sense of identity and purpose in life.

- **Second:** We should understand that in the work of finding our roots there are many things we can do, and that all of us should participate by selecting those ways that fit our personal circumstances at a particular time. All of the different things we do are expressions of love, devotion, and service to our ancestors who have gone before us. And he encouraged everyone to do something.

- **Third:** He said it would be desirable for each of us to think about the work of finding our family roots and stories as a personal assignment. And that all of us should use wisdom and order in our quest and have a total personal activity that does not exceed what is wise for his or her current circumstances and resources. (*Ensign,* June 1989, p.6)

Let us then use wisdom and order in our journey to find our family roots and stories. And may it help promote a sense of belonging that ties generations together, help us gain a sense of identify and purpose in life, and help teach us how to love...how to be more Christ like.

Most people do not know how to start to trace their own family roots and stories, or what has already been done by others. This book was written because we need help to learn *how* to do the work. And we need it *simple, easy* and *quick.* We need to know the exciting, easy way today to connect with our ancestor's lives and stories, and learn about our heritage. This illustrated guidebook was written for this express purpose.

Getting Started

Maybe you're curious about the idea of learning about your family history, but don't know where to start. Maybe you've listened to amazing stories from your grandfather, scoured old family photo albums, and attended family reunions. Now what? What records should you look for? What can they tell you about your ancestors and heritage? And what has already been done by others?

I hope this family history guidebook/ resource book offers a convenient, easy step-by-step approach to answering these questions, and learning how to trace your family roots. I hope you find this expanded, updated Third Edition helpful, inspiring, and to your liking. And I hope it offers a convenient, easy step-by-step approach to learning and doing the work. Get started today tracing your own family roots and stories and discover new meaning in your life and the thrill of uncovering new found treasures.

Paul Larsen

Family History Insights - 1

Spencer W. Kimball
© by Intellectual Reserve, Inc.

Connected With Our Past

"Whether we recognize it or not, we are connected with our past... people who care nothing for the past usually have no thought for the future and are selfish in the way they use the present." Spencer W. Kimball, World Conference of Records, 1980

Thich Nhat Hanh

Continuation of Your Ancestors

"If you look deeply into the palm of your hand, you will see your parents and all generations of your ancestors. All of them are alive in this moment. Each is present in your body. You are the continuation of each of these people." Thich Nhat Hanh, Vietnamese Zen Buddhist monk, teacher, author, poet and peace activist. *A Lifetime of Peace,* 2003, 141

Shirley Abbott

Weight of History

"We all grow up with the weight of history on us. Our ancestors dwell in the attics of our brains as they do in the spiraling chains of knowledge hidden in every cell of our bodies." Shirley Abbott

Mark Twain

Politics and Family History

"Why waste your money looking up your family tree, just go into politics and your opponents will do it for you." Mark Twain (Samuel Clemens) (1835-1910), Author & humorist

John H. Groberg
© by Intellectual Reserve, Inc.

Receive Strength and Guidance

"So often we think of our responsibility to do something for those who have gone before. We need to understand that probably one of the most important benefits of preserving our heritage is what it does for us today. If we want our problems to be solved, one of the surest ways of doing that is to search for our past, for therein we receive strength, guidance, and understanding. [You] are giving an added eternal dimension to your lives as you learn and study the past. We can receive strength and help from those who have gone on before. To raise our families today, we need to do family research and genealogy." John H. Groberg, Chairman of the Olympic Events Executive Committee, Press Conference 2002

Pliny the Younger

Deserve to be Remembered

"It is a noble employment to rescue from oblivion those who deserve to be remembered." Pliny the Younger (AD 61-112), Author and philosopher

Edmund Burke

Reflecting on Ancestors

"People will not look forward to posterity, who never look backward to their ancestors." Edmund Burke (1729-1797), Irish statesman & author

CHAPTER 2

3-Easy Steps
Follow These 3-Easy Steps to Begin Building Your Family Tree and Connect to Your Ancestors

STEP 1 - Identify Your Ancestors Using Your Family

The success of tracing your family roots and stories increases when families work together. Family members will often have information to share, or they may be willing to help you look for information. Your relatives may remember important events and dates that have not been recorded. They may have family heirlooms, records, mementos, photographs, and other valuable items. They may have interesting family stories to tell, and they can sometimes direct you to others who knew your ancestors or to other relatives you may not know.

INSIDE THIS CHAPTER:

2 Where do I Start?

Suggested Activities

- Purchase family history software to help you if you haven't already and learn the basics *(see Chapter 5: Family History Software)*.
- Start writing down what you know about your family.
- Print out a blank *pedigree form* and *family group sheet* on your computer to make it easier.
- Call relatives to find out if someone has already compiled a family history or other records that might contain the information you're looking for. Ask them to e-mail a GEDCOM file of their information. This is a great head start.
- Look around your house for documents that might provide new information or verify the information you already have. Keep copies of everything you find in your search. It may not seem important now, but it will in the future.

Family History Insights - 2

Boyd K. Packer
© by Intellectual Reserve, Inc.

Collect Everything About Your Life

"Get a cardboard box. Any kind of box will do. Put it someplace where it is in the way, . . . anywhere where it cannot go unnoticed. Then, over a period of a few weeks, collect and put into the box every record of your life..... Collect diplomas, all of the photographs, honors, or awards, a diary if you have kept one, everything that you can find pertaining to your life; anything that is written, or registered, or recorded that testifies that you are alive and what you have done." Boyd K. Packer, *Liahona,* Aug. 2003, 15

Gaius Sallustius Crispus

A Light From Our Ancestors

"Distinguished ancestors shed a powerful light on their descendants, and forbid the concealment either of their merits or of their demerits." Gaius Sallustius Crispus (86-34 BC), Roman historian

Samuel Adams

An Inheritance From Our Ancestors

"The liberties of our country, the freedom of our civil constitution, are worth defending at all hazards... We have received them as a fair inheritance from our worthy ancestors... [they] transmitted them to us with care and diligence." Samuel Adams (1722-1803), Founding Father

Traits from Ancestors

"A man finds room in the few square inches of the face for the traits of all his ancestors; for the expression of all his history, and his wants." Ralph Waldo Emerson (1803-1882), Poet and author

A Quotation from Ancestors

"Every book is a quotation; and every house is a quotation out of all forests, and mines, and stone quarries; and every man is a quotation from all his ancestors." Ralph Waldo Emerson

Made from Our Ancestors

"...a man represents each of several of his ancestors, as if there were seven or eight [ancestors] rolled up in each man's skin ... and they constitute the variety of notes for that new piece of music which his life is." Ralph Waldo Emerson

Gordon B. Hinckley
© by Intellectual Reserve, Inc.

Feel A Special Connection

"As you look into the [computer] you may be surprised to find names of your parents, of your grandparents, of your great-grandparents, and your great-great-grandparents, who have bequeathed to you all you are of body and mind. You will feel a special connection to those who have gone before you and an increased responsibility to those who will follow." Gordon Hinckley, National Press Club Speech, March 8, 2000

STEP 1 - Identify Your Ancestors Using Your Family

BEGIN BUILDING YOUR FAMILY TREE WITH WHAT YOU ALREADY KNOW

The information you gather about your ancestors gives you a greater appreciation of your heritage, the sacrifices your ancestors made for you, and a better understanding of what their life was like. Your knowledge of your forebears will increase, your family will grow closer, families will be strengthened, and the opportunity to learn more about your kindred dead will bless lives.

As you gather information about your ancestors, you are welding family links, and drawing yourself and your family closer to God. Your ancestors want to be found as much as you want to find them.

> Follow the 3-Easy-Steps to begin building your family tree and connect to your ancestors.

QUICK TIPS ON GETTING STARTED

1. Begin with a pedigree chart. It will be a road map for your Family history search. Create your own four generation pedigree chart. From memory, begin to fill in information on the lines indicating your father, your mother, your grandparents, and so on.

2. Start with yourself and what you already know about your parents and grandparents.

3. Work back one generation at a time, from the known to the unknown.

4. Be as complete as possible when you record information.

5. Don't be overwhelmed by the process.

6. Choose one of the commercially available family history software programs (See Chapter 5)

Write Everything You Know About Your Ancestors

Identifying your ancestors is fun and so much easier today. You can begin right now by picking up a pencil and writing down information on a piece of paper.

Begin with what you already know by writing information on yourself and work back one generation at a time. The most important family history information you already posses – your memories and the memories of your loved ones. Gather information about yourself, your siblings, your parents, your grandparents, and your great grandparents. Make a list of each member in your family that can help you identify your ancestors. Typically, information about your close relatives is readily available simply by talking to them, and searching through information in your home.

Write down specific information, such as: names, dates and places of important events such as birth, marriage, and death, ancestral village, occupation, etc. Try to gather 3-4 generations (or more) of information on your ancestors. Don't be concerned if you're missing information because you can go back and fill it in later.

> A *research log* is a comprehensive list of what you have already searched and what you plan to search next for an ancestor.

Why Keep a Research Log?

A research log is like a treasure map outlining your progress and documenting your search for your own family roots and stories. It can tell you what you have searched, what you found or didn't find, and save you time because you don't need to search the same source again. You can also tell your family or others what you have already searched, and help you decide on the next steps. Your family or others may want to look at the same sources as you did, so it's a quick way to provide confidence to others, and your records will be more complete. You can easily photocopy or print out a copy of your log. Don't go hunting for family history treasures without your map.

Forms and Computers Make It Easier

You can start just by writing information on paper. However, it's best to obtain a family history software program to help you keep things organized and print forms you can use to record your family information. These programs make the task of recording and organizing your information much easier. *Refer to Chapters 5 and 8 for more help.*

There are many useful forms, but the first forms of most value to you are a *Pedigree Chart, Family Group Record,* and *Research Log.*

Pedigree Chart

(Family Tree Chart) Lets you list your pedigree – your parents, grandparents, great grandparents, and so on.

Family Group Record

A tool to help you organize your research by families. Because information about an individual ancestor is most often found with information about your ancestor's siblings or parents, this form is a helpful organizational

Free Charts and Forms

You can also download family tree charts, pedigree charts, research logs, internet research logs, and other genealogy charts and forms for free on various web sites to help you record and track your research and keep your family history organized. Once you have installed a family history software program on your computer, you can print some forms using your computer program.

FamilySearch.org - www.familysearch.com.

On the front page, in the box titled *Start Your Family History,* click on *Forms,* then scroll down to each form and click on PDF.

About.com -

http://genealogy.about.com/cs/freecharts

Another excellent directory of free forms.

PBS Ancestors Series - www.byub.org/ancestors

You'll find fun PDF files for research questions, source notes, and charts. Scroll down the menu at the left of the screen and click *Free Charts.*

Family Tree Magazine -

www.familytreemagazine.com/forms/download.html

This magazine has created interesting forms that can help you access and organize your family history information.

tool. It includes room to write information found about a husband, his wife and their children.

Research Log

Helps keep track of the information you find. Include the name of the ancestor you are researching, the information you find, and the sources. This will help you remember what records you have searched and what information you found.

Look for More Information in Your Home

Look for sources in your home that might contain the missing or incomplete family

Suggested Activities

- Look at your pedigree chart and make a list of the records you need to verify the information you have gathered. You probably have some blank spots on your chart; think about what kinds of records you need to help you fill in those blanks.

- Look around your house for photographs, documents, old letters, journals, newspaper clippings, family Bibles—anything that might provide new information for your pedigree chart or verify the information you already have. Document your own life first by gathering records and information about your birth, marriage, graduation, military service, and so on. It is the same process you will eventually use to document the lives of your ancestors.

- Make copies of your original documents and organize your materials in labeled file folders. Enter any new information on your pedigree chart.

To Locate Living Relatives

Write to people with the same surname. Search the free "white page" Internet directories:

www.att.com/directory

www.switchboard.com

www.whitepages.com

www.peoplesearch.com

information you're seeking. Useful sources include: birth, marriage, and death certificates, family bibles, journals, letters, photo albums, funeral programs, obituaries, wedding announcements, family registers, church records, military records, legal

> Remember that records are created because of important life events.

Research Tip

Look for two kinds of records:

- Original (primary) records created by eyewitnesses at the time an event occurs.

- Compiled (secondary) records created by genealogists and historians, sometimes many years after an event has occurred.

First, check compiled records because someone may have already done much of the research you are trying to do. However, when using compiled records, try to verify the information you find there by then obtaining the original records and documenting the information.

papers, newspaper clippings, etc.

Add this information to your pedigree charts and family group records. It's important to record the sources of the information. This helps you and others know where the information came from. To do this, it's easier to use the *Notes / Sources* (or citations) function on your family history software program.

Choose a Family or Ancestor You Want to Learn More About

After gathering names, dates and perhaps some stories about your family, the next step is to choose a specific ancestor, couple, or family line on which to focus your search. Look for missing or incomplete information on your pedigree chart and family records. You could choose to learn more about your grandparents, or an ancestor you were named after. Start with the generations closest to you, and work your way back. The key here isn't

> Call relatives to find out if anyone has already compiled a partial or complete family history that might contain the record(s) you are looking for.

who you may choose to study; just that it is a small enough project to be manageable. This is especially important if you're just starting out building your family tree. People who try to do too much all at once tend to get bogged down in details. Identify questions you want to answer about your ancestor, such as: "When and where did he die?" Select one question at a time as the objective.

You can also check with local libraries, historical societies and genealogical societies to see if family histories are on file there.

Ask Relatives for Information

Make a list of relatives and the information they may have. Contact them – visit, call, write, or e-mail them. Be sure to ask specifically for the information you would like. Add the information to your pedigree charts and family group records. Record your relatives names, addresses, phone numbers, email addresses, relationship, and the date of your interview(s) in the *Notes* or *Sources* function of your family history software program.

> Family history is like putting together pieces of one big jigsaw puzzle with no boundary edges and an unpredictable number of pieces.

The Family History Jigsaw Puzzle

People like solving puzzles. But with the family history puzzle, you have to show that new pieces actually belong to your puzzle. It's fun! The first pieces you start with are *yourself* and *your spouse*. Then, hopefully, you will have both sets of your parents (4 pieces) and grandparents (8 pieces) that have at least some records of their birth and marriage dates and places. Then find the next 16 pieces – your great grandparents – to fit next to them. If you don't put the pieces together in just the right way, then you'll never get to see the final picture. To make sure your puzzle pieces end up in the proper positions you should use pedigree charts and family group sheets to record your research data and keep track of your progress.

Documenting Your Information

Citations and Sources

Information technology has been a great boon to tracing your own family roots and stories today. When tracing your family it is very important that you keep track of

Is Your Family Tree Naked?

Noted genealogist Helen Leary, CG, CGL, says, publishing or sharing your genealogy without citing sources is like sending it into the world naked. You should tell others where you obtained your information. The hundreds of hours you spent putting your family history together won't be respected unless you document your sources. Sources establish credibility. Citing and documenting sources is no longer important, it is *essential*.

Citing Sources

The six elements of a good source citation include:

- Author (who provided the information)
- Title
- Publisher (including location)
- Date of the information (usually the year)
- Location of the source you used (page number, library or archive) and the call number
- Annotations: These are optional comments by you about the source. [Place your comments in square brackets.]

Consistent formatting is useful, helpful, and even required in some cases, but for now, don't get hung up on the commas and colons. Just begin citing your sources, and cite them well enough that others can understand what you searched. *(See web sites below on where to find standardized formatting styles.)*

every piece of information. Taking time to document where you got your information will save you time later in your research and help prevent duplicating the research that you or others have already done.

This is important not only as a way to verify your data, but also as a way for you and others to go back to that source when future research conflicts with your original assumption. It helps you to easily go back to your previous source to see if you may have missed information or you want more details. It's also a way to let others know on which records you based your facts, i.e. did the birth date you have for your great-grandmother come from a published family history, a tombstone, someone's memory, or a birth certificate. With your sources documented, you and others can retrieve the same data bringing credibility and trace-ability to your family history.

Whether the source is a probate court record, a tombstone, an email, a website, a yellowed newspaper clipping, grandfather's diary, or a conversation with your grandmother, cite your sources. It doesn't matter if you take notes by hand, use a computer, make copies on a copier or dictate them into a recorder; you need to carefully cite your sources.

You should provide quality citations for your sources so you can remember where you found the information. This will also guide you to where to look for more information, and provide a trail for others to follow. Besides your own posterity, others with whom you share your information have the same desire and need to verify the facts which you have researched.

Any statement of fact, whether it is a birth date or an ancestor's surname, needs to

Here's an important point you should know about citing sources.

Citing Online Sources

When citing websites, emails, scanned image files, CD files, or other electronic media sources, the basics still apply but you must include instructions to help others find the work. Consider an annotation from you to help understand the source, i.e. [This website <www.myfamilyhistory.com> contains numerous hyper-links to other websites. On March 31, 2009, these were checked and found to be active and additional data on Jack Austin's will was found]. Whenever material in a citation is not obvious, an explanation in the annotation is appropriate. For examples of how to document these technology sources, see the referenced websites below.

Here's a book that is the best single source of information for documenting your family history.

have its own individual documented source. You should consider documentation of an information source just as important as finding and recording the information itself. Record enough information about the source, and tie it to the information in your history so someone else can retrieve it. Today's family history software will do this for you.

Cite Your Own Source

A citation must cite the source *you* used, not the one that someone told you existed in their citation. Another person's research, even cited, is hearsay until you can verify the source for yourself. For example, if a cousin tells you that she extracted your grandfather's birth information from his birth certificate, then your cousin is your source for the information, unless she provided you a photocopy, a scanned copy, or you actually verified her copy of the certificate.

EasyBibcom - www.easybib.com

A free web tool that automatically formats citations and bibliography based on your input.

Organize and Document As You Go

One of the most fundamental and important principles of family history research is to organize and document AS YOU GO! Organizing and documenting as you go is smart because it keeps the best information at your fingertips and saves time. Good documentation lays the groundwork for easier correlation and evaluation of sources. If you put off documentation until later, you may never do it. This results in information clog-ups. Failure to document starts a chain of confusion,

Evidence Explained

This must-have book for every genealogist conveys the principles behind source citation, the formats in which citation should be cast, and the fundamentals of evidentiary analysis itself. Whatever the source of information – courthouse land records, family Bibles, cemetery markers, microfilmed census registers, unpublished manuscripts, electronic e-mail, or a videotaped family reunion – you will find multiple examples of each in this book. It offers13 concisely explained points of genealogical analysis,

including: the distinction between direct and indirect evidence, and between quality and quantity, and the importance of custodial history. Elizabeth Shown Mills, published by Genealogical Publishing Company $49.95.

redundant searches, missing or overlooked evidence, and uninformed linkage decisions.

Source citations should become a habitual part of all of your research. Include notes, sources, facts and complete information in the original file so that the information posted is complete and adequately documented. Not only do you want to document all of your evidence and sources, but others reading your family history may want to retrace your path as well. They may want to visit the same places, access the same web sites, documents, books or microfilm, and experience the thrill of the trail that you enjoyed.

Where do you put your notes and source citations? If you're writing a family history, citations may be embedded in parentheses within the text, shown as footnotes (at the bottom of each page) or as endnotes (at the end of a chapter or the work). If you're keeping your genealogy in a computer software program, it allows for recording your notes and sources under each individual and event. Good documentation includes:

Research Logs – Fill in the purpose of

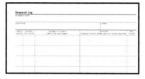

each search, and source data on logs *before* looking at the source because repository catalogs often describe the source better than the source itself which makes your trail easier to follow. It also helps to keep track of unsuccessful searches (negative evidence). After success, list where you file the copy. Good research logs serve as a guide to all the sources on a family researched successfully or unsuccessfully. They help avoid repeated searches of the same unproductive sources. Good logs help you pick up research after a pause. They assist in evaluation by starting your thinking about a source as you describe it on the log. Research logs are also the best place to document your thinking and research strategies. Write lots of comments to yourself about your search strategies, suggestions, questions, and discrepancies you have noticed.

Family Group Records – Compile a good family group record right at the start. Keep

up-to-date with source footnotes for every event. Cite ALL the known sources for that family in footnotes tied to the events they document. Add more than just birth, marriage, and death events on the family group record. Add all events like census, military service, and migrations to the family group record. Well-documented

and up-to-date family group records are the best source of ideas about where to search next. They show all the clues and background information needed to guess name variations, guess dates and places of events, and guess the most likely sources to document those events.

Photocopy Source Documents – If the repository will allow it, *always* make a photocopy. Photocopies are better than handwritten copies because photocopies show ALL the clues, including things you would ignore if you copied by hand. Cite the footnote information in the margin on the front of the copy. This starts your thinking about and evaluation of the source. On the back of the copy write the name of the file and file number where you will store this copy.

Well-Organized Files – Stay organized by completing paperwork and filing before starting another search. Start research on a family by preparing a new research log for the family and a well-footnoted family group record. Start each individual search by filling in part of your research log BEFORE the search. Give the date of the search, repository, purpose of the search (person and event you seek), and the source you will search. If the source does not have useful information put nil on the research log. Keep everything up-to-date. Don't start more research before doing all the paperwork and filing from the previous search.

Online Source Citations -
www.bedfordstmartins.com/online/citex.html

An excellent website for creating source citations particularly electronic media.

About.com Citing Sources -
http://genealogy.about.com/cs/citing

Tips on documenting your research and formats for citations, including citations for electronic genealogy sources and maps.

Why We Cite -www.ancestry.com/learn/library/
article.aspx?article=782

An article on quality citations for electronic sources such as web pages, email, mailing lists, and CD-ROMs by Mark Howells.

Creating Worthwhile Genealogies -
www.rootsweb.ancestry.com/~rwguide/
lesson12.htm

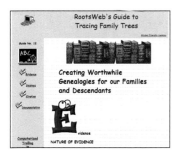

An interesting lesson on evidence, sources, documentation, and citation from RootsWeb's *Guide to Tracing Family Trees.*

Evaluate the Evidence

Family historians must also learn to weigh and evaluate evidence, especially conflicting evidence. Don't assume that if several pieces of information agree, the data must be correct. Such assumptions may lead to erroneous pedigrees which may create a dead-end to your family tree.

What is a GEDCOM?

A GEDCOM (**GE**nealogical **D**ata **COM**munications) is a type of file that takes family history information from one computer program and compresses it into a standard format which can be transferred into any other program. Importing and exporting a GEDCOM file is usually the best way to receive or send your information anywhere in the world via e-mail. You can receive from (import) or share (export) your information with other people, even if they use a different family history program. It was created by FamilySearch and The Family History Library in the mid-1980s to make it possible for people with different brands of software and computers to share their information.

To Create and Export a GEDCOM File

In most software programs, go to *File > Export to GEDCOM* and create a new file with a ".ged" file extension after the name. GEDCOM files can be uploaded to genealogy sites on the Internet, and can be adjusted for privacy and copyright concerns.

Steps to Import GEDCOM Files

When you import a GEDCOM file, all of the information from the GEDCOM file is added into your database file. To preview the data, you could import the GEDCOM file into an empty file. From there, you can correct or change information or select specific individuals and family lines to import into your actual database file. If you change information in the new file, you need to create a new GEDCOM file to import the information into your actual database.

■ From the *File* menu, select *Import.*
■ Select the drive and folder where the file is located.
■ Select the file.
■ Click *Import.*
■ Choose the import options that you want.
■ To import the file, click *OK.*

Where do I Start? 2

When receiving a new GEDCOM file, rather than merging the data back into your actual database file directly; always transfer it to a new, empty database file which you create.

After examining the new data, you can then import the records you wish into your primary family history database file. Even then, before you merge the new GEDCOM data, make a backup of your original database first.

GEDCOM Web Sites

There are many GEDCOM database web sites you can search for matches on names, dates, and locations; download the information; and share (or upload) your information.

FamilySearch.org - www.familysearch.org

Ancestry.com - www.ancestry.com

RootsWeb.com - www.rootsweb.com

GenServ.com - www.genserv.com

GenDex.com - www.gendex.com

GenCircles.com - www.gencircles.com

One Great Family.com - www.onegreatfamily.com

Remember to cite the specific sources *you actually used* in compiling your family history. "Source notes have two purposes: to record the specific location of each piece of data and to record details that affect the use or evaluation of that data." *(Evidence! Citation & Analysis for the Family Historian).*

If you have conflicting information, carefully examine it and sort it into either primary or secondary evidence. Primary sources are usually written records created at or near to the time of the event. Secondary sources are second-hand information that has come from some other person or record. Get as close to the original documents as you can as they are more likely to be correct. And don't blindly accept information you find in a book, CD, on the Internet, or from someone's memory.

One of the most important skills you can acquire will be learning to evaluate the accuracy of primary records and the relative reliability of secondary sources. Remember that most of the family history information you discover online is from a secondary source. You should consider it a *clue* to check out.

Family history is a fun, exciting and rewarding hobby that will bring you great happiness! But it may also bring many sighs of disappointment. Here are some guidelines to help keep you on the right track.

20 Tips to Help Keep You on the Right Track

Some practical Do's and Don'ts

The following suggestions may be helpful to keep you on the right track, and hopefully prevent misfortune when planting and growing your family tree. You need to be aware of some potential pitfalls (unforeseen or unexpected difficulties) when researching your family roots and stories. Here's some practical Do's and Don'ts for pulling everything together, saving you valuable time, and making your journey fun.

- **Begin with yourself** and your parents and work backwards on your pedigree, building on the supporting evidence you find, one generation at a time. Research is usually not difficult, but it does require understanding the basics. Basics are easily learned, and, with experience, productive and efficient research will become easier. Don't overwhelm yourself by taking on too much all at once. Take baby steps. Focus on one small step at a time, like one single family, or a single surname in a particular place.

- **It is important for you to understand the difference** between building your family tree through actual research in appropriate records vs. that of merely collecting names without supporting evidence to verify that your family tree is correct. Don't assume something is correct just because someone says so, or it's in print, or on the Internet. Verify it with documented research from multiple

Don't get sidetracked with multiple goals. Organize your overall search strategy and focus your efforts. Plan where you are going and keep track of where you have been.

Where do I Start? 2

sources (when possible) for every name, date, and place in your records.

- **Research is finding clues to lead you to records that prove relationships.** You build your case one or two facts at a time, and base continuing research on those proven facts. If the information you are working with is incorrect, then you are wasting your time. Do your research thoroughly as you go so that you can recognize your family among errors, misspellings, and various other imperfections.

- **Create a time line** of your ancestor's life listing all events in chronological order to view the whole picture. Then, log your progress. Write down supporting evidence for each event in the time line and the source of the evidence to keep you from duplicating the research. Make a *To Do* list of information you are seeking and the records that are available for the Surname or location you are searching. Start with www.familysearch.org and click on *Research Guidance* to help you locate records that may contain information about your ancestors.

- **Realize that you will encounter spelling variations of names.** Assuming that there is only one way to spell your family name can cause you to bypass good information. Consider anything remotely close to the name you are looking for. And

Do NOT enter surnames (last names) in all uppercase letters into your database. Enter women using their maiden name. If you don't know their maiden name, just use their first given names, i.e. "Grandma" is not a first name. Do not use titles (Dr., Mrs., Mr., Colonel, Rev., etc.) in name fields, but you can enter suffixes like Jr., Sr., III, etc.

be alert for the use of initials and nicknames. The older the time period in which you are researching, the less consistent your ancestors were about the spelling of their surnames. Some of them may have been illiterate, and could not tell the record keeper how their names were spelled.

- **Don't assume that "Jr" and "Sr" are father and son.** Usually they are, but sometimes they are not. They may be uncle and nephew, grandfather and grandson, cousins, or even no relation. These are merely titles to distinguish an older man from a younger one with the same name. To add to the confusion, these titles shift as "Sr" dies and "Jr" becomes "Sr", and a younger person often becomes "Jr". Without sufficient research in official records, one can not detect these changes and identities. It only takes one misidentification to cause you to spend years researching the wrong people.

- **Beware of compiled family data that does not support** documented names, dates, and places. Without evidence, one has nothing more than possible clues with which to try and find proof. However, even if existing Internet family trees contain likely errors, they may provide valuable clues − such as a date or place you had not known

about − that can give you new ideas for searching.

- **Always note the source of any material you copy.** Obtain copies of your proof documents as you find them. Finding information from multiple sources strengthens your case if it agrees, or indicates the need for deeper research if it disagrees. Studying the documents periodically often reveals clues previously missed.

- You may often encounter **conflicting information** that you will have to weigh against other evidence. Try to determine which is the most likely to be true. Periodically review and verify the conclusions you have reached concerning each of your ancestor's lives; this will help to prevent wasting time following blind alleys.

- **Try not to let your organizing get behind.** Establish a filing system for your papers from the start (using file folders, 3-ring binders, and your computer) and file each page of notes, photocopy, etc. as you acquire it. It's disheartening to rummage through a high stack of unfiled papers to find that copy of a birth certificate you desperately need.

- **Don't assume modern meanings** for terms used to describe relationships. For example, in the 17th century a step-child was often called a "son-in-law" or "daughter-in-law", and a "cousin" could

At times, if you feel like you're on your own in putting together your family history puzzle, remember that you're not alone. Your ancestors really are there pushing you in the right direction and cheering for you.

refer to almost any relative except a sibling or child.

- **Remember that indexes** to books rarely include the names of all persons mentioned in the book and, moreover, occasionally contain errors. If it appears that a book is likely to have valuable information, spend some time skimming its contents rather than returning it immediately to the shelf after a quick look at the index.

- **Collaborate with others searching the same names.** Advertise the surnames you are researching by submitting them to genealogical directories and surname lists on the Internet, such as RootsWeb Surname List at http://rsl.rootsweb.com. This will put you in touch with others who are researching the same surnames.

- **Learn who the siblings of your ancestor were** because it can often lead to the desired information you need. Example: Perhaps a death record is not available for your grandmother, but if you have documents that prove who her siblings were, then maybe their death records might give parent information, etc. There might also be a biography about some of them that would give family background information. Knowing who the siblings

Make frequent backups of your computer disks. Consider long-term storage of all your computer information with a secure online, automatic-backup company, such as www.mozy.com or www.carbonite.com.

and in-laws were can help sort out individuals with the same name.

- **Pay attention to your ancestor's neighbors,** witnesses to their legal transactions (marriages, deeds, etc.), guardians or godparents of their children, and other close associates. All persons in these categories may be potential relatives of your ancestor, and investigating them can provide clues for you to work with in developing your family tree. Your ancestors were part of networks of social acquaintances, business contacts, military comrades-in-arms, extended family, in-laws, neighbors, and, of course, family members. Use those people to help you find your ancestors.

- ***Death records*** usually contain parent information and various other important data. Death records usually are found in the county in which death occurred. Examples would include death while traveling, visiting, hospitalized, in prison, etc. outside his or her county of residence. ***Probate records*** can prove family relationships that may be found nowhere else. If there was property to be distributed, probate records would be found in the person's county of residence. It's also possible that additional probate records might be found in other counties/states where the deceased owned property.

- **Wills don't always mention all children** of a deceased person. Often a child has already been given property and it simply does not

Genealogy Research Map -
www.thinkgenealogy.com/map

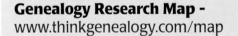

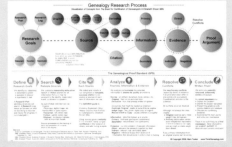

A popular research map which you can download for free from Mark Tucker's blog.

specify that in the Will. If the gift was real estate or other personal property, then there likely would be a deed. Wills are only a small part of probate records. Much, much more can be revealed in *estate records, inventories, bills of sale, administrator bonds, order books, etc.;* all heirs are likely to be named in estate settlements. Law suits among family members often occurred and these can be a goldmine of factual information on which to build. Knowing the names of siblings and in-laws helps you to recognize key people in the indexes. Develop your family group sheets so the information will be handy.

■ **Don't assume that family stories are completely true;** often there is partial truth in them but details have become distorted through the years. A common one might be "great-great grandma was an Indian". Someone may have said "she looked like an Indian", or, "she might have been an Indian", or "she lived near Indians". Always

When you trace your ancestors back to a foreign country, the records will be different but the process is the same.

seek out official records that can prove or disprove components of the story.

■ **Don't assume that children** in a pre-1880 census household (when relationships were stated) are children of the head of the household: They may or may not be. They may be nieces, nephews, step-children, grandchildren, or no relation. Study the ages and birthplaces of all household members. Other year's census records, probate, guardianships, deeds, etc. may help identify relationships and reveal the true children of the head of household. Understanding these relationships can be crucial to building your

Keep your family in historical context. Not only did the people around them impact their lives, so did political events and social trends.

family tree and can unlock pieces of the puzzle. Census records through 1840 can be very helpful when analyzed with other records, but they can also be misleading if you insist on "accounting" for everyone; various circumstances affected household members.

Elaine S. Dalton
© by Intellectual Reserve, Inc.

We Did This For You

"...[As] my husband and I...walked through the Old Pioneer Cemetery searching for the grave of an ancestor... I was touched by the peaceful solitude and spirit I felt. I walked through the trees and read the names on the gravestones, many of them children and families. I wept as my heart was turned to our forefathers.... In my mind I asked many questions: Why did they leave their comfortable homes and families? Why did they suffer persecution, sickness, even death? Why did they sacrifice all that they had to come to this place? ... As I sat silently contemplating this scene, the answer came forcefully yet softly to my mind and heart: *'We did this for you.'* Those words...reminded me that our ancestors...sacrificed everything so that past and future generations would [receive] eternal blessings.... I know that if we [connect with our ancestors], the joyful day will come when we shall meet our ancestors once again and be able to say to them, *'We did this for you.'*"
Elaine S. Dalton, Ensign, Nov 2004, 89

CHAPTER 3

3-Easy Steps
Follow These 3-Easy Steps to Begin Building Your Family Tree and Connect to Your Ancestors

STEP 2 - Add New Branches to Your Family Tree Using the Internet

3 Add New Branches

Computers, technology, and the Internet have revolutionized the way we do family history and genealogy today. We can search farther and faster than ever before, and we can record everything we find with just a few keystrokes. Computers allow us to discover, store, access, and share family history information with speed and convenience.

The Internet is an excellent and powerful tool for you to gather your family history information and share it with others. It's made up of millions of sites which are just files stored on computers around the world. Each site can contain any number of associated pages — each of which has an unique electronic address, i.e. *about.com.* It's estimated that more than two million separate web sites are devoted to genealogy / family history.

Suggested Activities

1. Enter all of the family information you've gathered–including info from your relatives–into your family history program; learn the basics of your software program.

2. Search for your ancestors using existing family tree web sites described herein, and discover the wealth of information available.

3. Import any new information into your family history database.

Family History Insights - 3

3 Add New Branches

Barack Obama, President

Greatness Must be Earned

"... greatness is never a given. It must be earned. Our journey has never been one of short-cuts or settling for less.... Rather, it has been...men and women... who have carried us up the long, rugged path towards prosperity and freedom. For us, they packed up their few worldly possessions and traveled across oceans in search of a new life. For us, they toiled in sweatshops and settled the West; endured the lash of the whip and plowed the hard earth. For us, they fought and died.... Time and again these men and women struggled and sacrificed and worked till their hands were raw so that we might live a better life. ... This is the journey we continue today. ... We must pick ourselves up, dust ourselves off, and begin again the work of remaking America." Barack Obama, Presidential Inaugural Address, Jan. 20, 2009

Richard Scott
© by Intellectual Reserve, Inc.

Decide to Do Something Significant

"Set aside those things that don't really matter in your life. Decide to do something that will have eternal consequences. Perhaps you have been prompted to look for ancestors but feel that you are not a genealogist. Can you see that you don't have to be anymore? It all begins with love and a sincere desire. ... This is...a monumental effort of cooperation on both sides of the veil where help is given in both directions. It begins with love. Anywhere you are in the world, with prayer, faith, determination, diligence, and some sacrifice, you can make a powerful contribution. Begin now. I promise you that the Lord will help you find a way. And it will make you feel wonderful." Richard Scott, *Ensign*, Nov. 1990, 7

Creating Memories

"Each day of our lives we make deposits in the memory banks of our children." Charles R. Swindol, pastor of the First Evangelical Free Church of Fullerton, California (1971-1994); radio host for *Insight for Living*; www.oneplace.com

Bryant Hinckley
© by Intellectual Reserve, Inc.

Influence of Your Dead

"The spirit and influence of your dead will guide those who are interested in finding those records. If there is anywhere on the earth anything concerning them, you will find it." Bryant S. Hinckley, *Sermons of Melvin J. Ballard,* Deseret Book, 1949, p 230

George Santayana

Nature's Masterpiece

"The family is one of nature's masterpieces." "Those who cannot remember the past are condemned to repeat it." George Santayana (1863-1952), Philosopher & poet.

Tend Your Roots

A family tree can wither if nobody tends it's roots. Unknown

J. Fielding Smith
© by Intellectual Reserve, Inc.

Become Acquainted with Ancestors

"It doesn't matter whether your computer is able to compile all the family group sheets for everyone that every lived on the earth, it remains the responsibility of each individual to know his kindred dead…[it is] each person's responsibility to study and become acquainted with his ancestors." J. Fielding Smith, *Turned to the Fathers*, 184

Lemons and Bad Apples

Any family tree produces lemons, nuts, and a few bad apples. Unknown

Heritage of the Past

"The heritage of the past is in the seed that brings forth the harvest of the future." National Archives, Washington. D.C.

STEP 2 - Add New Branches to Your Family Tree Using the Internet

SEE IF SOMEONE HAS ALREADY FOUND INFO ON YOUR ANCESTORS

When you're tracing your family roots and stories, why re-plow a field that has already been plowed? You are most likely not the only—or the first—person searching for and building your family tree. So see if someone has already found information on your ancestors. You can save yourself hours of work, verify information that you already know, make connections between generations, and help you determine which ancestors to search for. Most web sites allow free searches, but some may require a fee or just registration. If you don't have a computer or an Internet connection at home, you can use one at a Family History Center, or your local library or university.

Some of the most useful websites offer invaluable databases of existing family trees, vital information and transcribed census records, such as *FamilySearch.org* and *Ancestry.com;* others are collections of links to other sites, such as *Cyndi'sList.com* and *Linkpendium.com;* some are more specific with genealogies from people or about a specific group of people, such as *GenServ.com* and *AfriGeneas.com;* others offer useful data such as land records, like *The Bureau of Land Management (BLM.gov),* and some specifically help you to learn how to do family history, such as *DearMYRTLE.com* and *Genealogy.About.com.*

We are living in exciting times because old records are being indexed to electronic formats at an ever increasing rate. This is changing family history dramatically. An enormous number of old records still exist which are very difficult to research right now because they have not been digitized, but sometime in the future essentially all old records will be converted to electronic formats. This means that we will most likely be able to connect with ancestors and solve family history problems in the near future that may still be very difficult today.

Research Tip
Keep in mind possible alternate spellings of your surname as you are researching.

First, Search Existing Family Tree Web Sites

There are many wonderful web sites with existing family tree databases to help you determine if someone has already found information on your ancestor. Here's the best of the Internet; they may also serve as web links to the entire Internet to help you find other family history web sites. *See also Chapters 6 and 7, Best of the Internet Family History Web Sites, for more details.*

FamilySearch.org - www.familysearch.org

Free family history, family tree, genealogy records and resources from around the world. A web site that provides access to the world's largest collection of free family history information all in one place—from U.S. census data to the parish records of tiny European villages. It's a powerful computer software system to help you learn about your ancestors. You can do significant research online and also discover what records you need to search to find your ancestors in record-breaking time. It provides easy access for the gathering and sharing of family history information. *FamilySearch* provides access to these family tree databases: Pedigree Resource File, Ancestral File, International Genealogical Index, and Record Search (pilot). In addition, it offers a free copy of PAF *(Personal Ancestral File)*, a family history software program that allows you to record and publish your family history. *See information on "New FamilySearch" in Chapter 7.*

Ancestry World Tree -
www.ancestry.com/trees/awt

Rootsweb WorldConnect -
http://wc.rootsweb.ancestry.com

Ancestry World Tree and Rootsweb WorldConnect are free collections of user-submitted GEDCOMs (family trees). You can access World Tree and World Connect from two different websites, but either way, it is the same program and the same set of trees. The database contains more than 480 million names in family trees submitted by users. This is a leading provider of private Web sites for connecting families, with over 1.25 million paid subscriptions and more than 10 million people using its Web resources every month. The Generations Network includes *MyFamily.com, Ancestry.com, Genealogy.com,* and RootsWeb.com providing both free and paid subscription.

GenCircles Global Tree -
www.gencircles.com/globaltree $$$

A popular place for searching and submitting family trees. Surnames from over 90 million ancestors can be searched for free, and if you've submitted your own GEDCOM file you can use their "matching technology" to pair the people in your pedigree with those already on file. They allow you to interact with your data and with other researchers in new ways, such as, posting messages on your file and on individuals in your file. The integrity of your data will not be compromised in any way and you can delete these messages at any time. By doing this, you can have others immediately interacting with you.

One Great Family.com -
www.onegreatfamily.com $$$

A family history program that allows everyone to combine their knowledge and data to build one huge, shared database. Using sophisticated, patented technology, OneGreatFamily is linking all of the family trees together into one shared, worldwide database with shared multimedia, notes, research, biographies and citations. The idea is to leverage the effort and research of all users rather than duplicating research that others have already done. They have over 180 million ancestors worldwide.

MyTrees.com - www.mytrees.com $$$

Contains a pedigree-linked database with over 370 million names, share your family tree

To use these comprehensive Web sites and indexes, think about what you know about a specific ancestor or surname and then look in the appropriate categories.

Research Tip

If you are trying to find information on a Quaker couple married in Virginia in 1766, you could look in categories for marriages, Virginia, Quakers, or Colonial records. They can also help locate information about an ancestor's culture, traditions, homeland, and history.

worldwide, build your own family tree on-line, and store family history pictures online for display with your family tree.

Family Tree Searcher.com -
www.familytreesearcher.com

Enter your ancestor information just once to search existing family trees at nine online family tree databases.

This free service creates the best family tree searches based on your ancestry. They also include hints for searching your family tree.

Search for a Family History That has Been Published

Family histories are books that give genealogical information about one or more generations of a particular family. Libraries and genealogical societies have been collecting published family histories for years. You can often find family histories in libraries in the area where your ancestors lived. Your family's stories might be among them. Compiled stories and histories can be an amazing source of information about the lives of your ancestors. They provide stories and interesting information that help you really connect with your ancestors. They are usually very well-researched for tracing your family roots; however, you still need to verify that the information is accurate and documented.

Family History Library Catalog -
www.familysearch.org > *Library* > *Library Catalog*

The Family History Library has an extensive collection of published family histories. First, do a catalog *Surname Search.* The search will list family histories in the Library's collection that contain the surname. You can then arrange to view the actual histories at your local Family History Center. The microfilm or microfiche from the Family History Library can be loaned to you for free at your local Family History Center. There is a small postage fee.

If the family histories do not contain information about the family you want using a *surname,* search for records from the *place* where your ancestor lived. Then, look for published family histories on other web sites or at public archives and libraries.

How to Use the Online Family History Library Catalog

The Family History Library Catalog™ describes the books, microfilms, and microfiche in the Family History Library in Salt Lake City. The library houses a collection of genealogical records that includes the names of more than 3 billion deceased people from throughout the world. It is the largest collection of its kind in the world, including: vital records (birth, marriage, and death records from both government and church sources); census returns; court, property, and probate

Research Tip
Use the Family History Library's free Research Guidance for the state/county where your ancestors came from. It gets you quickly oriented to what's available to help you.

records; cemetery records; emigration and immigration lists; printed genealogies; and family and county histories.

When you want to look at actual records of the people you are researching, you can visit the Family History Center nearest you and order copies of the records from the main library in Salt Lake City. To locate the nearest family history center, click on *familysearch.org,* then *Find a Family History Center,* or you may call 800-346-6044 in the United States and Canada.

Using the Family History Library Catalog

Go to www.FamilySearch.org

■ Click the *Library* tab > *Library Catalog.*

■ Search in the catalog for your surname and various places that your ancestors lived, looking for information that might be relevant to your research. Choose from the various searches including:

Place - To locate records for a certain place such as city, county, state, etc. Search either by town/city, county, state/country. Each jurisdiction has different records available, so it is important to search all jurisdictions for your area (i.e. both the city and county records). Click *Film Notes* to see the microfilm number.

Surname - To locate family histories which include that surname. A list of family histories with that surname will be shown. Click on a title to see the detailed information. Review the notes to decide if this history is one that would

include your ancestor. Click View Film Notes to see the microfilm number for this record.

Keyword Search - To find catalog entries about records that contain a certain word or phrase. You can use this to search for keywords in titles, authors, places, series and subjects.

Title Search - To find catalog entries about records that contain a certain word or combination of words in the title.

Film/Fiche Search - To find the titles of items on a specific microfilm or microfiche in the Catalog.

Author Search - To find the author details record for a person, church, society, government agency, and so forth identified as an author of a specific reference. It lists titles linked to the author and may include notes and references.

Call Number Search - To find an item by its call number (the number used to locate items on the shelves in the Library).

3 Add New Branches

Where to Search Chart

OBJECTIVE	RECORD TYPES	
To obtain information about the following...	Look in the Family History Library Catalog, Locality and Subject sections for these type of records...	
	First look for:	**Then look for:**
Age	Census, Vital Records, Cemeteries	Military Records, Taxation, Obituaries
Birth date	Vital Records, Church Records, Bible Records	Cemeteries, Obituaries, Census, Newspapers, Military Records
Birthplace	Vital Records, Church Records, Census	Newspapers, Obituaries, Military Records
City or parish of foreign birth	Church Records, Genealogy, Biography, Obituaries, Naturalization & Citizenship	Emigration and Immigration, Vital Records*, History
Country of foreign birth	Census, Emigration and Immigration, Naturalization and Citizenship, Vital Records*	Military Records, Church Records, Newspapers, Obituaries
County origins & boundaries	History, Maps	Gazetteers
Death	Vital Records, Cemeteries, Probate Records, Church Records, Obituaries	Newspapers, Military Records, Court Records, Land and Property
Divorce	Court Records, Divorce Records	Newspapers, Vital Records*
Ethnicity	Minorities, Native Races, Societies	Church Records, Emigration and Immigration, Naturalization and Citizenship
Historical background	History, Periodicals, Genealogy	Church History, Minorities
Immigration	Emigration & Immigration, Naturalization & Citizenship, Genealogy	Census, Biography, Newspapers, Church Records
Maiden	Vital Records, Church Records, Newspapers, Bible Records	Military Records, Cemeteries, Probate Records, Obituaries
Marriage	Vital Records, Church Records, Census, Newspapers, Bible Records	Biography, Genealogy, Military Records, Probate Records, Land and Property, Nobility
Occupation	Census, Directories, Emigration and Immigration, Civil Registration, Occupations, Probate Records	Newspapers, Court Records, Obituaries, Officials and Employees
Parents, children, & other family members	Vital Records, Church Records, Census, Probate Records, Obituaries	Bible Records, Newspapers, Emigration and Immigration, Land and Property
Physical description	Military Records, Biography, Court Records	Naturalization, Civil Registration, Church Records, Emigration & Immigration, Genealogy, Newspapers
Place-finding aids	Gazetteers, Maps	Directories, History, Periodicals, Land & Property, Taxation
Place of residence when you know only the state	Census, Genealogy, Military Records, Vital Records, Church Records, Directories	Biography, Probate Records, History, Land and Property, Taxation
Places family has lived	Census, Land and Property, History	Military Records, Taxation, Obituaries
Previous research	Genealogy, Periodicals, History	Biography, Societies, Nobility
Record-finding aids	Archives and Libraries, Societies, Genealogy	Periodicals
Religion	Church Records, History, Biography, Civil Reg.	Bible Records, Cemeteries, Obituaries, Genealogy

3 Add New Branches

What is a Family History Center?

Typical Family History Center

Family History Centers (FHC) are local branches of the Family History Library located in Salt Lake City, Utah, and there are some 4,500 centers worldwide. The library houses a collection of genealogical records that includes the names of more than 3 billion deceased people. It is the largest collection of its kind in the world, including: vital records (birth, marriage, and death records from both government and church sources); census returns; court, property, and probate records; cemetery records; emigration and immigration lists; printed genealogies; and family and county histories.

Since many people are not able to travel to Salt Lake City to use the library, local Family History Centers make the library's resources accessible to those interested in finding their family roots. They enable you to research the vast holdings of the library including its computerized indexes. Family History Centers provide FREE access to top important websites, such as:

   Footnote.com

   Godfrey Memorial Library (Godfrey.org)

   FamilySearch.org

   WorldVitalRecords.com

   KindredKonnections.com (My Trees.com)

HeritageQuestOnline.com (available in 1400 FHC in No. America)

Ancestry.com (Regional centers only)

Family History Centers also provide access to the vast family history records via the Internet, and most of the *microfilms* (a roll of film that contains reduced photographic images of various records) and *microfiche* (rectangular sheets of microfilm on which information is arranged in rows and columns) in the library to help you identify your ancestors.

Millions of records are stored on microfilms and microfiche. You can order microfilms and microfiche to view at your local Family History Center. The vast records available on microfilm and microfiche are currently being scanned and indexed and you can search the records online that are completed so far at www.familysearch.org > Search Records > Record Search. Join thousands of volunteers around the world who are helping to make more free records available online through www.FamilySearchIndexing.org.

Everyone is welcome at a Family History Center at no cost to use their resources. Most of them are maintained in meetinghouses of the Church of Jesus Christ of Latter-day Saints (Mormon). When you want to look at actual records of the people you are researching, you can visit the Family History Center nearest you and order copies of the records from the main library in Salt Lake City. They provide friendly, knowledgeable volunteers at the centers to assist you without cost or obligation. To locate the nearest family history center, click on: www.familysearch.org, then click on: *Find a Family History Center;* or you may call 1-800-346-6044 in the United States and Canada.

Search Other Sources For a Published Family History

Libraries and genealogical societies have been collecting published family histories for years. You can often find family histories in libraries in the area where your ancestors lived. Your family's

stories might be among them. Compiled stories and histories can be an amazing source of information about the lives of your ancestors that help you really connect with them. Here are some additional resources you can use to locate published stories about your family:

Library of Congress -
www.loc.gov/rr/genealogy

One of the world's premier collections of U.S. and foreign genealogical and local historical publications.

Ancestry.com - www.ancestry.com > *Search* > *Stories, Memories, Histories*

Selected histories that profile families from all fifty U.S. states, Canada, and the British Isles going back to the 1700s.

Suggested Activities

■ Search for an ancestor using existing family trees on a comprehensive web site.

■ Download the information you've found to your computer, import into your database, and synchronize the new information with your existing database records.

■ Then, print a new pedigree chart for your review

Do I Need An E-Mail Address?

Q. I do not have e-mail or Internet access at home, but I would like to register on the Internet with various family history websites. They tell me I have to have an e-mail address to register. What can I do?

A. You must have an e-mail address in order to register with family history websites. There are several providers who offer free e-mail addresses that you can set up and access from a computer at a Family History Center, your library, or a university. These providers can be found by searching the phrase "free e-mail" in an online search engine (see *Search Engines* below).

> Another way to find out about your family tree and connect with others who may be doing the same research as you is to visit free *message boards and forums.*

Message Boards

You can post surname queries, ask questions, or just network with fellow genealogists. They allow people with common interests to "meet" and share their information. They cover a wide range of topics—surnames, localities, adoptions, occupations, etc. You may find a group devoted to your family name or a particular locale where one of your ancestors lived. If you find someone that you would like to contact, send them an e-mail. Go to these web sites:

Ancestry / Rootsweb -
http://boards.ancestry.com
(Over 161,000 different boards)

GenForum - http://genforum.genealogy.com
(Over 14,000 online forums)

About Genealogy -
http://genealogy.about.com/cs/surnamequery
(One of the most active)

Cyndi's List Queries -
www.cyndislist.com/queries.htm
(Links to web sites)

BBC - www.bbc.co.uk/messageboards
(Popular collection of UK-based message boards)

GenSource Common Threads -
www.gensource.com (To find others researching your family name)

> When you find existing family trees online, published family histories, or information on message boards, you need to evaluate the information to determine if it is reliable and accurate.

Research Tip

Just because the information is printed in a book or available on the Web doesn't necessarily mean that it is factual. Work to organize and document your information as you go to verify the information.

WorldCat - www.oclc.org > *WorldCat*

Online Computer Library Center (OCLC) hosts WorldCat, the window to the world's libraries. WorldCat is a global network of library content and services that uses the Web to let you be more connected.

HeritageQuestOnline.com - www.heritage questonline.com > *Search Books*

Find information on people and places in over 23,000 family and local histories. It is available free through your local library with your library card, and free at some Family History Centers.

Cyndi's List.com - www.cyndislist.com/lib-state.htm

Web links to State Libraries, Archives, Genealogical & Historical Societies.

SEARCH OTHER RECORDS FOR MISSING INFORMATION

Search Engines

Use "search engines" to see if someone has posted information on the Internet about your ancestors and descendants of your ancestors. You may find family Web sites, pedigree charts, personal histories, cemetery records, etc. The good thing about using a search engine to find missing information is that they will typically search millions of Web pages within seconds. The bad thing is that they will search millions of Web pages. The sheer number of results can be overwhelming.

Generally, searching information on the Internet using a search engine requires a little finesse. For example, searching the term *'genealogy'* using Google.com or Yahoo.com will result in about 160 million hits. Obviously, this is overwhelming and far too many to handle, so before you begin searching for information you need to be very specific about what information you are searching for. Also, understanding that some web sites are *databases* of information, while others are *directories* that will lead you to other useful web sites will help you to find the information you seek.

Using search engines and finding information and resources need not be complicated—all you need is to unleash the simplest math you know of to help you get the results you want. How do you do that? You *add, subtract* and *multiply* to do better searches. One of the best ways to focus your search is to use the add or plus symbol (+) and/or the subtract or minus symbol (-) to let the search engine find only the pertinent pages relating to your search. You multiply by using the quotation symbols (" ").

Search Engines

A Web search engine is designed to search for information on the World Wide Web. Information may consist of web pages, images and other types of files. Some search engines also mine data available in newsbooks, databases, or open directories. Unlike Web directories, which are maintained by human editors, search engines operate algorithmically or are a mixture of algorithmic and human input. You can use a search engine to find many helpful sites. Some of the major search engines include:

Google.com - This is currently the most popular and the one to beat: bigger, deeper, faster, more relevant and richer in features than all the other search engines. It enables users to search the Web, Usenet, and images. Features include PageRank, caching and translation of results, and an option to find similar pages.

Yahoo.com - The first Web directory and still one of the most popular search sites on the Internet. Features: personalized content and search options, chatrooms, free e-mail, clubs, and pager. It has become a true portal and content site.

Dogpile.com - Puts the power of all the leading search engines together in one search box to deliver combined results. The process is more efficient and may yield more relevant results.

Live.com - The fourth most used search engine (formerly MSN Search) offers some innovative features, such as the ability to view additional search results on the same web page and the ability to dynamically adjust the amount of information displayed for each search-result (i.e. just the title, a short summary, or a longer summary).

Ask.com - Provides relevant search results by identifying the most authoritative sites on the Web. It goes beyond mere link popularity (based on the sheer volume of links pointing to a particular page) to determine popularity among pages considered to be experts on the topic of your search.

Beginning each keyword with a plus (+) symbol tells the search engine to find pages that include all of the words that you enter, not just some of them. For example, if you are looking for the surname GATES, Google brings up over 92 million pages which match your search request. But if you were really looking for information on Bill Gates, typing in +bill +gates narrows the results considerably (by 60 million pages) because you only want pages that contain both names.

Moreover, including the minus (-) symbol allows you to search for pages that exclude specific words or phrases. For example, typing (-fences -BBQ -robert -scholarship) excludes all pages with information on "gates and fences, Gates BBQ equipment, Robert Gates, and Gates scholarships". Another example, if you're searching the surname RICE, but want to exclude all the pages relating to food and cooking you type *rice -food -cook -recipe.*

Using the quotation symbols (" ") allows you to find results containing the exact phrase you specify, i.e. *"hans larsen quaker" +1776.*

Google Your Family Tree -
www.GoogleYourFamilyTree.com

Dan Lynch

This new book by Dan Lynch is written in a friendly, informative, and non-technical way, but still conveys the depth of power contained within each major part of the Google service. If you have ever used Google (or any Internet search engine) and experienced frustration with millions

How To use Free Research Guidance

- Go to www.familysearch.org
- Click Research Helps > Guidance on the top bar
- Notice the Research Assistant on the left side bar. She will tell you what to do for each step. Read what she has to say and then select a place.
- Follow the Research Assistant's instructions and select an event and date range.
- You will then be given your "Search Strategy." Again, follow the instructions of the Research Assistant and choose a record.
- Continue through this site, reading and following the instructions from the Research Assistant. Use your Search Strategy as your "homepage" for this site, and make use of the many links available.

Free Research Guides and Outlines

The Family History Library has developed many comprehensive brochures and guides about researching ancestors around the world. The **Research Guides** describe how to use a particular source of family history information, and **Research Outlines** describe the records and strategies that can be used to pursue family history research in a specific geographic location or particular type of record. They are invaluable to help find your family roots, and you can access them online and download for FREE at *FamilySearch.org > Research Helps > Guidance > Document Type.* Click on PDF under each desired title to view or print the document.

Consider starting with the one titled, **Tracing Immigrant Origins,** a 49-page outline of tips, procedures, and strategies. Using the above described navigation, click on *Research Outline* and scroll down to *Tracing Immigrant Origins.* You can review the *Table of Contents* and click on the subject you want.

of listings resulting from your query, you are about to discover a true breakthrough. He dissects more than one hundred powerful commands and features of Google, but maintains a focus on how they can be used specifically to conduct family history research. It teaches you about many of the other capabilities of Google including: Language Tools, Google Books, Google News Archives, Google Images and Videos, Google Alerts and Google Maps. It includes special tips for finding people, places, and even filters for searching through different time periods.

Using Free Research Guidance, Research Outlines, & Research Guides

When you're online in *FamilySearch.org,* click on *Research Helps > Guidance* on the top bar on the front page. This unique feature guides you in finding copies of original records, such as censuses and birth records, based on where the person lived and the time of his or her birth, marriage, or death. You select the place and time, and Research Guidance provides a list of recommended things to do and records to search in priority order.

Research Guidance is designed to help you develop a "search strategy" for your research. Once you have provided a place, event and time period, you will be given a list of records to search, in a recommended searching order. Each record will give step-by-step instructions, tips, descriptions and addresses or web links to lead you directly to that record. There are many links on this site so do not get frustrated if you get lost. Always go back to your search strategy.

Many forms and guides are available in *Research Helps > Articles* which help you plan, record, and analyze your research. You can download and print these free forms and guides.

Census Records

A Snapshot of History
Building Blocks of Your Research

The census has proven to be a great resource for family historians. There are few other records that help you track your ancestors throughout their lifetime. Census records can place entire families at a specific point in time and are one of the best sources to explore. You may want to consider starting with the federal census records—especially those since 1850—because they provide the best information. There is a 72-year privacy cap on census and military records so the records that are now available for research span the years 1790-1930; the census is taken every ten years.

From 1790 to 1840, the census takers asked few questions, thus limiting the value these

> To search the census schedules, convert all the surnames you want to track into their corresponding Soundex codes.

Census Tips

Searching the census is a multiple step process and each step must be done in order. First, however, you should learn about the Soundex as this is the most important piece of the puzzle. To use the census soundex to locate information about a person, you must know his or her full name and the state or territory in which he or she lived at the time of the census. It is also helpful to know the full name of the *head of the household* in which the person lived because census takers recorded information under that name.

Census Web Sites

Ancestry.com - www.ancestry.com > *U.S. Census Collection* (scroll down) $$$

This site offers the most census information available online – a Herculean effort that took a team of experts and workers a combined 6.6 million hours of labor. The information details more than just names or population numbers. It includes people's moves across the country, their race, marital status, assets, residence, schooling and other personal information. U.S. census records available at this time include: 1790, 1800, 1810, 1820, 1830, 1840, 1850 (including slave schedules), 1860 (including slave schedules), 1870, 1880, 1890 (fragment, census substitute, and veteran's schedules), 1900, 1910, 1920, 1930. Canadian census records are available at www.ancestry.ca and include the schedules for 1851, 1871, 1891, 1901, 1906, 1911 and 1916. Preview available for free, but you must subscribe to see any details. $19.95/month. Free at some Family History Centers.

FamilySearch Record Search - www.familysearch.org > *Search Records* > *Record Search pilot*

FamilySearch provides free family history, family tree, and genealogy records and resources from around the world, including census records. Many new and updated census records are becoming available regularly with increasing frequency with many on-going indexing projects by 170,000 volunteers, and are now currently available to search on the new Record Search pilot. In addition to census records, you can also search other worldwide record collections (birth, death, marriage, pension, church, tax, military, baptism, christening, burial, funeral, and civil registration records) currently in process of being indexed. Millions of new records are being added every month. You can join thousands of volunteers around the world who are helping to make more free records available online. Find out more at www.familysearchindexing.org.

Heritage Quest.com - www.heritagequestonline.com

Contains U.S. Census indexes and images, but only indexes "Head of Household". It is available free through your local library (you can log-on at home) with your library card, and free at some Family History Centers.

World Vital Records.com - www.worldvitalrecords.com $$$

Various census images and transcriptions from 1790-1930. Free at Family History Centers.

Find My Past.com - www.findmypast.com $$$

1841, 1861, 1871, 1891, 1901 and 1911 UK Censuses. It's free to search but to view the original images requires you to be a paying member. 1841 and 1861 Censuses are free at www.FamilySearch.org > *Search Records* > *Record Search pilot.*

Footnote.com - http://www.footnote.com $$$

Explore and search the new interactive 1860 and 1930 US Federal Censuses, and leave a

comment, photograph, story, or a document on a person's record. Free at Family History Centers.

Census Online.com - www.census-online.com

Guide to online census records with over 45,000 web links.

Genealogy.com - www.genealogy.com/genealogy/uscensustxt_popup.html

Detailed introductory summary of each U.S. Census

U.S. Census Bureau.gov - www.census.gov

Census dates for countries and areas of the world: 1946 to 2004. Shows the dates of census enumerations over the past half century, as well as projected or scheduled enumerations in the near future for countries around the world.

Census Links.com - www.censuslinks.com

Non-commercial directory of international census transcriptions published on the Internet.

records have for us today. Starting in 1850, however, more information was gathered by the census takers. For example, enumerators listed the names, ages, and gender for all persons living in the house, whereas prior censuses only listed the heads of household.

One of the basics of family history research is to start with yourself and work backward in time, moving from the known to the unknown. So start your search with the most current 1930 census. *See the comparison charts below for more information.*

Census Tutorial - http://census.byu.edu

Designed to help individuals with little or no previous census research experience to learn

how to effectively search and utilize the U.S. Federal Census schedules.

Key Tips for Census Success - www.lostcousins.com > Help & Advice (in left column)

Here's a web site with an excellent article on census tips.

U.S. CENSUS COMPARISON CHART

Year	Ancestry.com* Soundex search Advanced Search Ranked Search (best results first)	Genealogy.com* No soundex search	Heritage Quest Free - Only available through your local library; No Soundex search, Advanced Search	FamilySearch.org Free - Soundex search
1930	Every-name	No Index	Head-of-Household 5 states (CT, DE, MD, TX, and VA)	
1920	Every-name	Head-of-Household (partially completed)	Head-of-Household 35 states	Every-name
1910	Every-name	Head-of-Household	Head-of-Household	
1900	Every-name	Head-of-Household	Head-of-Household	Every-name
1890	Every-name (fragment) Substitutes**	Head-of-Household	Head-of-Household	
1880	Every-name		No Index	Every-name
1870	Every-name	Head-of-Household	Head-of-Household	Every-name (in-process)
1860	Every-name + Slave schedules	Head-of-Household	Head-of-Household	Every-name (in-process)
1850	Every-name Head-of-Household + Slave schedules	No Index	No Index	Every-name (in-process) +Mortality schedule +Slave schedule
1840	Head-of-Household	No Index	No Index	
1830	Head-of-Household	No Index	No Index	
1820	Head-of-Household	Head-of-Household	Head-of-Household	
1810	Head-of-Household	Head-of-Household	Head-of-Household	
1800	Head-of-Household	Head-of-Household	Head-of-Household	
1790	Head-of-Household	Head-of-Household	Head-of-Household	
STATES	Individual states			Individual states

* Browse the census indexes for free, but you must subscribe to see details. Free at some Family History Centers.
** The Ancestry 1890 Census Substitute is a collection of replacement data for the 1890 census information that was destroyed in a fire in Washington D.C.; less than 1% of the schedules survived enumerating only 6,160 individuals. With the aid of the National Archives and the Allen County Library, this database is the first definitive online substitute for the missing 1890 census. It includes fragments of the original 1890 census that survived the fire, special veteran's schedules, several Native American tribe censuses for years surrounding 1890, state censuses (1885 or 1895), city and county directories, alumni directories, and voter registration documents.

UK / BRITISH ISLES CENSUS COMPARISON CHART

Year	Ancestry.com* Soundex search Advanced Search Ranked Search (best results first)	FindMyPast.com	Heritage Quest Only available through your local library; No Soundex search, Advanced Search	FamilySearch.org Soundex search
1911		England and Wales Every name & address		
1901	Every name	Every name & address		
1891	Every name	Every name & address		
1881	Every name	Every name & address		Every name
1871	Every name	Every name & address		
1861	Every name	Every name & address		Every name (provided by FindMyPast.com)
1851	Every name	Every name & address		(In process)
1841	Every name	Every name & address		Every name (provided by FindMyPast.com)

CANADA CENSUS COMPARISON CHART

Year	Ancestry.ca* Soundex search Advanced Search Ranked Search (best results first)	Canadian Genealogy Centre www.CollectionsCanada.gc.ca/ genealogy/index-e.html	FamilySearch.org Soundex search
1916	Every name: Manitoba, Saskatchewan and Alberta	Every name	
1911	Every name	Every name	
1906	Every name: Manitoba, Saskatchewan and Alberta	Every name Northwest provinces	
1901	Every name	Every name	
1891	Every name	Every name	
1881		Every name	Every name
1871	Ontario Index, Head-of-Household - Free	Ontario Index	
1861		Every Name	
1851	Every name	Every name	

* Browse the census indexes for free, but you must subscribe to see details. Free at some Family History Centers.

3 Add New Branches

The Soundex Indexing System

Soundex is a phonetic algorithm for indexing names (last name) by sound, as pronounced in English. The soundex coding system was developed so that you can find a surname even though it may have been recorded under various spellings. In the Soundex code, all surnames are reduced to a letter followed by three digits: the letter is the first letter of the name, and the digits encode the remaining consonants. A simplified list of rules follows:

Number	Represents the Letters
1	B, F, P, V
2	C, G, J, K, Q, S, X, Z
3	D, T
4	L
5	M, N
6	R

Disregard the letters A, E, I, O, U, H, W, and Y. Surnames that sound the same, but are spelled differently, like SMITH and SMYTH, have the same code and are filed together. Both ROBERT and RUPERT return the same code "R163" while RUBIN yields "R150". JONES would be reduced to JNS which converts to J520. Note that if less than three characters follow the first letter; zeroes are used as place fillers. The name LEE would be reduced to just L and the Soundex code would thus be L000. As a final example, HENDERSHOT would be reduced to HNDRST and the Soundex code would be H536. Note that the code stops after the fourth character, even if there are consonants remaining.

For more information go to:
www.archives.gov/publications/
general-info-leaflets/55.html

> Census research is usually very rewarding and provides a snapshot of an individual or a household at a specific time and place in history.

Census Tutorial

It can also be frustrating if you don't understand how to effectively search the census. Learn how to search the census with the census tutorial on page 57, and acquire valuable tips for census success using these resources to ensure your success.

> Here are some websites that will automatically convert any name you type into the Soundex code for that name.

Soundex Converter

www.searchforancestors.com/soundex.html

www.jewishgen.org/JOS/jossound.htm

http://resources.rootsweb.ancestry.com/cgi-bin/soundexconverter

Top 10 Search Tips for Census -
http://genealogy.about.com/od/census/a/census_search.htm

Kimberly Powell has compiled some good census search tips that you need to read.

Many new and updated census records are becoming available regularly with increasing frequency due to on-going indexing projects, and are now available mostly on FamilySearch.org and Ancestry.com.

Immigration / Emigration

Tracking Your Ancestors Voyage

Where did your ancestors originate from? As our ancestors emigrated from one country to another, information about their lives were recorded on passenger lists and government documents. These documents can help you learn where your ancestors originated from, when they left, where they went, and who they traveled with. You can often find the age, occupation, place of residence, town of destination and the names of family members.

American Family Immigration History Center - www.ellisislandrecords.org

The Ellis Island site contains the immigrant arrival records stored in the Ellis Island Archives containing some 22 million immigration records from 1892-1924 available for free searching. There are an estimated 100 million Americans who have at least one ancestor who entered the U.S. through Ellis Island. Information about each person was written down in ships' passenger lists, known as "manifests." Manifests were used to examine immigrants upon arrival in the United States. Searching the archives can help you write your own family's story. On this site you'll find: *Passenger records* (giving passenger name, date of arrival, ship of travel, age on arrival, and more); *original manifests* showing passenger names and other information; and *ship information,* often with a picture, giving the history and background of each ship that brought the immigrants.

One-Step Search Tools - http://stevemorse.org

Some people have been frustrated at not being able to locate a particular ancestor in the Ellis Island Archives or other passenger lists. Transcribing millions of foreign-sounding names and places written in often difficult-to-decipher handwriting on pages that were frequently faded, smeared, or otherwise damaged was difficult. And many of the names were perhaps faithful replications of misspellings in the original records. Dr. Stephen Morse developed his own specialized search form that enables us to search the immigration databases in more ways that are faster and in some cases more useful: by passenger, "sounds-like" using the last name, town search, Jewish passengers, ancestor's village, date, and damaged images which are not indexed. If at first you don't succeed, try using different names (or spellings) your ancestor may have used, last-name only searches, switching the first and last names in your search, and by approximating their arrival date.

CastleGarden.org - www.castlegarden.org

Free access to an extraordinary database of information on 10 million immigrants from 1830 through 1892, the year Ellis Island opened. Over 73 million Americans can trace their ancestors to this early immigration period.

U.S. Citizenship and Immigration Services - www.uscis.gov

This website has a page for guiding us to records. Click on the *Site Map* on

3 Add New Branches

The small passenger list manifest page showing your ancestor's name in the Ellis Island Archives can be enlarged by clicking on the small magnifying glass icon to the side of the photo.

When you click on the button, *Add to Your Ellis Island File,* you are given the opportunity to save any searches you have done on this website, saving you valuable time for future searches.

the top bar. There are lots of good tips, guides and information. It explains ports of entry, their records and has links to each state with a port, as well as U.S. cities with ports of entry from Canada. The *Immigration Arrival Records* page has links to passenger ship lists including Ellis Island and other ports.

Awesome Genealogy.com Directory -
www.awesomegenealogy.com/Genealogy/immigration.shtml

A directory of immigration links, including naturalization, oaths of allegiance, passenger lists, ports, ships and ethnic immigration.

Ancestor Roots Directory -
www.academic-genealogy.com/ancestorroots informationdatabases.htm

A directory of links to Immigration databases (scroll down to Immigration).

Tracing Immigrant Origins - www.family search.org > *Research Helps* > *Articles* > *Sorted by Title* > *T*

A Research Outline that introduces the principles, search strategies, and various record types you can use to identify an immigrant ancestor's original hometown. These principles can be applied to almost any country.

Article About Immigration -
www.genealogy.com/00000388.html

Links and information about the immigrant experience and finding records related to immigration.

Not all immigrants came to America through Ellis Island. It was the busiest port of entry, but there were many other entry points in the U.S., including Baltimore, Detroit, New Orleans, Philadelphia, San Francisco, etc.

Research Tip

Don't get discouraged if you don't find your ancestors in the Ellis Island database.

AncestorsOnBoard.com –
www.ancestorsonboard.com $$$

This site offers a complete collection (24 million records) of all UK outbound passenger lists 1890-1960 for all voyages made from any British port. You can search for free but there is a fee to view the full records.

Ancestry's U.S. Immigrant Collection –
www.ancestry.com $$$

Ship passenger lists, naturalization records, ship photos and much more.

Canadian Genealogy Centre -
www.collectionscanada.gc.ca/genealogy

Canada's documentary web site offers immigration and naturalization databases in both official languages, as well as vital, census, military, and land record databases.

Military Records
Track Your Ancestors Footsteps Through History

History of battles and wars, and military records–service or pension records, bounty land records, muster rolls, discharge lists, fatalities, and prisoner of war records–are some of the most interesting and helpful records available to assist you in tracing your own family roots and stories. Military records contain large amounts of biographical information, from the color of a person's eyes to the day-by-day muster rolls that track your ancestor's footsteps through history. There are numerous opportunities to learn the stories of your ancestor's courage and sacrifice with hundreds of military record databases.

Revolutionary War Pension Files -
www.heritagequestonline.com

Index and supporting file images to participation in Revolutionary War. It is available free through your local library with your library card, and at some Family History Centers.

Every war in American history has military records that are very valuable in family history research. All servicemen have records (regardless of rank) from private to general.

3 Add New Branches

U.S. Military Records Chart

War	Conflict Years	Approx. Birth Years	Locate Records at	Look for
Revolutionary War (250,000+ servicemen, 50,000+ casualties)	1775-1783	1726-1767	www.HeritageQuestOnline.com (check with your local library, or available at some Family History Centers)	Muster Rolls Pension Files Bounty-land Warrants (applications)
			www.Footnote.com $$$	Muster Rolls, Pension Files, Service Records
			www.Ancestry.com >*Military Collection* $$$	DAR Linage Books Bounty Land Warrants
			www.Dar.com	DAR Patriot Index
			www.RoyalProvincial.com	Loyalist Records: Muster Roll Index, Regimental Documents, Land Petitions, Postwar Settlement Papers
War of 1812 (530,000 servicemen, 2,000 casualties)	1812-1815	1762-1799	www.Ancestry.com > *Military Collection* $$$	Service Records Pension Application Index Bounty-land Warrants
			http://Labs.FamilySearch > *View All Collections*	Louisiana, War of 1812 Pension Lists
Mexican War (100,000 servicemen, 13,000 casualties)	1846-1848	1796-1831	www.archives.gov/research/military/mexican-war.html	Microfilmed indexes to military service and pension files available from your local Family History Center
			www.militaryindexes.com	
			www.olivetreegenealogy.com > Military	
Civil War (2.8 million+ servicemen, 510,000+ casualties)	1861-1865	1811-1848	Civil War Soldiers and Sailors System - www.itd.nps.gov/cwss	Service Records, Regimental Histories, Battle Descriptions Prisoner Records
			www.Ancestry.com >*Military Collection* $$$	Soldier Index, 1890 Veterans Schedules (partial records only), Pension Index
			www.Footnote.com $$$	Confederate Service Records Union Pension Records (click: Browse by Historical Era > Civil War > Title > Civil War Pension Index)
			www.familysearch.org http://Labs.FamilySearch.org > *View All Collections*	NARA Confederate Service Records, Civil War Pension Index
			www.CivilWarData.com $$$	Pension Indexes, Rolls of Honor, State Rosters
			www.Archives.gov/genealogy/military > Civil War	Union Pension Index links Confederate Pension Records (by State Archive links)

Spanish-American War (280,564 servicemen, 2,061 casualties)	1898	1848-1881	www.spanamwar.com	Rosters Historical info
			www.accessgenealogy.com > *military records*	Spanish American War
			Archival Research Catalog http://arcweb.archives.gov	Spanish American War
Philippine Insurrection (125,000+ servicemen, 4,200 casualties)	1899-1902	1849-1885	www.ancestry.com > *Military Collection*	1900 Census (use Military & Naval Forces as the state of residence)
			www.heritagequestonline.com	Use Military & Naval Forces as the state of residence
			www.Archives.gov/genealogy/ military > *Philippine Insurrection*	Phiippine Insurrection information
World War I (24 million+ registered for draft; 4.7 million+ served, 116,516+ casualties)	1917-1918	1872-1900	www.ancestry.com > *Military Collection*	WWI Draft Registration Cards
			www.Archives.gov/ genealogy/military > *World War I*	Draft Registration Cards
World War II (16.5 million+ servicemen, 400,000+ casualties) The majority of WWII records are not publicly available yet.	1941-1945	1877 1925	www.ancestry.com > *Military Collection $$$*	WWII Draft Registration Cards Army Enlistment Records POW Records
			http://Labs.FamilySearch.org > *View All Collections*	United States, WWII Draft Registration Cards (In process)
			www.Archives.gov/ genealogy/military > *World War II*	Army Enlistment Records
Korean War (33,642 casualties)	1950-1953	1900-1936	www.Archives.gov/genealogy/mi litary > *Korean War*	Electronic records - The majority of records are not publicly available yet.
Vietnam War (110,000+ casualties)	1964-1972	1914-1955	www.Archives.gov/genealogy/ military > *Vietnam War*	Casualty Lists
			www.Footnote.com	Vietnam Veterans Memorial database

Ancestry, Footnote and HeritageQuest are free at some Family History Centers. HeritageQuestOnline is also searchable free through subscribing libraries; check your local library whether you can log on from home via the library's Web site using your library card.

3 Add New Branches

Daughters of the American Revolution.org - www.dar.org

A volunteer women's service organization dedicated to promoting patriotism, preserving American history, and securing America's future through better education for children.

Sons of the American Revolution.org - www.sar.org

A historical, educational, and patriotic non-profit corporation that seeks to maintain and extend the institutions of American freedom, an appreciation for true patriotism, a respect for our national symbols, the value of American citizenship, and the unifying force of one nation and one people.

American Civil War -
http://sunsite.utk.edu/civil-war and www.cwc.lsu.edu

Directory of web links to hundreds of civil war web sites and databases.

Civil War Soldiers and Sailors - www.itd.nps.gov/cwss

Index of Civil War service records by the National Park Service.

WWI Draft Cards - www.ancestry.com > Search > Military Records

Index and images of draft registration cards. Free at some Family History Centers.

WWII Army Enlistment and Other Military Records - www.worldvitalrecords.com > Record Types

Free at Family History Centers.

American War of Independence (1775-1783)

American Revolution - www.lineages.com

Revolutionary War - www.revwar.com

United States Military Records - www.rootsweb.com/~rwguide/lesson14.htm

Cyndi's List: Military Resources - www.cyndislist.com/milres.htm

Virtual Museum of the Revolutionary War - www.home.ptd.net/~revwar/museum.html

The War for American Independence - www.home.ptd.net/~revwar

National Archives and Records Administration - www.nara.gov/genealogy/genindex.html

Sons of the American Revolution - www.sar.org

Daughters of the American Revolution - www.dar.library.net

Web Links to Major Repositories - www.familysearch.org > Search Records > Web Sites

Library of Congress - www.lcweb.loc.gov

Suggested Activities

Look at your pedigree chart and determine if you have any ancestors who may have served in the following wars: French and Indian War 1754-1763; Revolutionary War 1775-1783; Indian Wars late 18th and 19th centuries; War of 1812, 1812-1815; Mexican-American War 1846-1848; Civil War 1861-1865; Spanish-American War 1898; Philippine Insurrection 1899-1902; World War I 1917-1918; World War II 1941-1945; Korean War 1950-1953; Vietnam War 1965-1973.

Footnote Military Records -
www.footnote.com > Browse

An online repository for original historical documents relating to the Revolutionary War, Civil War, WWI, WWII, US Presidents, historical newspapers, naturalization documents, and many more. The documents are made possible by their unique partnership with The National Archives. They recently released the first ever interactive World War II collection, which includes an interactive version of the USS Arizona Memorial, WWII Hero Pages, and WWII photos and documents previously unavailable on the internet. Their Hero Pages is an easy way to create a tribute or memorial to war heroes. It features an interactive timeline and map, a place to upload photos, documents and letters, and a place to share stories about individuals who fought in WWII. All the indexes are free to search which includes names, places, topics, a list of documents and a small image of the document, but a membership is required to view the full image. Free at Family History Centers. $11.95/month, $69.95/year.

Court, Land and Financial Records

Add Interest to Your History

Court and land records, wills and other financial documents are those kept by town, county, and state officials regarding property owned, sold or bequeathed to others. Court records may often be overlooked but are valuable to help you find information to assist you in your research and add interest to your history. Land records, such as deeds, provide evidence of specific places your ancestor lived at a specific time. Other court records dealing with finances and estates usually provide interesting information such as the value of your ancestor's property, and may list related family members.

Ancestor Search.com -
www.searchforancestors.com

Free land records search.

Bureau of Land Management - www.blm.gov

The Official Land Patent Records Site. This site has a searchable database of more than two million Federal land title records for Eastern Public Land States, issued 1820-1908, including scanned images of those records indexing the initial transfer of land titles from the Federal government to individuals.

World Vital Records.com -
www.worldvitalrecords.com > Record Types

A collection of various court, land, and probate records. Membership is required, but is free at Family History Centers.

Public Records Online - www.netronline.com

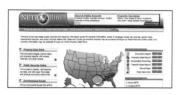

Links to available state & county Tax Assessors' and Recorders' offices. Online public records may include copies of deeds, parcel maps, GIS maps, tax data, ownership information and indexes. Some Recorders' offices have marriage and birth records available online.

Freedman's Bank Records - www.heritagequestonline.com

Includes information for nearly 500,000 African Americans from the post-Civil War era. You can search this database for free at Heritage Quest by first logging onto your local library online, or go to www.family-search.org > Search Records > Record Search (select USA region)

Libraries, Archives and Organizations

Rich Sources of New, Unique Information

Even though the Internet contains a seemingly endless depth of information for tracing your own family roots and stories, sooner or later you may want to visit a library or archive to find records that you can't find as yet on the Internet. It's difficult to physically visit the library in every town in which your ancestors may have lived, but most libraries around the world now have their library catalogs and collections online, so their information is becoming increasingly available to us. You can quickly know whether that library has the information or title you want, if it's available by interlibrary loan, or found in a nearby branch library. It's fast, convenient, and time-saving.

The Family History Library - www.familysearch.org

The library houses a collection of genealogical records that includes the names of more than 3 billion deceased people. It is the largest collection of its kind in the world, including: vital records (birth, marriage, and death records from both government and church sources); census returns; court, property, and probate records; cemetery records; emigration and immigration lists; printed genealogies; and family and county histories.

National Genealogical Society - www.ngsgenealogy.org

Founded in 1903 as a non-profit organization, the National Genealogical Society (NGS) is a dynamic and growing membership of individuals and other groups from all over the world that share a common love of genealogy. Whether you're a beginner, a professional or somewhere in between, NGS can assist you in your research into the past. The NGS is one of the important genealogical societies in the U.S., and is an excellent site for learning genealogy standards and methods.

National Archives & Records (NARA) - www.archives.gov

NARA is America's national record keeper. It is the archives of the Government of the United States that is responsible for safeguarding records of all three branches of the Federal Government. NARA provides ready access to essential records of what the Federal Government does—why, how, and with what consequences.

Library of Congress - www.loc.gov

The Library's mission is to make its resources available and useful to the American people and preserve a universal collection of knowledge and creativity for future generations. Since its founding in 1800, it has amassed more than 119 million items and become one of the world's leading cultural institutions. Just a few of the vast sections of the library include:

American Memory - http://memory.loc.gov

A gateway to rich primary source materials relating to the history and culture of the United States. The site offers more than 7 million digital items from more than 100 historical collections.

America's Story - Here you can discover

what Abraham Lincoln had in his pockets on the night he was assassinated. Or you can read about Buffalo Bill Cody and his "Wild West" show; the heroism of Harriet Tubman, who helped many slaves escape bondage; the music of jazz great Duke Ellington; or the inventions of Thomas Edison. Click on *Jump Back in Time* and find the settlers who landed on Plymouth Rock. Or jump to a more recent age and read about be-bop, a type of music invented long before hip-hop. Do you know what happened on the day you were born? You can find out here.

Research Tools - www.loc.gov/rr

Offers many databases and links to resources. Specifically, you should access the *Local History and Genealogy* page - www.loc.gov/rr/genealogy.

American Treasures - www.loc.gov/exhibits/treasures

An unprecedented permanent exhibition of the rarest, most interesting or significant items relating to America's past, drawn from every corner of the world's largest library.

Allen County Public Library - www.acpl.lib.in.us

One of the leading genealogy departments in a public library.

The following web sites are directories of genealogy libraries and archives.

Library Directories

Cyndi's List.com - www.cyndislist.com/lib-b.htm

Directory of Genealogy Libraries in the U.S. - www.gwest.org/gen_libs.htm

WorldCat - www.oclc.org > *WorldCat*

The window to the world's libraries. WorldCat is a global network of library content and services.

LibDex - www.libdex.com

An easy-to-use index to 18,000 libraries worldwide, library home pages, Web-based library catalogs, Friends of the Library pages and library e-commerce affiliates.

3 Add New Branches

Major Family History Libraries

Family History Library, Salt Lake City, Utah - www.familysearch.org. The largest genealogical library in the world houses 2 million rolls of microfilm and more than 270,000 compiled family histories.

Library of Congress, Genealogical Room, Thomas Jefferson Annex, Washington, DC - http://lcweb.loc.gov/rr/genealogy/

U.S. National Archives and Records, Washington, DC - www.archives.gov/index.html

U.S. National Archives Library, College Park, Maryland - www.archives.gov/research_room/genealogy/index.html

National Genealogical Society Library, Arlington, Virginia - www.ngsgenealogy.org

New England Historic Genealogical Society Library, Boston, Massachusetts (Specializes in data about New England and NY, and the states to which they migrated.) - www.newenglandancestors.org

Daughters of the American Revolution Genealogical Library, Wash., D.C. - www.dar.org/library/library.html

Palatines to America National Library, Columbus, Ohio (ancestors from all German-speaking lands) - www.palam.org

New York Public Library, New York, New York - www.nypl.org

Newberry Library, Chicago, Illinois - www.newberry.org

Allen County Public Library, Ft Wayne, Indiana - www.acpl.lib.in.us

> Become familiar with local libraries, historical and genealogical societies, and Family History Centers in your area.

Use state and national resources after you have thoroughly explored what is available to you locally which will save you time and money.

DAR Library - http://dar.library.net

Daughters of the American Revolution library, one of the largest genealogical libraries in the world, is an essential destination when researching your family history. Since its founding in 1896, the library has grown into a specialized collection of American genealogical and historical manuscripts and publications.

Repositories of Primary Sources - www.uidaho.edu/special-collections/other.repositories.html

A listing with Internet links of over 5300 websites describing holdings of manuscripts, archives, rare books, historical photographs, and other primary sources for the research scholar.

LibDex - www.libdex.com

An easy-to-use index to 18,000 libraries worldwide, library home pages, Web-based library catalogs, Friends of the Library pages and library e-commerce affiliates.

African American Roots

Many people have interesting challenges in doing ethnic research. This may be particularly true of African American research. However, many African Americans, believing they are descendants of slaves, falsely assume that records relating to the lives of their ancestors are non-existent. This is not necessarily the case today due to the availability of new information on the Internet and the compilation of records by thousands of people.

Freedman's Bank: A New Era in Black Genealogy - www.heritagequestonline.com

Freedman's Bank Records is a unique searchable database documenting several generations of African Americans immediately following the Civil War. You can access the Heritage Quest database for free using your local subscribing library online (and your library card), or access Heritage Quest for free at your local Family History Center. Or you can search the records for free at http://search.labs.familysearch.org >*View All Collections.* You can also purchase the CD for a nominal fee at www.ldscatalog.com > (do a quick search for *Freedman*). $6.50

Congress chartered the Freedman's Savings and Trust Company in 1865 with the primary objective to assist former slaves and African-American soldiers with their new financial responsibilities. Ideally, this bank would be a permanent financial institution for savings deposits only and assist families with the challenges they faced in their transition from slavery to freedom. It was also designed to provide a place, safe from swindlers, to deposit money while individuals learned personal finance management skills. But mismanagement and outright fraud caused the bank to collapse in 1874, dashing the hopes and dreams of many African Americans. Bank deposits totaling more than $57 million were tragically lost.

Reginald Washington of the National Archives and Records Administration said, *"An idea that began as a well-meaning experiment in philanthropy had turned*

A Rosetta Stone

William Alexander Haley, chairman of the Alex Haley Center, said,

"The Freedman's Bank records may be more than just an historical record. They may be the Rosetta Stone – the piece that allows you to go in and make the connection."

It's difficult for us who are not the descendants of slaves to fully comprehend the sense of pain and loss of identity for African-Americans from this bleak time in history. We have never tried to piece together our ancestry from families who howled in pain as they were sold away from each other. Or who cannot find their grandparents in a census because they were considered only a possession. Or had no surname except for one they borrowed from a 'master' who claimed them as property.

However, we can take comfort in knowing that there are no wounds too great for Divine healing, and that the Lord can transform devastating failure into healing blessings.

into an economic nightmare for tens of thousands of African Americans."

A Silver Lining

Now, nearly 140 years later, there is a silver lining to the disaster. In an effort to establish bank patrons' identities, bank workers at the time recorded the names and family relationships of account holders, sometimes taking brief oral histories. Many of the records documented family relationships and relatives who were sold into slavery to other locations. In the process, they created the largest single repository of lineage-linked African-American records known to exist.

It contains more than 480,000 names, documenting several generations of former slaves. Remarkably, the records of an institution that caused so much pain among African Americans following the Civil War now hold keys for their posterity to discover their roots. For the 8 to 10 million Americans who have ancestors whose names are recorded in the Freedman Bank Records, these records now cast a new light on their ancestry.

FreedmensBureau.com -
www.freedmensbureau.com

U.S. Freedmen Bureau Records of Field Offices, 1865-1872. This database contains African-American records relating to the Freedmen's Bureau from the following field offices: Washington, D.C., Florida, Georgia, New Orleans, North Carolina, Tennessee, and Virginia. Information available in the database includes: name, record type, year, and field office location.

Afro-American Historical and Genealogical Society - www.aahgs.org

Strives to preserve African-ancestored family history, genealogy, and cultural diversity by teaching research techniques and disseminating information throughout the community. Their primary goals are to promote scholarly research, provide resources for historical and genealogical studies, create a network of persons with similar interests, and assist members in documenting their histories.

African-American Genealogy Group -
www.aagg.org

A valuable resource for searching African-American roots.

Cyndi's List.com - www.cyndislist.com

Perhaps the best known index website; lists over 265,000 links to sites to help you with research; over 180 different categories. Contains hundreds of links to websites for doing African American research (search

"African American"). The general site links are categorized as follows: General Resource Sites; History & Culture; How To; Libraries; Archives & Museums; Locality Specific; Mailing Lists, Newsgroups & Chat; Maps, Gazetteers & Geographical Information; Military; Newspapers People & Families; Professional Researchers, Volunteers & Other Research Services; Publications, Software & Supplies; Records: Census, Cemeteries, Land, Obituaries, Personal, Taxes and Vital; Slavery; and Societies & Groups. Each category is helpful, but the "How To" category helps you find a place to get started.

Footnote African-American Collection -
http://go.footnote.com/blackhistory

View more than a million photos and documents from the National Archives found nowhere else on the internet. These newly digitized records provide a view into the lives of African Americans that few have seen before and cover subjects including slavery, military service, and issues facing African Americans dating back to the late 18th century. These records will help you to better understand the history and sacrifice that took place in this country.

AfriGeneas.com - www.afrigeneas.com

A searchable database of surnames for researching families of African ancestry. They offer a guide to family history resources around the world, and a mailing list of information about families of African ancestry. They also have impressive links to other websites to do research.

African American Cemeteries -
http://africanamericancemeteries.com

Listing of African American cemeteries created by the Millenium Project Coalition.

Christine's Genealogy Website -
www.ccharity.com

An excellent site about African-American history and genealogy.

Guide to Black History -
http://search.eb.com/blackhistory

Encyclopedia Britannica's *Guide to Black History* features a timeline, Eras in Black History; a numerous collection of articles; related Internet links to history, culture, literature and music; and a study guide.

National Archive Resources -
www.archives.gov/genealogy/heritage/index.html

Directory of web links to African-American resources.

Articles at Ancestry.com > *Featured Collections (scroll down) > African American Family History* -
www.ancestry.com/learn/ContentCenters/content Center.aspx?page=AfricanAm&sp=articles

Dr. Roseann Hogan has written a 3-part series of articles called *African American Research.* She says

that searching for African American families involves two distinct research approaches which correspond to the change in the legal status of African Americans in the U.S. before and after the Civil War. The first two articles discuss basic and general research techniques. In the third article, several case studies are presented to illustrate useful resources in building an African American family history. These case studies show that it is possible to discover precious information on African American families.

African American Research Guide -
www.familysearch.org > *Research Helps > Articles*

FamilySearch and the Family History Library have developed a comprehensive, 18-page *Research Guide* about African American research: *Finding Records of Your Ancestors: African American 1870 to Present.* This publication explains the best ways to search public records to find African American ancestors as well as U.S. ancestors of any heritage. Covering 1870-present, it explains the most useful records for that time frame, provides an introduction to basic research tools and strategies for finding records, and gives a

3 Add New Branches

> Begin at home to find information about yourself and work back one generation at a time.

Research Tip

Interview relatives for family history stories. Enter the information that you have gathered on a pedigree chart, family group record and research log. Join an African American genealogical society. Learn about African American history and the records that are available to you.

3 Add New Branches

case study that illustrates each step of the research process.

You can download and print it online for *free* at www.familysearch.org. Click on the *Research Helps >Articles* button on the top bar, click on *Sorted by Title* in the left hand column; find *African American: Finding Your Ancestors* and click on *PDF*. They also offer a 6-page *Quick Guide to African American Research* at the same web site location. It describes strategies for discovering your ancestors in various periods of history, the most useful records and indexes to search, and specific information you need to trace your ancestors.

Slave Voyages.org - www.slavevoyages.org

The Trans-Atlantic Slave Trade Database has information on almost 35,000 slaving voyages that forcibly embarked over 10 million Africans for transport to the Americas between the sixteenth and nineteenth centuries. It offers a chance to rediscover the reality of one of the largest forced movements of peoples in world history. It documents the slave trade from Africa to the New World from the 1500s to the 1800s. The names of 70,000 human cargo are also documented (slaves' African names).

MySlaveAncestors.com - www.myslaveancestors.com

A small resource center by professional genealogists who understand the needs of beginning researchers. They offer a sound strategy for tracing your African-American roots, plus some professional help if you desire.

Lowcountry Africana.net - http://lowcountryafricana.net

This free site focuses on records that document the family and cultural heritage

of African Americans in the historic rice-growing areas of South Carolina, Georgia and extreme northeastern Florida, home to the rich Gullah/Geechee culture. It will be a treasure trove of primary documents, book excerpts and multimedia for exploring and documenting the dynamic cultural and family heritage of the Lowcountry Southeast.

Afro-Louisiana History and Genealogy - www.ibiblio.org/laslave

A free site providing information on 100,000 Louisiana slaves 1719-1820 compiled by Gwendolyn Midlo Hall, Ph.D.

Documenting the American South - http://docsouth.unc.edu

This rich site from the University of North Carolina is especially strong on the African-American experience, including such collections as The Church in the Southern Black Community, Colonial and State Records of North Carolina, and North American Slave Narratives. It provides access to texts, images, and audio files related to southern history, literature, and culture. It currently includes twelve thematic collections of books, diaries, posters, artifacts, letters, oral history interviews, and songs.

Afriquest.com - www.afriquest.com

A new free database (beta) for African and African American genealogy and history which is a cooperative volunteer effort by The USF Africana Heritage Project, WeRelate, and IDEAS4.

Hispanic / Latino Americans

There are lots of great resources for tracing your Spanish language heritage family roots and stories especially in Spain or Latin American countries. Tens of millions of Spaniards emigrated from Spain to Mexico, Puerto Rico, Central and South America, Latin America, North America and Australia. Tracing your Hispanic roots may, eventually, lead you to Spain, where genealogical records are among the oldest and best in the world.

Mexico Research Guide - www.familysearch.org > *Research Helps > Articles*

The Family History Library has also developed a comprehensive 68-page *Research Outline* about Mexican family history records to search.

Cyndi's List of Hispanic Sites - www.cyndislist.com/hispanic.htm

Catalog of genealogical sites arranged by topic and country. Includes web links to Internet sites; mailing lists; people and families; news groups; publications, and transcriptions of records; societies; and villages, and colonies.

Suggested Activities

■ Regardless of your ethnic background, historical events affected the lives of your ancestors, and learning about those events can help you in your family history search. Using the dates and places on your pedigree chart, create a simple time line that shows some of the historical events that your ancestors may have experienced, such as the Civil War, or the Great Depression.

■ Locate history books about those events that will help you better understand the lives and experiences of your ancestors. For African American research, three main historical eras influenced African American records:

• Civil War and Reconstruction (1861-1877)

• Segregation (1896-1954), and

• Civil Rights Movement (1954-1970).

Mexico GenWeb - www.rootsweb.com/~mexwgw

Index of helpful genealogical sites arranged by region and country.

Hispanic Genealogical Resources - www.genealogiahispana.com

Directory of Hispanic web links in Spanish and English.

Hispanic Genealogy.org - www.hispanicgen.org/links.html

Valuable web links to Hispanic genealogy by the Colorado Society of Hispanic Genealogy.

Historical Map Collection - www.davidrumsey.com

The David Rumsey Historical Map Collection has over 18,460 maps online. The collection focuses on rare 18th and 19th century North American and South American maps and other cartographic materials which can be used to trace your family roots.

Spain and Latin America Archival Guide - http://aer.mcu.es/sgae/index_censo_guia.jsp

In Spanish.

3 Add New Branches

Hispanic Roots Television -
www.rootstelevision.com > Hispanic
Genealogy (right hand column)

An online television
network featuring on-
demand videos
absolutely free.
The Hispanic
Roots Channel features free genealogy family
history videos focused on Hispanic, Latino,
South American, and Mexican research.

Society of Hispanic Ancestral Research -
http://home.earthlink.net/~shharmembers/net
working.htm

A non-profit all-
volunteer organiza-
tion with the specific
goal of helping
Hispanics research their family history.

Genealogy of Mexico - http://members.
tripod.com/~GaryFelix/index1.htm

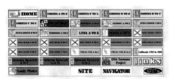

A comprehensive
resource of Spanish
genealogy information
including lists of
soldiers and settlers
serving in expeditions as far back as 1519, conquis-
tadores serving under Cortez, and names of the
first Spanish settlers in California.

Native Americans

The history and heritage of the Native Americans
who inhabited the American continent is a
significant part of the American story. Some
people want to trace their Indian family roots
and stories to learn more about from whom and
where they came. Some may want to become
a member of a federally recognized tribe. Others
may just want to verify a family tradition that
they descended from an American Indian.

Searching for American Indian ancestors has
become much easier today, but much of the
information may be inaccurate or incomplete.
First, determine the tribal affiliation of your

ancestor(s), and do some basic homework on
tribal history. Then, search for your ancestor in
official records created by the numerous Indian
agencies. These are the primary sources for
documenting that your ancestor was recognized
by the federal government as a member of a tribe.

How to Trace Indian Ancestry -
www.doi.gov/ancestry.html

U.S. Department of
Interior's website
on tracing your
Indian ancestry.

Indians.org - www.indians.org

List of federally
recognized U.S.
tribes and
locations.

Carolyne's Genealogy Helper -
www.angelfire.com/tx/carolynegenealogy

Valuable articles
and a blog by
a professional
genealogist on
tracing your Native American roots.

Cyndi's List.com - www.cyndislist.com >
Native American

Numerous links
to web sites for
tracing your
Native American
family roots.

Native American Genealogy -
www.accessgenealogy.com/native

Free message boards,
searchable Indian
rolls, and maps.

American Indian Help Center -
www.amerindgen.com

Native American
Indian help for all

tribes for beginners and experienced researchers.

Footnote.com Native American -
www.footnote.com $$$

Footnote is an online repository for original historical documents. Some areas are free, while others can be freely searched and then viewed with a paid subscription. They have nearly 900,000 Native American records currently. Free at Family History Centers.

Native American Internet Index -
www.hanksville.org/NAresources

Directory of web links and blog for Native American web sites.

Asia Web Sites

Map Resources - http://geography.about.com/od/findmaps/u/maps.htm

The Internet is home to a vast collection of world maps, country maps, state maps, city maps, street maps, road maps, physical maps, political maps, and every type of map possible. This page provides resources for maps along with information to learn how to best use maps and map tools.

Cyndi's List.com - www.cyndislist.com/asia.htm

Numerous links to web sites for tracing your Asian family roots and history.

Early Arrivals Records -
http://casefiles.berkeley.edu

Online searchable index to casefiles for early immigrants to San Francisco and Hawaii. You

won't find the actual case files on this website; you will have to travel to the NARA office in San Bruno, California to see the records themselves.

Asian-American Web Links -
www.archives.gov/genealogy/heritage/index.html#asian

From the National Archives and Records Administration.

AsiaGenWeb - www.worldgenweb.org > AsiaGenWeb

Part of the WorldGenWeb, this site links to genealogical information sources in 26 Asian countries.

Angel Island.org - www.angelisland.org

Describes the processing of Asian immigrants through Angel Island in San Francisco Bay. Learn the history of this California port and locate and search passenger lists.

Chinese Americans - www.angel-island.com

An oral history of Chinese American detainees.

Japan GenWeb -
www.rootsweb.ancestry.com/~jpnwgw

This web site contains links to Japanese genealogical web sites in English, Spanish and Japanese. Research on Japanese family heritage can also be done according to Japanese prefecture.

Japanese Research -
www.genealogy.com/00000376.html

Contact information, web sites, and books to assist in Japanese genealogy research.

Other Ethnic Resources

JewishGen.org - www.jewishgen.org

Searchable data bases for Jewish given names in fifteen nineteenth century European regions, including links to the new local vernacular names adopted in ten foreign countries. Thus, for each European region, these databases include the Hebrew, Yiddish, and local and other-European-country secular names used, as well as new names in foreign countries. These databases of linked European and foreign- country given names allow Jewish genealogists to define all of the Jewish and vernacular names which an ancestor may have used in Europe and in his new country of immigration. Their *Family Tree of the Jewish People* contains data on over 3 million people.

Jewish Shoah Foundation Holocaust Survivors - http://college.usc.edu/vhi

An archive of nearly 52,000 videotaped testimonies from Holocaust survivors and other witnesses videotaped in 56 countries and in 32 languages.

Jewish Holocaust Memorial -
www.yadvashem.org

Yad Vashem, Jerusalem, is the Jewish people's memorial documenting the history of the Jewish

people during the Holocaust period, preserving the memory and story of each of the six million victims. Contains 68 million pages of documents, nearly 300,000 photographs along with thousands of films and videotaped testimonies of survivors, and 112,000 titles in many languages, and thousands of periodicals.

Center for Jewish History - www.cjh.org

A Jewish historical and cultural institution to foster Jewish knowledge and to make the historical and cultural record of the Jewish people readily accessible to scholars, students and the broad public.

Jewish Genealogy Publisher -
www.avotaynu.com

The leading publisher of products and information of interest to persons who are researching Jewish genealogy, Jewish family trees and Jewish roots.

Jewish Cemetery Association - www.jcam.org

Provides free access to more than 50,000 Jewish names for genealogy searches or visitation information. You may search by individual name (first or last).

National Archive Resources -
www.archives.gov/genealogy/heritage/index.html

Directory of web links to various ethnic resources. Includes: United Kingdom and

Ireland; Australia and New Zealand; Canadian and French-Canadian; Eastern European and Russian; Hispanic: Central and South America, Mexico, Caribbean, West Indies; Jewish; Western European; and more.

Cyndi's List.com - www.cyndislist.com > *Topical Index > Ethnic Groups and People*

Numerous links to web sites for tracing many Ethnic heritages.

Federation of East European Family History Societies - http://feefhs.org

An umbrella organization that promotes family research in eastern and central Europe without any ethnic, religious, or social distinctions. It provides a forum for individuals and organizations focused on a single country or group of people to exchange information.

Russian & East European Studies - www.ucis.pitt.edu/reesweb

Directory of Internet resources for the Balkans, the Baltic states, the Caucusus, Central Asia, Central Europe, the CIS, Eastern Europe, the NIS, the Russian Federation, and the former Soviet Union.

Directory of Irish Genealogy - http://homepage.tinet.ie/~seanjmurphy/dir

Information, links, FAQ, advice, and articles about tracing Irish ancestors.

WorldGenWeb.org - www.worldgenweb.org

A non-profit, volunteer based organization dedicated to providing genealogical and historical

records and resources for world-wide access.

Additional Ways to Do Research Online

Here are additional ways to do research, gather information, and share your family roots, stories, photos, and heritage using the Internet.

Social Networking Sites

One of the Newest Connection Tools

Social networking refers to a class of web sites and services that allow you to connect with friends, family, and colleagues online, as well as meet people with similar interests or hobbies. At these web sites you can connect with your family, swap stories and recipes, share family photos, and build collaborative family trees. You and your extended family can collaborate and share information on your shared family tree. Some of the sites use advanced technologies like wikis (type of website that allows you to add, remove, and sometimes edit the available content), RSS (timely updates or web feeds from favored websites that you subscribe to), mapping, and online family tree building to help you connect with your family and ancestors. All of these family history social networking sites have great appeal, wonderful capabilities, and are private and secure. Here are the most popular social networking sites to explore.

Geni.com - www.geni.com

This free, simple interface allows you to create a family tree online and then invite family members to join the family tree and add other relatives. Family members can share photos and work together to create profiles for common ancestors. New features including video sharing and tree merging. Combined with existing features such as photo sharing, calendar, timelines, and news, the site provides a complete suite of free tools for families to build their family tree, preserve their history, and stay in touch in a private, secure environment.

FamilyHistoryLink.com - www.familyhistorylink.com (beta)

Free family service to connect with other researchers and preserve your family history. A one stop location to get everything that is happening with your family members including status updates, news, blog posts, photos, videos and more. You can organize your family and find and connect with other family members, upload and organize all your family photos and view photos from the rest of your family, build or upload your family tree and share it with your family, email your entire family and stay updated with everyone.

We're Related - http://tinyurl.com/75f6rk

A free application on Facebook (owned by FamilyLink.com) to help you stay in touch with your families through photo sharing, a news feed, birthday reminders, etc. You can also build your family tree.

MyFamily.com - www.myfamily.com

In a secure, password-protected environment, you can create online family photo albums, share family news, maintain a calendar of family events, and more. There's also a toll-free phone number to record your family stories and memories.

The basic site is free which includes uploading 100 MB per member per month (with unlimited storage space) and complete backup protection. You can upgrade for extra features such as: Ad-free, professionally-designed and customizable themes, your custom domain, and 1 GB per member of monthly uploads (10x more than basic) for only $29.95 per year total.

MyHeritage.com - www.myheritage.com

A host of free genealogy tools enable you to create your family's own meeting place on the Internet where you can share family photos, post your family tree online, trace the family's medical history and keep track of important family events. Plus, free genealogy software and a genealogy search engine help you expand your family history research. Home to more than 28 million family members, 5 million family trees, and 300 million profiles available in 34 languages.

GeneTree.com - www.genetree.com

A DNA-enabled networking site designed to help people understand where their personal histories belong within the greater human genetic story. Creates unparalleled opportunities for unlocking genetic heritage and identity, connecting with ancestors and living relatives, and sharing meaningful information and experiences to help preserve family histories. You can build and collaborate on family trees, and share digital videos, photos and memories. This site also offers a genealogy DNA testing service, and notifies you of a DNA connection with others in the database, providing the opportunity to make a connection with that individual if you wish.

Genes Reunited.com -
www.genesreunited.com

The UK's no.1 family tree and genealogy site with over 9 million members. It's free to build your family tree online, search for your ancestors in 500 million names in family trees, census, birth, marriages, death and military records, and send messages to other members to discover a shared family history and find new relatives.

Our Story.com - www.ourstory.com

Allows you to create a visual timeline, collaborate with family and friends, and document every moment of your loved ones' life with video, pictures, and story-telling. The site also offers ways to share with anyone you want and backup these memories on CD, DVD and books.

WeRelate.org - www.werelate.org

Wiki-based Web site—sponsored by the Foundation for On-Line Genealogy in partnership with the Allen County Public Library—allows you to easily create profile pages for your ancestors. Others can view these pages and add information, ornadd profiles for their own ancestors. Source citations and scanned images of original documents can be added to document the information.

KinCafe.com - www.kincafe.com

A free family network to connect, bond and cherish loved ones. You can build and link family trees together, remember birthdays and anniversaries, share your photo albums, family calendar, blogs and other family treasures with all who care most. You manage whether to allow your friends and relatives to see your family's content.

Famiva.com - www.famiva.com

This free social network for families offers a secure, password protected place for you and your relatives to connect and collaborate. You can share photos and stories, work together to build an online family tree, explore family maps, and more.

Mailing Lists
Share Info with Others with a Common Interest

RootsWeb Mailing Lists -
http://lists.rootsweb.ancestry.com

Mailing lists are free discussion groups where individuals with a common interest share information with each other by e-mail. All subscribers can send e-mail to and receive e-mail from the list. There are thousands of family history / genealogy mail lists. This is the oldest and largest index of family history mail lists (about 30,000 currently) which is organized in categories: Surnames, USA, International, and Other.

Newsgroups
Discussion Groups with Common Interest

Discussion groups are stored on the Internet until you request the messages. There are dozens of newsgroups and tools that will search these messages. For more information, see the following web pages:

www.rootsweb.com/~jfuller/gen_use.html
www.genhomepage.com/communications.html
www.cyndislist.com/newsgrps.htm

Surnames and Family Associations

Individual Family Surnames

RootsWeb Surname List -
http://rsl.rootsweb.com

Allow users to register the surname they are currently researching. By checking these lists, searchers often find others looking for the same surnames. Every day, dozens of connections are made between relatives using these lists. Contains over 1,200,000 surnames.

Finding Your Ancestors -
http://genealogy.about.com/library/weekly/aa041700a.htm

A guide to internet search techniques for the surnames in your family tree. There are many wonderful family history Web pages on the Internet which remain undiscovered because people just don't know how to locate them. These pages may contain just the valuable information that you are looking for - family trees, stories, photographs, cemetery transcriptions, wills, etc.

Suggested Activities

- Review the information you already have on your pedigree chart to help you decide what new information to look for.

- Use your computer to network with others who may be working on the same family line you're working on.

- Verify the information you find online because it may not always be correct.

Surname Finder - www.surnamefinder.com

Providing easy access to resources for 1,731,359 surnames.

Queries

Requests for information about a specific ancestor, couple, or family. Besides accepting queries, most sites allow you to search the queries left by others. These include www.usgenweb.org, www.genforum.com, and www.query.genealogytoolbox.com.

Help (or Lookup) Lists

USGenWeb.org - www.usgenweb.org

Provides e-mail addresses of people for each county in the U.S. willing to look up information for you at no charge. These are volunteers who do quick searches in various books, records, and record offices as a public service.

Random Acts of Genealogical Kindness -
http://raogk.org

A global volunteer organization with over 4000 volunteers in every U.S. state and many international locations have helped thousands of researchers. Their volunteers take time to do everything from looking up courthouse records to taking pictures of tombstones. All they ask in return is reimbursement for their expenses (never their time) and a thank you.

CHAPTER 4

3-Easy Steps
Follow These 3-Easy Steps to Begin Building Your Family Tree and Connect to Your Ancestors

STEP 3 - Connect With the Lives of Your Ancestors

DISCOVER YOUR FAMILY HERITAGE, STORIES, AND PHOTOS

Family history is more than just names and dates. You should learn more about who your ancestors really were, where they lived, and what they did. You should try to gain information and an understanding of each of your ancestors if possible. Finding your roots and stories helps you gain a sense of belonging, and an understanding of who you are and where you come from.

The Internet is the perfect tool for opening a window to the past and connecting with the lives and stories of your ancestors. Discover more than you ever imagined about the lives of your ancestors that made you who you are today.

INSIDE THIS CHAPTER:

4 Connect with Ancestors

Suggested Activities

1. Consider ways your family can best honor and pay tribute to your ancestors and inspire your children to know them.

2. Establish a new tradition in your family for honoring your ancestors which can be perpetuated from generation-to-generation.

3. Create a timeline of one or more of your ancestors lives combined with historical events to get to know the times in which they lived.

4. Visit the cemetery and gravesite of an ancestor(s) to better connect with them.

Family History Insights - 4

Alex Haley

Knowing Who You Are

"Knowing who you are and what responsibility you have towards your family forces your behavior to be consistent with your family values. It passes right down across the generations." Alex Haley, press conference, Freedman's Bank CD, 2001

Daniel Webster

Connecting the Past with the Future

"Those who do not look upon themselves as links connecting the past with the future do not perform their duty to the world." Daniel Webster (1782-1852), statesman

George Washington

The Graciousness of Heaven

"The success, which has hitherto attended our united efforts we owe to the gracious interposition of Heaven. And to that interposition let us gratefully ascribe the praise of victory, and the blessings of peace." George Washington, "To the Executive of New Hampshire, Nov. 3, 1789," *Writings*, 30:453

Boyd K. Packer

Find the Time to Connect to Your Ancestors

"There somehow seems to be the feeling that genealogical work is an all-or-nothing [activity]. That is not so. Genealogical work is [a hobby] for every [one]. And we may do it successfully along with all the other responsibilities that rest upon us. ... You can fulfill your [ambition to trace] your kindred dead...without forsaking your other responsibilities. ... You can do it without becoming a so-called 'expert' in it.

There is an old Chinese proverb which states: 'Man who sits with legs crossed and mouth open, waiting for roast duck to fly in, have long hunger.' Once we started, we found the time. Somehow we were able to carry on all of the other responsibilities. There seemed to be an increased inspiration in our lives because of this work. But the decision, the action, must begin with [you]. ...

The process of searching...[is] worth all the effort you could invest. The reason: You cannot find names without knowing that they represent people. You begin to find out things about people. When we research our own lines we become interested in more than just names. ... Our interest turns our hearts to our fathers—we seek to find and to know and to serve them." Boyd Packer, Bookcraft, 1980, pp. 223-30, 239-40

Monte J. Brough

I Felt a Connection with My Ancestors

"Spiritual blessings do come to people who are involved in this [family history] work! ... Thirty-five years ago I was...in England. My mother had been pursuing her grandmother's family history, but she knew nothing more than that her grandmother had been born in a little place called Philly Green, England. My mother had never been able to locate this town. ... As I was driving...I saw a little sign that said "Philly Green." Several weeks later, I returned and drove down a winding country lane until I came to a quaint little village with a church that had been built in 1174. I went out into the cemetery and looked at each headstone. During the next few hours, I had the privilege of finding the headstones of my great-grandmother's family members. I'll never forget how I felt that day standing in that cemetery in that beautiful place in England. I felt a connection with my ancestors, particularly with my great-grandmother, who as a seventeen-year-old girl left her family in England and moved to [America]. What a great experience! This kind of joy really can come to every[one]." Monte J. Brough, *Ensign*, Dec. 1994, 16

Connect With the Lives of Your Ancestors

DISCOVER YOUR FAMILY HERITAGE, STORIES, AND PHOTOS

Published family histories can help you make connections between generations. Timelines of your ancestor's lives in context with historical events–along with photographs of the times in which your ancestors lived–can provide an interesting perspective and add life to your story. Historic newspapers and periodicals provide unique insight and a rare opportunity to understand the culture and customs of how your ancestors lived. Online gazetteers (geographical dictionaries) and place databases help you discover the geographic location of the place your ancestors called home–their village or town and cemetery.

Discovering your ancestor's health history can be a useful tool to aid you in interpreting patterns of health, illness and genetic traits for you and your descendants. Learning how to care for your precious photos will help preserve the past for future generations. And perhaps discovering that you descended from royalty or related to someone famous may just 'make your day'.

Finding your family roots–and the stories, values and traditions about your ancestor's lives–can help you better understand them.   But it also helps you better understand yourself, and gives you a

Benefits of Connecting With the Lives and Stories of Your Ancestors

- **Knowledge** of your forebears will increase
- **Better Understand** your ancestors and yourself; the opportunity to learn more about your kindred dead will bless lives
- Gain a **Greater Appreciation** of your heritage, the sacrifices your ancestors made for you, and a better understanding of what their life was like
- **Gain Strength** from learning about how your ancestors met challenges in life
- Unite, weld, and **Strengthen Bonds** between family members forever; your family will grow closer
- Promote a **Sense of Belonging** that ties generations together, and foreshadows your belonging in the eternal family of God; your desire and willingness to honor your beloved ancestors prepares you to belong to Him who is our Father
- **Discover** within yourself a reservoir of patience, endurance, and love that you will never find without the deep commitment that grows from a sense of real belonging
- Gain a **Sense of Identity and Purpose in Life**
- Draw yourself and your family **Closer to God**
- Your ties with the eternal world suddenly become very real, **Sharpening Your Life's Focus** and lifting your expectations
- Exerting such immovable loyalty to your forebears teaches you how to love– indeed, how to be **More Christ-like**

greater appreciation of your heritage and the sacrifices they made for you. Many of your ambitions and challenges in life are the same as theirs. You gain strength from learning about how your ancestors met life's troubling challenges.

Doing family history work helps unite your family, and strengthens bonds between your family members. Knowledge of your forebears will increase, your family will grow closer, families will be strengthened, and the opportunity to learn more about your kindred dead will bless lives. As you learn more about your ancestors, you weld eternal family links, and draw yourself and your family closer to God. It's a wonderful opportunity to find your family identity. And help promote that identity in your children and grand children.

Appreciating Your Heritage

Reflecting on the Past

Who were your ancestors? Each of us has hundreds of thousands of ancestors as part of our unique heritage. And each and every one of your ancestors had to exist in order for you to exist. Each one of them and everything they were have contributed to your being. Their genes are in you; their blood runs in your veins. You not only inherited their genes, but many of their physical traits, values and attitudes have been passed down to you from one generation to another showing up in the way you look, think, and act. The choices made by your ancestors over the generations have influenced the way you live and think. In many ways, your ancestors have affected your life and molded your destiny. They are a part of who you are today. It took thousands of years of people having children with the right person at the right time to get to your existence.

Your ancestors are more than just a bunch of lifeless names and dates on a chart. They made a huge difference in who you are. And still do! But it is strange how little most of us know about them or the times in which they lived. Most certainly, many of your ancestors lived a life of deprivation and hardship. Most of them sacrificed much for their posterity. Many left behind beloved family members, plush homelands, and previous possessions to come to often a barren, undeveloped strange land so that their descendants could have a better life. By tracing your own family roots and stories, you can come to appreciate your heritage more and more, and know and honor your forefathers as you discover what their lives were like.

Some people find great joy in discovering an ancestor's diary, journal or letter to help find their roots and collect their family traditions and stories. But usually it's the small bits of information from many different sources that help bring your ancestors to life. Everyone has his own unique history and family stories. And finding your family roots and treasured stories is one of the most meaningful ways you can honor your ancestors. You can honor those who have gone before by learning more about them and following in their footsteps. And you should be grateful for the rich abundance you enjoy today because of their great sacrifices and efforts. They helped forge a life that is so much better for you than anything they might have even dared dream about for themselves.

They deserve your recognition and honor for the determination and fortitude they portrayed in leaving the comfort of their home and emigrating to the New World to forge a new life. Your ancestors labored long and hard, built their own home with their own bare hands, and raised a family and created their own livelihood. They became pilgrims and pioneers and cowboys who etched out a new life for themselves. They had great dreams and aspirations which wielded a profound influence on the future, just like you. You should honor your forbears for who they were, what they accomplished, and even the mistakes they made. One of the great lessons—maybe the principal lesson—of doing family history is learning from the mistakes of your ancestors. Tracing your family roots and connecting to your ancestors can be one of the most intellectually stimulating, absorbing, and fulfilling ways you will ever find to spend your valuable time.

Tools to Help Reflect on the Past

Here are some good tools that may help bring your ancestors to life. They can help you gain an insight into understanding their heritage, lifestyle, traditions, and what it was like "way back when".

Generation Maps.com -
www.generationmaps.com $$$

An easy to use, very affordable, genealogy chart design and printing service. They offer personalized working charts, beautiful decorative charts, custom heirloom charts, and a printing service for charts you've created. Now you don't have to fill in a chart yourself – just send your genealogy computer file and/or your digital photos, tell them how you want it to look, and it arrives on your doorstep for a very reasonable price. They can help you get your research out where you can see it and surround your family with a sense of their heritage. It's also a wonderful, easy way to explain to your family members the research that has been accomplished.

Making of America -
http://moa.umdl.umich.edu and
http://moa.cit.cornell.edu/moa

This is a joint project between the University of Michigan and Cornell University which provides free access to a large collection of 19th century books, journal articles, and imprints available on two websites. Two separate online archive sites put digitized books at your fingertips. The first collection contains some 8,500 books and 50,000 journal articles; the second site covers

267 monograph volumes and more than 100,000 journal articles.

Library of Congress - www.americaslibrary.org

The Library of Congress in Washington, DC is the largest library in the world and has millions of amazing things that will surprise you. This is a site that teaches American history in a manner that is appealing to both adults and older children. Their **"America's Story"** section contains many documents, letters, diaries, records, tapes, films, sheet music, maps, prints, photographs, digital files, and other materials from the past, and wants you to have fun with history while learning at the same time. They want to show you some things that you've never heard or seen before. You can look at pictures of American inventors, listen to Thomas Edison's voice extracted from an early recording, watch vaudeville acts filmed about 100 years ago, and even watch a film clip of Buffalo Bill Cody's Wild West show made in 1902. Their **American Memory Collection** at http://memory.loc.gov/ammem offers more than seven million digital items from more than one hundred historical collections.

Reminisce.com - www.reminisce.com $$$

A nostalgia magazine, written by its readers from around the country and published bi-monthly. Advertising-free with real-life stories and family album photos—recalling times from the Roaring Twenties to the Fabulous Fifties—take a trip down memory lane. A magazine that brings back the good times. $14.98

Everyday Life Book Series -
www.writersdigest.com $$$

Everyday Life in Colonial America from 1607-1783 describes home

life, agriculture, cooking, transportation, dealing with the natives, and details about their courageous struggles to carve out a new life for themselves in North America. (Dale Taylor, Writers Digest Books, Cincinnati, Ohio, 2002). $16.99

Everyday Life in the 1800s discusses homes, furniture, travel, money, occupations, health and medicine, amusement, courtship and marriage, slavery, crime, and cowboy life out West. (Marc McCutcheon, Writers Digest Books, Cincinnati, Ohio, 2001) $16.99

Everyday Life during the Civil War describes many aspects of life in both the North and South, including housing, clothing, military uniforms, weapons and insignia, camp life, newspapers, etc. (Michael J. Varhola, Writers Digest Books, Cincinnati, Ohio, 1999) $16.99

Honoring Your Ancestors

To honor means to regard with great respect; to have an attitude of admiration or esteem; any expression of respect or of high estimation by words or actions; to revere; to manifest the highest veneration for in words and actions.

We honor our ancestors for many reasons but also because they were brave, courageous men and women who fought stalwartly. During the American Revolutionary War they were outnumbered, outgunned, and ill-equipped, yet they successfully defeated the greatest military and naval power of the 18th century. Our forefathers believed that "all men are created equal, that they were endowed by their Creator with certain unalienable rights, that among these are life, liberty and the pursuit of happiness." They believed in consent of the governed, the right to bear arms and self-defense, and in limited interference by government.

They were good people who believed in the sovereignty and guardianship of Almighty God. Their motto became *"In God We Trust"* which was declared on all of our national coins. All of the Founding Fathers of our nation shared in common a belief that a people cannot maintain liberty

without dependence upon the Almighty.

Thomas Jefferson (1743-1826), Founding Father, 3rd President

When Jefferson penned the Declaration of Independence he mentioned God twice. Before Congress would sign it, members insisted on two more references to God. Thus, these four instances appear: the *Author of nature* and nature's laws; the *Creator* who endowed in us our rights; the *Judge* to whom we appeal in witness that our motives for independence spring from a dear love of liberty and a deep sense of our own proper dignity; and *Providence,* to declare that God is on the side of Liberty, and that those who trust in liberty will therefore prevail.

The words of one of our patriotic American hymns, *America* (My Country, 'tis of Thee), by Samuel Francis Smith reflects this vision:

Samuel Francis Smith (1808-1895), Baptist Minister, journalist, author

Our fathers' God to Thee,
Author of liberty,
To Thee we sing.
Long may our land be bright
With freedom's holy light;
Protect us by Thy might,
Great God our king.

We honor best those who have gone before when we serve well in the cause of right and truth. We should walk as they walked and embrace the truths they believed. It is not enough to just care for their grave sites and monuments. We should emulate their lives...and their faith.

Once you get to know your ancestors, you invariably develop a sense of belonging to them. So it's natural to want to pay tribute to and honor them. Many of us may lovingly write a family history or plan a family reunion which helps us reach out to others and ensure that the memory of our ancestors will survive. But there are countless ways you can pay tribute to the value of the precious insight and wisdom of those who have gone before us.

Ancestor Feast

© Intellectual Reserve, Inc.

Here's an idea to honor your departed ancestor on the anniversary of their birth or death–have an ancestor feast. Set an extra plate at the table, lit by a candle, and surrounded by a photo of your ancestor. Serve that person's favorite dishes, their signature recipes, or foods that reflect their cultural heritage. What were some of the special dishes they made that left a lasting impression on you? Have your children help in selecting and preparing foods for this commemoration. The flavors and aromas associated with a relative's favorite foods are a concrete way to keep memories alive. And if not an entire meal, baking or cooking something just like mom, dad, or grandma did can be just as effective a way to pass something of that person along to your own children.

Plant a Memory Garden

Here's a lovely and lasting tribute. Plant a small garden in honor of an ancestor. Consider having a small tree, such as a Japanese maple or weeping cherry as the centerpiece. Designate an annual ritual of adding something to the garden in the late spring or early summer of each year. If space allows, place a bench near this garden for sitting, meditating, and remembering.

How Would You Like to Be Honored?

Someday, each of us will be someone's ancestor. How would you like to be honored? Is it enough to just keep up the gravestones and monuments to our ancestors? That must undoubtedly be done, but it's only a part of the honor that we owe to our gallant ancestors. What would honor them the most of all?

Reverend John Weaver from the Freedom Baptist and Dominion Ministry wrote: *"The greatest honor that we could bestow upon our ancestors is to follow them in their faith, maintaining their cause, and fighting for the same truths and principles they tenaciously held. The greatest honor my grandchildren and great grandchildren can bestow upon me is to follow in the faith, principles, and truth that I communicate and teach."* (Pastor John Weaver - Freedom Baptist and Dominion Ministry; www.virginials.org/honoring.htm)

Megan Smolenyak's Books -
www.honoringourancestors.com

Megan Smolenyak has been an avid genealogist for 30 years. She was the lead researcher for the PBS *Ancestors* series, and did most of the research for PBS's *They Came to America.* She is skilled in many aspects of family history research, and is the author of several best-selling books on family history, including:

Honoring Our Ancestors
In Search of Our Ancestors
They Came to America: Finding
*   Your Immigrant Ancestors*

In her book, *Honoring Our Ancestors,* Megan discusses ways in which different cultures honor their ancestors and heritage. You'll find stories of people who built a Viking ship and sailed across the Atlantic, devoted decades to collecting slavery memorabilia, passed a diaper down through four generations, conducted ancestral scavenger hunts, and painted an 80 by 30 foot mural. She offers suggestions on many possible ways to creatively honor and pay tribute to our own ancestors and learn to appreciate our heritage. The heartwarming stories found in her book will inspire you in your quest for your own roots.

We should honor the ancestors who touched our lives and to pay tribute to the loving people who came before us. And we can help inspire our children to honor our ancestors so that they can also gain strength from the past.

Timelines and History

Add Life to Your Family Story

Timelines are chronological listings or graphics of historical events. Timelines are a great visual way to put all your historical research into perspective and discover the "rest of your family's story", but can also help you identify gaps where you may need more information on your ancestor's life. You may want to place each ancestor in a timeline at least once in every decade of their lives using some kind of official documentation. See if a major world event or disaster may have affected the lives of your ancestors. Check out these exciting software tools to help you quickly and easily create and customize historical timelines. Historical events help you place your ancestor's lives in context with history so you can get to know the times in which they lived.

Genelines -

www.progenygenealogy.com/genelines.html $$$

A powerful research and story-telling tool, lets you SEE your ancestor's lives in time. By bringing together elements of time, history and family relation-ships on visual timeline charts, Genelines can bring your family history to life, and even help you find new directions for your family. Different versions of the

software let you use the visual timeline charts with various popular genealogy software programs, including Legacy, Ancestral Quest, Family Tree Maker, Personal AncestralFile and GEDCOM. $29.95

Timeline Creator.com -

www.timelinecreator.com $$$

See history unfold with this easy-to-use software that enables you to easily and efficiently create historic timelines. You add you own events, choose fonts and icons, and add clipart images if you wish. $29.95

Timeline Maker.com -

www.timelinemaker.com $$$

A robust software application to build quality timeline charts instantly. Features include: Unlimited chart themes/styles, seamless integration with Microsoft PowerPoint®, exclusive sharing capabilities, and output to a range of graphic files, PDF and HTML. Not specifically designed for genealogy, though many do use it for that. $49.95 download.

OurTimeLines.com - www.ourtimelines.com

This site helps you create free, person-alized timelines for your ancestors that show how their life fits into history. You can generate as many timelines as you like, and if you're into creating your own family web site, you can insert the timelines into your own pages.

TimeLine Tool -

www.learningtools.arts.ubc.ca/timeline.htm

This free web-based template from the University of British Columbia allows you to

quickly construct an interactive timeline with audio and visual effects. It uses built in Flash (animation), PHP and XML.

WhoWhatWhen Timelines -
www.sbrowning.com/whowhatwhen/index.php

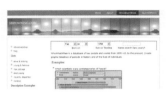

A database of key people and events from 1000 A.D. to the present which allows you to create graphic timelines of periods in history and of the lives of individuals for free.

U.S. Twentieth Century Timeline -
http://history1900s.about.com/library/weekly/aa110900a.htm

A free decade-by-decade timeline of the entire U.S. 20th century.

Din Timelines.com - www.din-timelines.com

A large world history timeline that follows the rise and fall of civilizations all over the world, from circa 5000 BC, to the 1940s.

Time Capsule: On This Day in History -
www.dmarie.com/timecap

What was it like back then? Go to this website and learn what happened on any date. They currently have data online for the years 1800 through 2005, although data for the years 1800 - 1875 may be spotty. You can select specific headlines, birthdays, songs, TV shows, toys, and books for the selected date.

World History.com - www.worldhistory.com

A new free social history web site that offers interactive maps, timelines, videos, geocoded photos, museum artifacts, genealogy and much more. Their goal is to compile the history of the world and display it in such a manner that people of all ages and backgrounds can be interested in history. Both the content and the manner in which that content is displayed are unique. It's organized as events, people, groups, places, and artifacts; all of which can be interconnected, and displayed in unison; the content originates from www.wikipedia.org, visitors who join, museums, historical societies, and other organizations. Visitors can upload GEDCOM files which will geocode the information, and display it on an ancestor map and timeline. This gives a unique perspective of your own personal history. Not only can you see your ancestors on a map with a timeline, but you can see the nearby events that occurred and the famous contemporaries of your ancestors. You can then share with others, create biographies for your ancestors, attach your ancestors to historical events, and add artifacts and other family heirlooms to events and people. They will also allow other websites to use the data found on this website for free.

Mayflower History.com -
www.mayflowerhistory.com

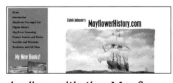

The Internet's most complete, thoroughly researched and accurate web site dealing with the *Mayflower,* the Pilgrims, and early Plymouth Colony.

Finding Mayflower Families -
www.genealogymagazine.com/finmayfam.html

An excellent magazine article on how to do

research on your pilgrim ancestors. Several good books are mentioned, to help further your study.

eHistory.com - www.ehistory.com

Serves up more than 130,000 pages of historical content, 5,300 timeline events, 800 battle outlines, 350 biographies and thousands of images and maps. A favorite resource here for Civil War buffs is, incredibly, the searchable 128 volumes of *The War of the Rebellion: A Compilation of the Official Records of the Union and Confederate Armies.* This series is the authoritative reference to army operations during the Civil War.

HyperHistory.com - www.hyperhistory.com

An interactive combination of lifelines, timelines, and maps covering over 3,000 years of world history, plus numerous web links to other sites.

Best of History Web Sites.net - www.besthistorysites.net

An award-winning portal that contains annotated links to over 1000 history web sites (the best sites for Prehistory, Ancient/Biblical History, Medieval History, American History, Early Modern Europe, World War II, Art History, Oral History, and maps) as well as links to hundreds of quality K-12 history lesson plans, history teacher guides, history activities, history games, history quizzes, and more.

How Old Was I When ...? - www.frontiernet.net/%7Ecdm/age1bd.html

Do you need help putting your life into perspective? Go to the *Age Gauge* and enter your

own birth date. You'll quickly learn how much older or younger you are than assorted celebrities, how old you were when Kennedy was assassinated, when man first walked on the moon, etc.

Online Sources for European History - http://eudocs.lib.byu.edu/index.php/Main_Page

These free links from BYU library connect to European primary historical documents—ancient, medieval, renaissance, and modern times—that shed light on *key historical happenings* within the respective countries and within the broadest sense of political, economic, social and cultural history.

Western History Photography Collection - www.photoswest.org

This searchable selection of over 120,000 images from the collections of the Denver Public Library and the Colorado Historical Society documents the history of Colorado and the American West. Bring your Old West family history to life with scenes of American Indians, pioneers, railroads, mining, frontier towns, ranch life, scenery, news events and more.

Library of Congress.com - www.loc.gov

The Library of Congress is the nation's oldest federal cultural institution, and serves as the research arm of Congress. It is also the largest library in the world, with more than 119 million items on approximately 530 miles of bookshelves. The collections include more than 18 million books, 2.5 million recordings,

12 million photographs, 4.5 million maps, and 54 million manuscripts. The Library's mission is to make its resources available and useful to the Congress and the American people and to sustain and preserve a universal collection of knowledge and creativity for future generations.

America's Story Online -
www.americaslibrary.org

The Library of Congress has millions of amazing things that will surprise you. This is a site that teaches American history in a manner that is appealing to both adults and older children. The Web site contains many documents, letters, diaries, records, tapes, films, sheet music, maps, prints, photographs, digital files, and other materials from the past, and wants you to have fun with history while learning at the same time. They want to show you some things that you've never heard or seen before. You can look at pictures of American inventors, listen to Thomas Edison's voice extracted from an early recording, watch vaudeville acts filmed about 100 years ago, and even watch a film clip of Buffalo Bill Cody's Wild West show made in 1902.

American Memory Collection -
http://memory.loc.gov/ammem

Perhaps you're curious to look at the world through your ancestor's eyes. Thanks to the *American Memory Collection* of the Library of Congress, now you can. This site offers more than seven million digital items from more than one hundred historical collections.

More Library of Congress

Catalogs, Collections, and Research Services - http://lcweb.loc.gov/library

Online Exhibitions - http://lcweb.loc.gov/exhibits

Economic History -
http://eh.net/hmit/ppowerusd

To determine the value of an amount of money in any year compared to another.

Manuscript Collections -
http://lcweb.loc.gov/coll/nucmc/nucmc.html

National Union Catalog of Manuscript Collections.

Daughters of the American Revolution.org -
www.dar.org

A volunteer women's service organization dedicated to promoting patriotism, preserving American history, and securing America's future through better education for children.

Sons of the American Revolution.org -
www.sar.org

A historical, educational, and patriotic non-profit corporation that seeks to maintain and extend the institutions of American freedom, an appreciation for true patriotism, a respect for our national symbols, the value of American citizenship, and the unifying force of e pluribus unum that has created, from the people of many nations, one nation and one people.

American Civil War - http://sunsite.utk.edu/civil-war and www.cwc.lsu.edu

A comprehensive portal to everything

about the civil war dedicated to preserving America's cultural heritage.

Civil War Soldiers and Sailors -
http://www.itd.nps.gov/cwss

CWSS is a database and historical information about servicemen who served on both sides during the Civil War; a cooperative effort by the National Park Service and partners. It enables you to make a personal link between yourself and history.

U.S. National Archives.gov - www.archives.gov

The National Archives and Records Administration (NARA) is America's national record keeper. It is the archives of the Government of the United States that is responsible for safeguarding records of all three branches of the Federal Government. NARA provides ready access to essential records of what the Federal Government does--why, how, and with what consequences.

UK National Archives -
www.nationalarchives.gov.uk

UK government records and information; 180,000 microfilm and microfiche, and 300,000 commercial trade catalogs.

National Archives Online Catalogue -
http://catalogue.pro.gov.uk

Ellis Island.org - www.ellisisland.org

Contains some 22 million immigration records from 1892-1924 available for free searching.

You'll find passenger records, original manifests, and ship information, often with a picture, giving the history and background of each ship that brought the immigrants. *(See more details in Chapter 3.)*

The Smithsonian Institution Libraries -
www.sil.si.edu

The most comprehensive museum library system in the world unites 20 libraries into one system supported by an online catalog. The Libraries offers its treasures to the nation through book exhibitions, lectures, special tours, and a well-designed public website. Collections include: 1.5 million printed books, of which 40,000 are rare books, 2,000 manuscripts, 180,000 microfilm and microfiche, and 300,000 commercial trade catalogs.

Color Landform Atlas -
http://fermi.jhuapl.edu/states/states.html

You can also view new U.S. maps and imagery that have never before been posted to the internet. You will see 3-D maps, high resolution maps, registered maps, as well as maps of Mars, Europe, Asia, all of the continents, and more.

U.S. Census Bureau.gov - www.census.gov

Serves as the leading source of quality data about the nation's people and economy.

U.S. Citizenship and Immigration Services -
http://uscis.gov

The History, Genealogy and Education section

provides interesting information about immigration history, about immigration in our history and about how to find out more about immigrant relatives.

Ancestry.com - www.ancestry.com > *Search* $$$

You can search their vast *Historical Records, Stories and Publications, Photos and Maps,* and *Other Resources* databases. You can also search the Allen County Public Library's famous periodical database, *Periodical Source Index, the Genealogical Library Master Catalog,* bibliographic references to over 200,000 family histories, genealogies, town and county histories, and other records held by libraries across the United States. There is a fee to become a member. Available free at regional Family History Centers.

U.S. Geological Survey - http://geography.usgs.gov

Confronts some of the most pressing natural resource and environmental issues of our Nation. Observing the Earth with remote sensing satellites, geographers monitor and analyze changes on the land, study connections between people and the land, and provide society with relevant science information to inform public decisions. Geographic names information.

Photographs, Videos and Scrapbooking

Preserving the Past for Future Generations

Google's Photo Organizer - http://picasa.google.com

Find, organize and share your photos. Picasa is a *free* software download from Google that helps you: Locate and organize all the photos

on your computer, edit and add effects to your photos with a few simple clicks, find, organize and share your photos.

PicaJet.com Photo Manager - www.picajet.com

Award winning digital photo album software with powerful sharing features. PicaJet offers direct import from your camera, image sharing via email or Web gallery, automatic photo enhancement, personal ratings and categories, as well as printing features. The photo organizer allows you to view your images by rating, keyword, or date/timeline and you can categorize your images by simple drag and drop. In addition, it offers editing features to correct red-eye, cropping, image sharpening, and level adjustment. Additional features include direct CD/DVD burning, an image search engine, slide show maker, and a tool to generate a Web gallery.

Easy Media Creator - www.roxio.com $$$

Besides helping you transfer your old records and tapes onto CD, DVD, iPod, or PSP it can also help you edit videos, make calendars, postcards, and help you get the most out of your digital videos, music and photos. $79.99

Dead Fred.com - www.deadfred.com

The original online orphaned-photo site has grown to more than 89,000 old pictures and over 10,000 surnames. Your ancestors might be waiting for you here.

Ancient Faces.com - www.ancientfaces.com

A visual genealogy website that has thousands of old photos that adds a face to your lists of names and dates.

Genealogy Photo Archive -
http://genealogyregister.com

A free genealogy database of family photos containing online vintage photographs. Many of these photos have been submitted by visitors to help you find your ancestors and surnames. Others were found in antique stores and flea markets, and posted here in hopes of reuniting them with family members. Your ancestors could be among these genealogy photos.

Family History Photo Gallery -
http://jsmagic.net/kith

A gallery of free family history graphics and photos for your own family web site and other uses.

Caring for Your Collections -
www.loc.gov/preserv/careothr.html

Need advice on the care of books, photos, videos, and other media in your collections? The Library of Congress site contains publications that answer many questions about the care, handling and storage of your valuable collections.

Talking Story.com - http://talkingstory.com

A professional video service that assists you in preserving your loved one's important memories and stories for generations to come on Video and DVD. The service is high quality and low pressure. They work with you and/or you loved ones to ensure that the process and the product are wonderful keepsakes.

Family Photoloom.com -
www.photoloom.com $$$

A dynamic web application that connects your photos, genealogy, stories, and documents to create truly seamless family history. You can organize your pictures around your family history (and into albums), index family relationships, and tag faces and resource documents. You can literally browse your pictures by simply clicking on an individual and every picture of him/her will appear in the portrait window. Plus it helps protect your family photos and documents from loss or damage by storing them on secure servers to give you security and peace of mind. Private, safe and secure. Unlimited image uploads and invited guests. 5GB storage space. Free trial. $39/year.

Newspapers and Periodicals
What Was Their Life Like?

Historical newspapers, magazines and other periodicals can open a window to the past about the lives of your ancestors, and are excellent sources of information about their heritage and stories. They provide a wonderful, untapped resource for events not recorded elsewhere, and affords you a rare opportunity to understand the times in which your ancestors lived and their daily activities.

For example, *obituaries* may include place and date of birth, names of siblings, parents, and other surviving relatives, occupation, and military service. *Society news* columns may include such tidbits as birthdays, job promotions, wedding announcements, and personal news. You might find in *public announcements* information on forced land sales, professional services, runaway slaves, and missing relatives. *Legal notices* may include proving of wills, divorce proceedings, proving of heirs, and the settlement of estates. *Military news* and *school news* are additional columns that you should also consider.

Historical newspapers can also add context through the breaking news of the day, gossip columns or local news, entertainment listings, and advertisements. Don't forget to evaluate the information you find against that provided from other sources.

Google Historical News Search -
http://news.google.com/archivesearch

Google enables you to search through more than 200 years of historical newspaper archives. Their News Archive Search provides an easy way to search and explore historical archives, and create a timeline of selected stories from relevant time periods arranged chronologically. These are web links to articles on other sites, both free and subscription. You may want to use *Advanced Search* to narrow the results.

GenealogyBank.com -
www.genealogybank.com $$$

Search over 127 million historical newspaper articles and find obituaries, marriage notices and often surprising facts about your ancestors. With more than 2,500 historical newspapers, you'll find not only names, dates, places and events, but also learn about the everyday challenges and moments of triumph that defined the lives of your ancestors. You can search for free, but you need to subscribe ($9.95) to view the details. New content added monthly.

NewspaperArchive.com -
www.newspaperarchive.com $$$

Access to more than 93 million historical newspaper pages for the U.S., Canada, United Kingdom, Ireland, Denmark, Germany, South

Africa, and Japan, including rare content from small towns, currently over 1,000 million articles, over 3 billion names. Membership is required. $9.99/month or $59.99 annually.

WorldVitalRecords.com -
www.worldvitalrecords.com $$$

Exclusive access to the Small Town Newspaper Coll-ection, a searchable digital archive that features small-town newspapers back to 1846. They currently offer over 1 million pages and adding more than 100,000 pages each month. $14.95/month

U.S. Newspaper Program -
www.neh.gov/projects/usnp.html

A cooperative national effort among the states and the federal government to locate, catalog, and preserve on microfilm newspapers published in the United States from the eighteenth century to the present. You can access the database through participating libraries across the country.

Library of Congress - www.loc.gov/rr/news

An extensive newspaper collection of over 9,000 U.S. newspaper titles, 25,000 non-US newspaper titles, 7,000 current periodicals, 6,000 comic books, and 1 million government publications.

Godfrey Memorial Library -
www.godfrey.org $$$

Offers access to many historic newspapers, including the London Times, 19th century US

FamilySearch.org - www.familysearch.org
>Library

This site offers thousands of microfilmed newspapers from around the world which can be ordered through your local Family History Center for free (small postage fee). Use the *Place Search* button in the Family History Library Catalog for your ancestor's location to find what newspapers and other records have been microfilmed.

Ancestry's Newspaper Collection -
www.ancestry.com/newspapers $$$

You can search a large collection of digitally available, large and small newspapers beginning in the early 1800s and some extending into the 2000s. Membership is required. $19.95/month. Free trial.

The Olden Times.com -
www.theoldentimes.com

Historic newspapers online for free from the 18th to 20th century from the U.S., England, Scotland, Ireland, and Australia. Search for your surnames in the index and click on the link to complete scanned copies.

Grave Sites / Obituaries / Death Records

Visiting cemeteries is a very rewarding part of connecting with the lives of your ancestors.

newspapers, and early American newspapers.

Your ancestor's tombstone is one of the few remaining physical evidences of the life they lived. There is nothing in discovering your family roots and stories that will connect you to your ancestor more than to stand in the one place on earth which contains their mortal remains, and to touch their gravestone inscription. It is an once-in-a-lifetime, inspiring experience. Check out these free cemetery and obituary listings.

Find a Grave.com - www.findagrave.com

Find the graves of ancestors, create virtual memorials, add 'virtual flowers' and a note to a loved one's grave, etc. Browse descriptions and photos of graves of thousands of famous people from around the world. The site also lists over 12 million grave records.

Tombstone Transcription Project -
www.rootsweb.ancestry.com/~cemetery

Volunteers from across the U.S. have uploaded transcriptions and photos from thousands of cemeteries.

DeathRecords ObituarySearch.com -
www.deathrecordsobituarysearch.com

Complete and accurate official U.S. death records and obituary records; more than 300 million records.

DeathIndexes.com - www.deathindexes.com

A directory of links to websites with online death indexes, listed by state and county. Included are death records, death certificate indexes, death notices & registers, obituaries, probate indexes, and cemetery & burial records.

National Archives.gov -
www.archives.gov/research/alic/reference/vital-records.html

Hot links to vital records collections at the National Archives.

Interment.net - www.interment.net

The most popular resources for finding a lost burial.

Maps, Charts & Geography

Mapping Your Ancestry; Discover the Place Your Ancestors Called Home

Google Maps - www.maps.google.com

A popular, free web mapping service that offers street maps (U.S., Australia, Canada, Japan, New Zealand, and Western Europe), satellite maps for the whole world, and a hybrid map (a combination of satellite imagery with an overlay of streets, city names, and landmarks). It's easy to use and offers options for customization. It's easy to locate current places (including small towns, libraries, cemeteries and churches), but they're not historic listings. You just enter keywords, and you see the results as markers on a map. You can search for cities, states, landmarks, or even types of businesses. Their *My Maps* feature allows you to create your own personalized maps. You can plot multiple locations on a map; add text, photos and videos; and draw lines and shapes. You can then share these maps with others via email or on the Web with a special link.

Generation Maps.com -
www.generationmaps.com $$$

The next generation of online genealogical charts. Pick out the chart you want from decorative to work charts, upload your genealogy files and/or digital photos, and it arrives on your doorstep. Janet Hovorka also has a genealogy blog at http://thechart chick.blogspot.com.

Community Walk.com -
www.communitywalk.com

A free website that allows you to create your own personal maps using Google Maps. You can add location markers and route markers, upload lots of photos and videos for each location, display content from other websites, leave comments, and show your map on a website or blog.

TriggerMap.com - www.trippermap.com

A web service that allows you to put a flash based world map on your own website or blog. It automatically searches your photos at the free Flickr photo service for location information and plot the photos on your own map, on your own website. It works well for documenting family history travels and vacations. The free version is limited to 50 locations.

Family Atlas - www.rootsmagic.com $$$

Family Atlas software is a fun and easy way to map your family history. Trace your ancestor's migration around the world and pinpoint the sites of important family events. Import your family data directly from your genealogy software, then automatically add markers to create personalized maps. Print maps or save them to several graphics formats.

USGS Gazetteer -

http://geonames.usgs.gov/pls/gnis/web_query.gnis_web_query_form

Enter a place name to find out where it is located. Also has other uses, such as finding the location of every church, school, or cemetery in a particular county.

Color U.S. Landform Atlas -

http://fermi.jhuapl.edu/states/states.html

You can view new maps and imagery that have never before been posted to the internet. You will see 3-D maps, high resolution maps, registered maps, as well as maps of Mars, Europe, Asia, all of the continents, and more.

USGenWeb - www.usgenweb.com

Contains resources and queries for a specific state or county in the USA.

Bureau of Land Management -

www.glorecords.blm.gov

The Official Federal Land Patent Records Site provides access to Federal land conveyance records for the Public Land States, and image access to more than two million Federal land title records for Eastern Public Land States, issued between 1820 and 1908. Land east of the Mississippi that wasn't in one of the original colonies belonged to the U.S. government and was sold originally to the first settlers.

U.S. City Directories.com -

www.uscitydirectories.com

City Directories, arguably one of the most over-looked resources by genealogists, have been around since the 1700s. This web site attempts to identify all printed, microfilmed, and online directories, and their repositories, for the United States. Sponsored by Genealogy Research Associates.

Worldwide GenWeb - http://worldgenweb.org

Resources and read/post queries that relate to a specific country.

Zip Code Lookup - www.usps.com

Find a ZIP+4 Code for an address or all cities in a zip code.

Canadian Genealogy Centre -

www.genealogy.gc.ca

Genealogical resources in Canada. The Centre contains the complete updated integration of genealogical content from the former Web sites of the National Archives of Canada, the National Library of Canada and the Canadian Genealogy Centre. It is a single window providing access to genealogical resources in Canada.

ArchiviaNet -

www.collectionscanada.ca/archivianet/0201_e.html

The National Archives of Canada's online research and consultation tool provides access to a variety of information resources related to

the actual archival holdings. It allows a number of different means of exploration of the fonds and collections by offering the option of searching by theme or by type of document.

National Library of Canada -
www.nlc-bnc.ca/genealogy/index-e.html

A wealth of published materials of interest to genealogists researching their Canadian ancestors. Collections include published histories of Canadian families and communities, transcriptions and indexes of parish registers, cemetery records, Canadian newspapers and directories, journals of Canadian genealogical and historical societies, genealogical reference tools, government publications including genealogical data, and much more.

Places in Canada - www.johncardinal.com/ca

This site includes place information and mapping resources for 28,898 places in Canada. You

Be sure to note *when* medical conditions occur. For example, did Grandpa have diabetes as a child, or did it develop later in his adult life?

Privacy Concerns

Remember to respect everyone's privacy as you gather medical information. The information is only for you, your health care professional, and your descendant's use. You shouldn't publish this information as part of your family web site.

How To Begin a Medical Pedigree

Start by writing down what you already know. Write down the health facts for yourself, and then go back one generation at a time. Consider recording the following information:

- Birth and death dates
- Cause of death
    - Ethnic background (some genetic diseases occur in particular ethnic groups)
    - Birth defects
    - Major illnesses such as cancer, heart disease, diabetes, etc.
    - General patterns of ill health, like respiratory problems
    - Chronic health problems like asthma, diabetes, or high blood pressure
    - General health routines (smoking, diet, overweight, etc.)
    - Allergies (food-related and environmental)
    - Emotional problems (depression, heavy drinking, anxiety, etc.)
    - Vision and hearing problems

can review a list of place names by province or territory. From there, you can navigate to a link to locate a place using Google Maps, Live Local, MapQuest, or Yahoo! Maps.

Geographical Names of Canada -
http://geonames.nrcan.gc.ca/index_e.php

Toponyms, or geographical names, are used by us all every day - to describe our surroundings and to tell others where we have been or where we plan to go. When we use maps we expect the names to help us identify features of the landscape, and perhaps even to throw light on the local history of an area. This site is the

Sources of Information

Sources for medical information can include your memory, your living relatives, and medical records. For deceased ancestors, search the following resources:

> Death certificates (dates and cause of death)
> Obituaries
> Pension and insurance documents
> Social Security applications
> Family bibles
> Diaries
> Old letters, etc.
> Military records

national data base to provide official names of mapping and charting, gazetteer production, and World Wide Web reference, and other geo-referenced digital systems.

Quebec Family History Society -
www.cam.org/~qfhs

A Canadian non-profit organization to foster the study of genealogy among the English speaking peoples of Quebec.

Canada GenWeb -
www.rootsweb.com/~canwgw

Contains resources and read/post queries that relate to a specific province or county in Canada.

UK Family History Online.net -
www.familyhistoryonline.net $$$

The Federation of Family History Societies (FFHS) which operates this pay-per-view site is

an international organization, established in the UK as a non-profit charitable company. It represents, advises and supports over 220 family history societies and other genealogical organizations world-wide, with a total Membership of over 180,000. Its principal aims are: to co-ordinate and assist the work of societies or other bodies interested in family history, genealogy and heraldry; and to foster the spirit of mutual co-operation, by sponsoring projects in these fields.

UK Origins.net - www.origins.net

Genealogy search for English, Scots and Irish origins, and is becoming recognized as a good web resource for genealogy in the British Isles.

Suggested Activities

■ Create a medical pedigree chart by listing the names of your ancestors, the illnesses from which they died, along with the dates of onset of the illnesses, and their death dates.

■ Talk to your living relatives about what they remember the causes of death were for your ancestors.

■ Verify the information they give you and find additional information for your medical pedigree by gathering death certificates. Copies of death certificates can usually be obtained through the public records office in the area where the death occurred.

■ Look around your house for other records that will help you build a medical pedigree such as obituaries, insurance documents, hospital records, etc.

4 Connect with Ancestors

Genealogy of the United Kingdom and Ireland - www.genuki.org.uk/big

Resources for England, Scotland, Wales, Ireland, Channel Islands and the Isle of Man.

European Search Engine: NedGen - www.nedgen.com

Trace your roots in Europe with this search engine dedicated to indexing personal homepages with online family trees in Europe.

East European Family History - http://feefhs.org

The Federation of East European Family History Societies is a very large collection of materials for people with ancestry in Eastern Europe.

Genealogy of Denmark - www-personal.umich.edu/~cgaunt/dk.html

Resources relating to Denmark.

Danish-American Genealogical Society - www.danishgenealogy.org

Danish immigration, genealogy books, photography, history, etc.

Four-generations of medical information are usually sufficient for genetic counseling.

Privacy Concerns

- Gather medical information on living as well as deceased members of your family. Information from your horizontal line (brothers and sisters, aunts, uncles and cousins) may be as important as information from your vertical line (parents, grandparents, and great-grandparents).

- Don't rely on family members' accounts of causes of death or illnesses in the family; document as much information as you can.

- Treat the information that you gather with discretion.

- Consult a physician or a genetic counselor if you have questions or concerns about the information you find in your family's medical history.

Distant Cousin.com - www.distantcousin.com/Links/Ethnic/Danish.html

A good directory of links to Danish genealogy.

Court, Land and Financial Records

Add Interest to Your History

Court and land records, wills and other financial documents are those kept by town, county, and state officials regarding property owned, sold or bequeathed to others.

4 Connect with Ancestors

Bureau of Land Management - www.blm.gov

The Official Land Patent Records Site. This site has a searchable database of more than two million Federal land title records for Eastern Public Land States, issued 1820-1908, including scanned images of those records indexing the initial transfer of land titles from the Federal government to individuals.

World Vital Records.com -
www.worldvitalrecords.com

A collection of various court, land, and probate records. Membership is required, but is free at Family History Centers.

Public Records Online - www.netronline.com

Links to available state & county Tax Assessors' and Recorders' offices. Online public records may include copies of deeds, parcel maps, GIS maps, tax data, ownership information and indexes. Some Recorders' offices have marriage and birth records available online.

Tracing Your Medical Heritage

A Useful Tool in Your Life

Tracing one's medical heritage is gaining more interest for people everywhere. What runs in your family? Long life? Twins? Blue eyes? Curly hair? Large nose?

Perfect health? Cancer? Heart disease? Many of the factors that determine your health today were inherited from your ancestors. For some people, the answers to these questions can literally be a matter of life and death.

For example, what if both of your parents died of heart disease or cancer and you pieced together a medical family history that showed deadly cancers or heart disease going back several generations on both your mother's and father's lines. Or perhaps some of your family lived long active lives well into their 90s, and it was not unusual on another side of your family for some to pass away in their 60s. Why the difference? What caused their deaths? Are there common health characteristics in family lines? What does this mean to you and your descendants?

The information on your medical pedigree can show doctors not only what to look for, but exactly where to look, and may help provide preventive treatment to save your life. Experts say that about 3,000 of the 10,000 known diseases have genetic links, and that many diseases "run in families," including colon cancer, heart disease, diabetes, alcoholism and high blood pressure. Creating a family health history can be a useful tool to aid you and your health care provider in interpreting patterns of health, illness and genetic traits for you and your descendants.

Family Health History: Medical Genealogy

Learn how to get started creating your own medical family tree to help determine your genetic predisposition to certain diseases, genetic traits and more. Trace your family's medical history and become better informed about health conditions that may affect your own health and that of your loved ones with help from these websites:

http://genealogy.about.com/cs/healthhistory
www.cyndislist.com/dna.htm
www.dcn.davis.ca.us/~vctinney/medical.htm

Organizing Your Health History

To organize your information, you can either enter it in your family history program as written text, or utilize special software program, such as *GeneWeaver,* (www.geneweaveronline.com) to create a medical genogram. A genogram is a schematic diagram of family relationships and diseases, which is used by your doctor to determine if there is a risk of inherited illnesses, which may lead to early detection and prevention.

Who knows, maybe the family health information you find today will help provide preventive treatment to save a life tomorrow.

Royalty and Nobility

Royal and Princely Families of the World

Records and other works about the genealogies, titles, and histories of the noble class: kings, dukes, duchesses, earls, etc.

Cyndi's List Royalty & Nobility -
www.cyndislist.com/royalty.htm

Web links to over 220 indexed web sites of royalty and nobility.

Wikipedia Biographies & Genealogies -
http://simple.wikipedia.org/wiki/Category: Royalty_and_nobility

Numerous web links to sites containing great biographies and genealogies of royalty.

Directory of Royal & Noble Genealogies -
www3.dcs.hull.ac.uk/public/genealogy/ GEDCOM.html

The genealogy of the British Royal family and those linked to it via blood or marriage relationships; contains the genealogy of almost every ruling house in the western world because of the inter-marriage that took place between them; over 30,000 individuals. It also contains the genealogy of the U.S. Presidents, and links to other royalty sites.

About.com Royal Families - www.about.com > *(search for royal genealogies and medieval history)* -or- http://historymedren.about.com/library/ who/blwwroyaldex.htm -or- http://genealogy .about.com/cs/royalgenealogies

Family trees and genealogy of kings, queens and royal families around the world; and Who's Who in Medieval History: Articles on Emperors, Kings, Princes, Dukes, Counts, Caliphs and others who governed cities, sovereign states, principalities or nomad nations.

The Crown of Russian Empire -
http://sunsite.cs.msu.su/heraldry

An introduction to the *Russian Royal House.* Here, you will find pictures of the Russian tsars as well as the genealogical tree of the family.

Non-European Dynasties -
www.almanach.be $$$

A compilation of about 2500 non-European Sovereign Families and rulers, such as the Emperors of China, Morocco, and Turkey (over 700 countries), available by subscription. $9.95/month

Antique Portrait.com -
www.antiqueportrait.com $$$

Contains prints for sell of original antique engravings spanning over 500 years and encompassing every major ruling family of Europe.

Nobility Royalty.com - www.nobility-royalty.com

The International Commission on Nobility and Royalty works to authenticate that one has a royal or noble bloodline, or that one is a true member of a royal family.

ABC Genealogy.com -
www.abcgenealogy.com/Royalty_and_Nobility

Website devoted to royalty and nobility in countries outside of Europe.

Heraldry and Arms

Coat of Arms, Family Crests and Emblems

The study of coats of arms–including the art of designing, displaying, and recording arms–is called heraldry. A coat of arms (or armorial bearings), in European tradition, is a design belonging to a particular person or group and used by them in a wide variety of ways. Historically, they were used by knights to identify them apart from enemy soldiers. Unlike seals and emblems, coats of arms have a formal description that is expressed as a blazon (or symbols). Today, coats of arms still continue to be in use by a variety of institutions and individuals. Nearly every nation in every part of the world has its own coat of arms. The American Great Seal is often said to be the coat of arms of the United States.

Intro to Heraldry -
http://genealogy.about.com/cs/heraldry/a/heraldry.htm -or-
http://genealogy.about.com/od/heraldry/Heraldry_Coats_of_Arms_and_Family_Crests.htm

Learn all about coats of arms and family crests, including which people were granted the right to bear arms, what the designs and colors mean, and how you can use heraldry to prove family relationships.

American College of Heraldry.org -
www.americancollegeofheraldry.org

Aids in the study and perpetuation of heraldry. Contains a lot of good information on heraldry and coats of arms.

College of Arms - www.college-of-arms.gov.uk

The official repository of the coats of arms and pedigrees of English, Welsh, Northern Irish and Commonwealth families and their descendants.

Learn more about heraldry and coats of arms, and help you locate your ancestor's coat of arms.

Rootsweb's Guide to Heraldry -
www.rootsweb.ancestry.com/~rwguide/ lesson19.htm

A good overview of heraldry (or armory) around the world.

Cyndi's List.com Heraldry -
www.cyndislist.com/heraldry.htm

Contains about 120 indexed web links to heraldry web sites.

Fleurdelis.com -
www.fleurdelis.com/coatofarms.htm

The meanings behind the symbols and a brief history of Heraldry.

Family Chronicle Article - http://family
chronicle.com/CoatofArms1.htm

Halvor Moorshead explains the process of obtaining legitimate armorial bearings: *Acquiring a REAL Coat of Arms - Parts I &II.*

Heraldry & Genealogy -
www.acpl.lib.in.us/genealogy/11heraldry.pdf

A document from the Allen County Public Library: Researching a coat of arms, guides and glossaries, with descriptions and illustrations.

Augustan Society.org -
www.augustansociety.org

An historical society working in the areas of European history, heraldry, genealogy and related fields. They maintain a Heraldry Collection including many rare books and pamphlets. In addition, the Society registers coats of arms and publishes a roll of arms.

Baronage Press - www.baronage.co.uk

A magazine devoted to genealogical and heraldic data.

British Heraldic Archive -
www.kwtelecom.com/heraldry

Heraldic Artist -
www.calligraphyandheraldry.com

The studio web site and gallery of Neil Bromley, a Heraldic Artist, Calligrapher, and Medieval Illuminator.

Heraldic Dictionary -
www.rarebooks.nd.edu/digital/heraldry/index.html

A dictionary to help understand written descriptions of armorials or coat of arms in order to identify the individual, family, or organization to which those arms belong.

Family History Insights - 4

Rex D. Pinegar
© by Intellectual Reserve, Inc.

The Seeds of Our Heritage

Etched in stone at the National Archives building in Washington, D.C., is this meaningful truth: *"The heritage of the past is the seed that brings forth the harvest of the future."* Two hundred years ago the seeds of our heritage were being planted by men and women of great spiritual drive and steadfastness of purpose. Seeds of devotion and willing sacrifice for a just cause, seeds of courage and loyalty, seeds of faith in God were all planted in the soil of freedom that a mightier work might come forth. In Richard Wheeler's *Voices of 1776* we read firsthand accounts of some of those who were engaged in this "planting" process. Their expressions stir our souls to a greater appreciation of the heritage we enjoy and upon which we must build. A young doctor of Barnstable, Massachusetts, recorded in his journal on the 21st of April, 1775, the following: *"This event seems to have electrified all classes of people … inspiriting and rousing the people to arms! to arms! … Never was a cause more just, more sacred, than ours. We are commanded to defend the rich inheritance bequeathed to us by our virtuous ancestors; it is our bounden duty to transmit it uncontaminated to our posterity. We must fight valiantly."* (Richard Wheeler, *Voices of 1776*, New York: Thomas Y. Crowell Co., 1972, pp. 33-34.) Rex D. Pinegar, "A Call to Arms," *Ensign,* Nov. 1975, 101

James E. Faust
© by Intellectual Reserve, Inc.

Unlock the Knowledge of Who You Really Are

"I encourage you...to begin to unlock the knowledge of who you really are by learning more about your forebears. ... Without this enriching knowledge, there is a hollow yearning. No matter what our attainments in life, there is still a vacuum, an emptiness, and the most disquieting loneliness. We can have exciting experiences as we learn about our vibrant, dynamic ancestors. They were very real, living people with problems, hopes, and dreams like we have today. In many ways each of us is the sum total of what our ancestors were. The virtues they had may be our virtues, their strengths our strengths, and in a way their challenges could be our challenges. Some of their traits may be our traits. ... It is a joy to become acquainted with our forebears who died long ago. Each of us has a fascinating family history. Finding your ancestors can be one of the most interesting puzzles you...can work on. James E. Faust, *Ensign,* Nov. 2003, 53

Just by Chance?

"Having been brought up in an orphanage, I knew very little about my family... [but] I wanted to...learn about my ancestors. One day, as I was preparing to go on a business trip to Canton, Ohio, I...called an older half-sister and asked her if she knew our grandparents' names and where they had been buried. She gave me their names and told me that when she was a child she would visit them in a town in Ohio called Osnaburg.... I was amazed because this was only a few miles from where I would be going. I was very excited...I said a prayer that I would be guided if there was anything for me to find. I found myself in front of a small cemetery.... I saw an elderly man coming toward me on the sidewalk. I walked up to him and told him about my search for the grandparents of Fanny and John Robert Gier. He directed me to a house in town. When I went there, I found a woman in her 80s, Gurtie Baker.... When I said my maiden name was Irene Gier, she began to cry. She said she knew Uncle Bobby had remarried and had other children but that she never expected to see any of them. It turned out her mother and my father were brother and sister. I left the home with pictures... of my father, all his siblings and his mother and father. She also gave me all their birth and death dates and told me where my grandparents were buried. Throughout the visit, she said several times, 'This didn't just happen by chance.' I agree." Irene Durham, Church News, 18 August 2007, 16.

CHAPTER 5

A Directory of Family History Software and Tools

Family history has become a real passion and big-time hobby for millions of people today all around the world. Alex Haley called it "a hunger, bone-marrow deep, to know our heritage". Family history helps you discover a sense of identity and family pride in your life. It can also help unite and strengthen bonds between family members.

Whatever your reason for tracing your own family roots and stories, genealogy software can become one of your most valuable and indispensable tools. Software helps you discover your ancestors, organize and store your information (such as family photos, scrapbooks, health and personal data, reunions, etc.), measure the progress of your research, share your information with family and friends, provide tons of tools to make it easier, and much more. Software programs today are fun and interesting for the whole family, and no longer just about names, charts, and graphs.

In this Directory, you'll learn where to find comprehensive reviews that will help you make an informed decision about which software is right for you. Selecting the right software program can make all the difference in how much satisfaction and information you will derive from your family history quest. And the right software will help make your journey fun and much easier.

Suggested Activities

1. Educate yourself about the different family history software programs available. Read the reviews herein of the various programs.
2. Try different free demos if you wish. Make a decision on which one(s) you want to purchase.
3. Go on a treasure hunt. Discover some of your buried treasure in the web sites provided.
4. Persevere in searching for your ancestors and understanding what their life was like.

5 Directory of Tools

Family History Insights - 5

Gordon B. Hinckley
© by Intellectual Reserve, Inc.

Increases Sense of Identity

As I learn more about my own ancestors who worked so hard, sacrificed so much, it increases my sense of identity and deepens my commitment to honor their memory. Perhaps there has never been a time when a sense of family, of identity and self worth has been more important to the world. Seeking to understand our family history can change our lives and helps bring unity and cohesion to the family." Gordon Hinckley, *Deseret News,* 17 Apr 2001

Woodrow Wilson

Know Where You Came From

"A nation [or family] which does not remember what it was yesterday, does not know what it is today, nor what it is trying to do. We are trying to do a futile thing if we do not know where we came from or what we have been about." Woodrow Wilson, 28th President of the United States (1913-1921)

Boyd K. Packer
© by Intellectual Reserve, Inc.

A Feeling of Inspiration

"Revelation comes to individual[s]...as they are led to discover their family records in ways that are miraculous indeed. And there is a feeling of inspiration attending this work that can be found in no other. When we have done all that we can do, we shall be given the rest. The way will be opened up." Boyd K. Packer, *Ensign,* Nov 1975, 99

No Progress Without Struggle

"If there is no struggle, there is no progress. Those who profess to favor freedom and yet renounce controversy are people who want crops without

Frederick Douglass

ploughing the ground." – Frederick Douglass (1818-1895), Abolitionist, author, statesman & reformer

John H. Widtsoe
© by Intellectual Reserve, Inc.

Help From the Other Side

"Those who give themselves with all their might and main to this work...receive help from the other side, and not merely in gathering genealogies. Whosoever seeks to help those on the other side receives help in return in all the affairs of life." John A. Widtsoe, *Utah Genealogical and Historical Magazine,* July 1931, p. 104

Lee Iacocca

Love Your Family

"No matter what you've done for yourself or humanity, if you can't look back on having given love and attention to your family, what have you really accomplished?" Lee Iacocca (1924-   ), former Chrysler CEO

Shall Not Have Died in Vain

"...that from these honored dead we take increased devotion to that cause for which they gave the last full measure of devotion – that we here highly resolve that these dead shall not have died in vain – that this nation, under God, shall have a new birth of freedom – and that government of the people, by the people, for the people, shall not perish from the earth." Abraham Lincoln, (1809-1865) Gettysburg Address

Abraham Lincoln

Which Software is the Best?

The most often asked question today by people interested in family history software is *"which one is the best?"* This question is difficult to answer because what is right for me may not work as well for you. Everyone has different needs and preferences. There may be features in a particular family history program that I may not use, e.g. web-site creation or multi-media scrapbooking, but may be very important to you.

Some people even use more than one program to meet their needs. For example, you may prefer a primary, heavy duty program for your everyday use, and a different program to generate well-designed charts. Each program has its own strengths and weaknesses; each program does certain things well and other things not-so-well.

And they are always changing and upgrading. New features and options are constantly being introduced. They offer a wide variety of options including the way they format data, the types of charts they print, their ability to help you organize your research, and their capacity to store photographs and documents. They can even assist you in your research by letting you keep a research log or to-do list right with your family data. With dozens of software programs, and hundreds of features available, which program(s) should I choose?

First of all – whether you're just starting out, or upgrading your existing software program – take some time and effort to make your decision; it's well worth it. You may want to consider making a list of features that you want or need, then prioritize that list to decide which are most important to you. As you gain more understanding and knowledge your list may change and grow.

> Here are some things to keep in mind as you decide which features you may want or need.

Software Features

■ **What do you want to do** with your family history information? Are you just looking for a basic program to organize names, dates and events? Some program basics may include: planning tools, data recording, analytical tools (search features, custom lists, flags, custom data fields, multiple note options, etc.), source documentation, reports, charts, publishing, multimedia, internet, portability, additional tools and convenience items.

■ **What about charts and reports?** Do you want to create beautiful family trees to decorate your home; do you want to include photos, audio and video with your data? What kind of charts and reports would you like your software to be able to print?

■ **Do you plan to create a family Web site** to share your information with family and friends? The popular software programs offer you the ability to upload your family tree data online right from your computer program, and help you create a simple family Web site.

■ **Will you want to write a family history book** using your information? Some software programs offer more features for printing a family history book than others.

■ **If you're a member of the LDS Church,** do you want to take your ancestors with you to the temple? If so, you will want to use software that helps track the special ordinance information.

Consider downloading one or more of the *free* family history programs, or trying the demo or trial versions of several programs to see how each one works for you; download and use several different ones to find the one that feels right. Many software vendors have free trial or demo versions available to try out. Some software companies offer their basic software for free, and then charge for the more advanced features. It won't take long for you to learn which ones offer the features you need and are the most intuitive for the way you work.

You may want to read reviews by experts and users' comments. You can do a Google search to find articles about a particular software

program and read users' comments. Also, look at the publisher's Web sites for details and other web sites for users' message boards and e-mails.

There are many excellent family history programs available to meet your needs. Get the scoop on all the latest versions of the most popular family tree software programs in this software roundup.

Popular PC Software Programs

Legacy Family Tree.com - www.legacyfamilytree.com **Free/$$$**

An easy-to-use, user-friendly, full-featured software program. Super-intuitive and includes all of the standard features you could want: GEDCOM import/export, a wide variety of reports, global search and replace, auto-

> You may want to read reviews by the experts on the dozens of software programs available before you purchase.

Reviews by Experts

Top Ten Reviews.com - http://genealogy-software-review.toptenreviews.com

Provides detailed product reviews, ranking, and side-by-side comparisons of ten family history PC software programs. They did not review or compare any free programs, web-based programs, or Macintosh programs, but they provide helpful buying guides, articles explaining how to get the most out of a product, and an easy way to buy them. Here's the criteria they used to evaluate the genealogy software they offer:

■ **Ease of Use / User-Friendliness –** It's easy for beginners and experienced computer users alike; the program should be well organized and easy to navigate.

■ **Ease of Installation & Setup –** The software should be straightforward and simple to install and setup on your computer, without any errors or confusing steps.

■ **Feature Set –** It should include all of the features necessary to research and organize your family tree including reports, charts, searching capabilities, web access and insightful ways to store data.

■ **Help/Documentation –** The developer should provide ample help in the form of FAQs, email and phone support, online course and product tutorials so anyone can learn to use the program and conveniently access customer support.

GenSoftReviews.com - www.gensoftreviews.com

A new site that allows people to review and rate all the software packages.

About.com Review - http://genealogy.about.com/cs/genealogysoftware/a/software_2.htm

Kimberly Powell, a professional genealogist, Web developer, and author of *Everything Family Tree*, did an excellent genealogy software review and ratings of popular software in 2007.

complete, even an alarm clock to help keep you focused. Powerful merge features and split-screen views. It automates the process of creating a family Web page, offers a fairly good Family History Book feature and even helps you print out custom Address Labels and Name Tags (complete with pictures or three-generation pedigree charts) for your next family reunion.

Includes sourcing, reports, merging, To Do list, slide shows, multimedia, Web pages, spell checking, import and export, etc. Lots of additional new features have been added to the new version, including Geo Location Database (about 3 million locations worldwide), U. S. County Verifier, Descendant View tab, Multiple Lines of Descent Report, Master Location List Mapping, privacy options, and international language reports. There is also a Calendar Creator that lets you create your own calendars, complete with pictures, birthdays, anniversaries and pictures. Standard is Free, Deluxe $29.95 (download). Beautiful charts require an extra add-on program. Certified by Family Search.

Family Tree Maker.com -
www.familytreemaker.com $$$

A popular family history program for building, customizing, searching and sharing your family history because it's easy to use, has wide distribution by Generations Network, and it's loaded with features. This new version is a major improvement

over the previous 2008 release and includes improved operating performance and a number of the new search and sourcing features. However, for those who are familiar with earlier versions, this new version has not yet realized it's full potential.

It has improved synchronization with and access to Ancestry.com. It also includes a powerful new global find and replace feature that searches text in facts, notes, media, sources, and tasks; updated charts and reports including new book layouts for charts, and new relationship, and data error reports; and ability to save and reuse publication templates, charts, and reports. The Web Search report will allow you to compare the search results side-by-side with the information in your data base, so you can quickly determine whether the information is relevant to you.

The Family View allows you to see three generations instead of two and up to eight children at once. Another update is the streamlined toolbar with more intuitive buttons. The Pedigree View allows you to quickly and easily navigate. You can view up to seven generations or as few as three. When navigating to other generations in your tree, animation will help you see how the tree is changing, so you won't get lost. $39.95

Personal Ancestral File - www.familysearch.org
click on *Download PAF* - Free

PAF is one of the most widely used and popular family history software programs today. It hasn't been updated for several years, but it's a powerful, full-featured, user-friendly, quality product making it perfect for novice users. And it's *free!* It is produced by FamilySearch that pioneered the use of family history software. You can use it to

record, organize, print, and share your family history information. It provides excellent reliable service. It has a nice selection of reports and charts and allows you to attach a person's picture with their information. It's easy to use, and has good support, including GEDCOM import and export.

It can also create a web page of your information. PAF allows you to create a computerized family tree, beginning with yourself and continuing with your parents, grandparents, and so forth. You can add, delete, or edit the information in your file; link families together, store the source of the information, add notes about people, print forms and lists, search for people in your database, and share your information with others. There is a User's Guide which provides seven lessons on how to use the program, plus navigation tips.

> PAF assigns each person in your database a *unique serial number.*

5
Directory of
Tools

A unique record serial number identifies each individual, and is unique worldwide which means that each individual in each of your database files has a number that is different from all other individuals in all other computer files in the world. The number does not change if you export a GEDCOM file and send it to another person. Therefore, you can send a GEDCOM file to another individual; he or she can import it into PAF, make changes to it, create another GEDCOM file, and send it back you. You can then use the Match/Merge feature to identify the records that you originally created, identify what changes the other person made, decide which information to keep, and merge the records. You cannot see a unique serial number on the Individual screen, and you cannot edit it.

PAF Support Software

These are add-on software programs to enhance the various functions of PAF.

PAF Companion -
www.familysearch.org **Free**/$$$

A utility program for Personal Ancestral File, it is designed to print a variety of high-quality genealogy charts and reports from PAF files. Basic version is Free; full version $6.75.

Family Insight -
www.ohanasoftware.com $$$

An essential tool for file management and a *FamilySearch Certified* PAF add-on. It synchronizes your PAF file and all GEDCOM files with the new *FamilySearch FamilyTree,* plus it compares or synchronizes with an online database or another file. Its the only program currently both Windows and MAC compatible which makes it easy to collaborate with others. It is a full-featured program that works directly with GEDCOMs from other genealogy programs. And it is superior in finding and combining duplicate records, making corrections to *FamilySearch FamilyTree,* cleaning up multiple pedigrees, and separating incorrectly combined individuals. It was awarded the FamilySearch 2009 Software Award for *"Best Person Separator"* and *"Best Standardizer"* (finding multiple instances of a place name in your file and correcting all of them at once). For LDS Church members, it also allows you to submit records for temple ordinances directly and reserve them. Free 60-day trial. $25.00

PAF Pal -
www.ohanasoftware.com **$$$**
Adds additional features that are not available in the PAF software. Expand or abbreviate states, provinces, and/or British counties, search and replace LDS temple codes, display statistics and reports. $18.00

AncestralQuest.com –
www.ancquest.com **$$$**

Because PAF was derived from AQ, if you're a PAF user looking for extra features, you'll find AQ will feel like PAF plus more. See more info below.

However, PAF does not synchronize data with the new FamilySearch (FamilyTree) and will not be upgraded. PAF users will need to purchase another software program or software add-on to do this. All major family history computer software programs need to make some enhancements or adaptations in order to work correctly (or synchronize) with FamilyTree. Therefore, FamilySearch is certifying minimum requirements for other vendor's software to make it easier for you to understand what a vendor may or may not be offering you to synchronize your records with FamilyTree. *See Chapter 6 for more details.*

RootsMagic.com - www.rootsmagic.com **$$$**

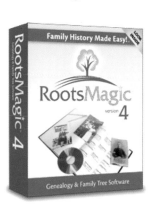

RootsMagic is an exciting full featured genealogy program produced by a developer of quality genealogy software for many years. It's one of the easiest to use family tree software available, yet is also one of the most power-

ful and offers something for everyone. It can generate professional looking web sites automatically from your data, in narrative format, pedigree chart format, family group sheet format, or a combination pedigree / family group sheet format. There are two main views: Tree View and Family View. You can add an unlimited number of facts for every person, and even create your own category if desired. You can add unlimited source citations and notes for every fact. You can print pedigree charts, family group sheets, four types of box charts, six styles of books, 27 different lists, mailing labels, calendars, photo charts, letter-writing templates, and seven different blank charts. It's fun to be able to output your information into a pedigree chart with links between the people. Certified by FamilySearch. $29.95

Ancestral Quest.com -
www.ancquest.com **$$$**

This software is easy-to-learn, fun to use and packed with powerful features, including a unique 'collaboration' capability and award winning name listing feature. The data entry process, layout, and navigation are easy and clean. It creates and uploads multimedia web pages, and you can upload family files to their servers and work on them simultaneously with family and friends. You can attach photos, and audio and video clips to individuals that allow you to create a memorable multi-media scrapbook. Because PAF was derived from AQ, if you're a PAF user looking for extra features, you'll find AQ will feel like PAF plus more. Certified by FamilySearch. $29.95

The Master Genealogist -
www.whollygenes.com $$$

Known by experts as "the one that does it all." Although it is written with professional

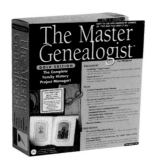

genealogical standards in mind, it comes with a tutorial and has more flexibility than its easy-to-use competitors. The learning curve is somewhat difficult, but it comes with everything you need to: manage volumes of research data, photos, and sources; organize a research trip, including "To Do" lists, reference material, charts, and forms; track your correspondence and expenses; be the hit of a family reunion; or publish a book, complete with table of contents, footnotes, multiple indexes, and bibliography. Silver $34.00, Gold $59.00

Genbox.com - www.genbox.com $$$

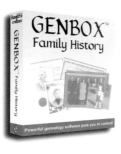

A complete, powerful and flexible genealogy software program that helps you organize your family genealogy research, store your family history data, enter proper source citations, and produce professional-quality family tree charts and genealogy research reports that you can preview and modify, then print or publish on the web on your own genealogy website. Offers you all the tools that you have been wishing for in your genealogy software with ability to link multimedia files to your family tree. Extensive data entry fields, customizable sources, helpful management tools, and beautiful reports and charts. The program seems to have essentially everything a genealogist needs, although due to its complexity beginners may find themselves somewhat overwhelmed. Someone with only basic skills may find it difficult to use. You can work with several databases at once, and the tools for helping you cope with different spellings of the same surname are excellent. Free trial. $29.95

DynasTree.com - www.dynastree.com - **Free**

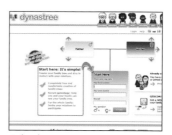

A new, fast-growing family network from the UK that offers free family tree software to create your family tree and stay in contact with your relatives. Their *Home Edition* is a genealogy and family tree program that offers secure, state-of-the-art usability and technology in multiple languages.

Family Tree Legends.com - www.familytreelegends.com - **Free**

Offers most of the features you would expect, but also offers an Internet-intelligent genealogy application. Their SmartMatching technology allows you to collaborate with other genealogists through a sophisticated, simple interface, and intelligently matches the ancestors in your file to all the ancestors in the Gencircles global tree. It also includes: GEDCOM merge and find duplicates, lots of reports which can be exported to Adobe PDF format, Spell Check which quickly and easily checks your spelling in your notes and can add custom words to the dictionary, search and replace places, sources, repositories, and addresses in convenient list windows.

The Next Generation (TNG) - http://lythgoes.net/genealogy/software.php $$$

A genealogy program that runs on web servers. It has most all the features one expects in any modern genealogy program, including a powerful database, easy methods of adding new data, relationship charts, timelines, and more. The major difference is that TNG is installed on a Windows, Apple or Linux web server; to use this software you must have a Web server that supports PHP and MySQL and so should not be considered by most people. It also is multi-user: multiple people can access the database and even add new data simultaneously. $29.99

Brothers Keeper - www.bkwin.org $$$

A shareware program that will help you organize your family history information and let you print a large variety of charts and reports. It's available in 15 languages or so. You can download it for free and then decide if you want to keep it. It's one of the most respected and successful shareware genealogical programs, and has been around a long time and has many dedicated users. $45.

Web-Based Software

When you want to work together with other family members or researchers to collectively research a family tree, free Web-based family history software may be a good option. Check out the following considerations.

Find My Past.com - www.findmypast.com

Family Tree Explorer is a new version of the original *Family Tree Builder* program. You can create a tree from scratch or upload a GEDCOM file. $14.95/month.

SharedTree.com - www.sharedtree.com - **Free**

An online family history and genealogy application that allows multiple people to collaborate on a family tree.

We Relate.org - www.werelate.org - **Free**

This free public-service Web site, created in partnership with the Allen County Public Library, allows you to create Wiki pages for your ancestors, collaborate online with relatives, and upload photos, scanned images and GEDCOM files.

Family Pursuit.com - www.familypursuit.com - **Free**

A new collaborative online genealogy management tool that allows people to work together in their efforts and to easily share their ideas and research. FamilySearch certified.

Genes Reunited.com - www.genesreunited.com

The UK's largest family history and social-networking website. You can become a cyber detective by building your family tree and posting it on the site and investigating which ancestors you share with other members. It currently has over 9 million members worldwide and over 500 million names listed.

Family Tree Builder - www.myheritage.com > Downloads

A powerful software program that MyHeritage members can download and use for free to build family trees, research family history and add content like photos and videos. Their Smart Matching™ technology constantly compares new family trees to the database of more than 300 million profiles to find matches and discover long lost family connections. Basic (up to 500 people and 100MB) Free, Premium (up to 2500 people and 500MB) $3.95/month, Premium Plus (unlimited) $9.95/month.

Mac Software

MyHeredis.com - www.myheredis.com $$$

A full-featured, snazzy-looking family tree software program developed for Mac which benefits from all the latest technology of Mac OS X. It's a multi-file, multi-window application, with no limits to the number of individuals, or generations, or data entry. One of its greatest strengths is its ability to create an assortment of attractive, fully customizable charts. Free demo version available. System requirement: Mac OS X version 10.1.3 or later. $69.

Reunion - www.leisterpro.com $$$

Reunion is one of the easiest-to-use programs with superb charting capabilities and many features. It helps you to document, store, and display information about your family. It records names, dates, places, facts, plenty of notes, sources of information, pictures, sounds, and videos. It shows family relationships in an elegant, graphic form – people and families are linked in an easy-to-understand fashion. Reunion makes it easy to publish your family tree information. You can automatically create common genealogy reports, charts, and forms, as well as birthday calendars, mailing lists, questionnaires, indexes, and other lists. Reunion even calculates relationships, ages, life expectancies, and statistics. It also creates large, high-resolution, graphic charts allowing complete on-screen editing of boxes, lines, fonts, and colors. Wall charts are one of its specialties. $99.

MacFamilyTree - www.synium.de/products/macfamilytree $$$

A popular genealogy application that sports a stunning, configurable user interface, animated charts, editable reports, powerful print and export options, visualize migration of your ancestors over centuries and continents, and built-in support for Google Earth. Data can be viewed and compared in a number of useful ways. You get ancestor and descendant charts, timelines and family charts, as well as the more typical family tree. There's a powerful 3D view that maps family members with flags pinned to a rotating globe. Its main claim to greatness is its editing tools. The *Family Assistant* is the software's hub where you can access an animated family tree that zooms and scrolls as you navigate through its branches, adding new ancestors as you go. $49.

Handheld Software

See Chapter 9 for information on handheld computer software.

Software Tools and Utilities

To Make it Easier

You can do much more than just keep track of your family tree with the following useful family history utility programs; including programs for writing your history, story-telling, creating timelines, creating your healthy history, smart research, organization, mapping, planning your family reunion, family tree charting, etc.

Personal Historian.com - www.personalhistorian.com $$$

A complete system for writing personal and family histories. This exciting program imports names, dates and events from your family history software, and the powerful writing analysis helps you make your history readable

and interesting to others. You can choose historical and cultural LifeCapsules to remind you of important events and give context to your history. The Timeline gives a visual description of your life in historical context. You can publish your completed history to your printer, word processor or PDF file. $29.95

Heritage Collector.com -

http://heritagecollector.com $$$

A comprehensive software management system that allows you to organize, work with, preserve, and find the many varied kinds of multimedia files you are using. It helps organize photos and documents, find anything in seconds, save hard drive space, achieve your information to CD/DVD, search your archive, create shareable slide shows, safeguard files with a backup system, unique photo identification, create "talking" photos, and print in many different formats. It has an easy way to name everyone in the photo or create a caption by creating a photo "hot spot." You also get a free 200 page family history e-guidebook. Download $74.95

LifeSteps - www.allaboutfamily.com $$$

LifeSteps is a system of maintaining all the information about a family's situation. The easy-to-fill-out forms cover medical issues, real estate and finan-

cial holdings, an inventory of household and personal valuables, and more. A fun section on family traditions allows users to list birthdays and other special family events, including how they are usually celebrated. Included in this program are simple-to-fill-out forms that cover information individuals will need in the event of an emergency. $9.95

Genelines -

www.progenygenealogy.com/genelines.html $$$

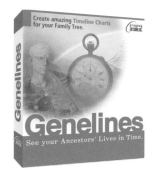

One of the most powerful research and storytelling tools available, Genelines lets you SEE your ancestor's lives in time. By bringing together elements of time, history and family relationships on visual timeline charts, Genelines can bring your family history to life, and even help you find new directions for your family research. With Genelines you can create amazing timeline charts. Genelines gives you a suite of seven distinctive, fully customizable timeline charts. These eye-catching charts are created from two sources – your genealogy database and an extensive library of history files – to illustrate your family lines along with any fascinating facts and interesting events you've found in the course of your research. $29.95 (download)

GeneWeaver - www.geneweaveronline.com $$$

A computer program for creating and maintaining your family health history using a medical genogram. A genogram is a schematic diagram of family relationships and diseases, which is used by your doctor to determine if there is a risk of inherited illnesses, which may lead to early detection and prevention. $39.95

Family Reunion Organizer -
www.family-reunion.com $$$

It's never been easier to plan your family reunion and a variety of family and neighborhood events as well. A checklist leads users through the steps involved in family reunion planning, including tracking a budget and expenses, creating a schedule, managing assignments, and even keeping a family address book. Print invitations, name tags, mailing labels and dozens of other items to make organizing your reunion a breeze. Free demo. $29.95

Passage Express -
www.passageexpress.com $$$

Software to transform your family history research into a professional looking multimedia presentation. Free Trial. $34.95

Ancestral Author -
www.ancestralauthor.com $$$

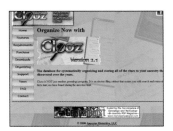

A program that constructs Adobe Acrobat PDF files from GEDCOM files, text files, images, and other sources of user input. It is used to create a family history and genealogy book based on the information stored in your files. It's simple to use, and creates high quality documents that you can print, email to family and friends, publish on the internet, or send

to a printer for printing into a bound book. The end result is a family history 'book' PDF file that contains a customized document of your genealogical research. It automatically creates a name index, and a list of sources. One of the great things about Ancestral Author is that the sections are hyperlinked. Click on a name in the index, and you are brought to the page on which that person appears. $24.95

Clooz.com Filing Cabinet -
www.clooz.com $$$

Clooz is a database for systematically organizing and storing all of the clues to your ancestry that you have been collecting over the years. It's an electronic filing cabinet that assists you with search and retrieval of important facts you have found during your ancestor hunt, showing you a complete picture of what you have and what you lack Once you import your information, you can assign documents to each person. Then, a report will show you all the birth and death certificates, wills, deeds, diary entries, or other documents that pertain to each individual. $39.95

Family Tree SuperTools -
www.whollygenes.com/supertools.htm $$$

Offers powerful wall charting features and many other exciting add-ons to users of many popular family tree programs. It works directly with the data from many programs without the need of an intermediate GEDCOM file. $17.95

FamilySearcher - http://myweb.cableone.net/kevinowen3/familysearcher.htm

A windows program that can read a GEDCOM file and display a list of all names contained in the file in a spreadsheet format. It is then possible to search the Internet IGI (International Genealogical Index) and the other resources at FamilySearch.org web site for any matching entries. Free

GenSmarts - www.gensmarts.com $$$

Works with your existing genealogy file and produces research recommendations. It helps you generate and track to do lists, print worksheets to record your search results, and plan research trips to libraries, court houses, etc. For online research sites, GenSmarts produces links that already have your ancestors name and specifics embedded - making it much easier to perform online record lookups. $24.95

GENMatcher -
www.mudcreek.ca/genmatcher.htm $$$

Quickly compares two genealogy files for matches, or one genealogy file for duplicates. It can show the comparisons side by side and save your work from session to session. $19.95

US Cities Galore -
www.uscitiesgalore.com $$$

Quickly find U.S. cities, towns, townships and counties. Copy and paste results into your

genealogy program. Reads and writes GEDCOM. $29.95

AniMap Plus - www.goldbug.com $$$

Just about every researcher deals with the problem of finding an old town that has long-since disappeared from the map. AniMap displays over 2,300 maps to show the changing county boundaries for each of the 48 adjacent United States for every year since colonial times. Includes all years, not just the census years. Maps may be viewed separately, or the program can set them in motion so you can automatically view the boundary changes. Maps of the full U.S. are also included showing all the changes in state and territorial boundaries from 1776 to the present. Each map includes a listing of the changes from the previous map making it simple to keep track of parent counties. $79.00

Map My Family Tree -
www.legacyfamilytree.com/MapMyFamilyTree-1.asp $$$

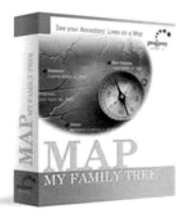

Genealogy mapping software that presents your ancestors' lives on a map. It plots all ancestral life events on customizable color maps. This allows you to see where your ancestors were born, married and died, plus track family migrations using the world and country maps. Then zoom into any part of the world to see detailed events in that particular location. $39.95

SmartDraw - www.smartdraw.com $$$

Uses templates and drag-and-drop capabilities to make it easy to draw professional-looking family tree charts, diagrams, genograms, and flow charts. Free trial download for 30 days. $197.

I Felt Two Hands From Behind

Hildo Flores of Piura, Peru traveled to the town of Zorritos in northern Peru to find the death dates and final resting place of his great-grandparents. He walked down every vault aisle and read every inscription in the cemetery. Still nothing. He knelt and prayed, then repeated his thorough search pattern. For a third time, he was unable to find them and now it was getting late. He would have to leave without finding them. He turned toward the front gate, ready to leave the cemetery when something wondrous happened. "Just as I took my first step, I felt two hands take hold of my head from behind and turn it towards a certain spot. My eyes rested on a small, dirty headstone that was level with the ground. I looked behind me to see who had grabbed my head, but no one was there. I walked to the headstone...and cleaned off the inscription." To his amazement, it was the very marker he was searching for! Hildo Rosillo Flores, *Ensign,* October 2007, 72

SnapGenie.com - www.snapgenie.com **Free**

Share the stories behind your photos. This program helps you easily build and share verbal narrated photo slide shows in a matter of minutes which you can share with family and friends. And best of all, it's free.

A Paper From Nowhere

Steve and Nancy Lealos made a trip to Delaware from their home in Alaska to spend two weeks researching Nancy's genealogy. They called and visited anyone and everyone with any information. They were at libraries, courthouses and other locations from the moment they opened until they closed. However, their hard work hit a dead end with Nancy's great-great grandfather and the time had come to go. "While I was taking some last photographs on a lawn, I happened to see out of the corner of my eye an older piece of yellow legal paper on the ground. As I picked up the paper, I was absolutely stunned to realize that I had in my hand a handwritten document that was at least 50 years old, written in ink without a smudge on it, that listed Nancy's great-great grandfather, his parents, his wife's family and continuing back even further with parents, husbands, wives and children, with dates, places, etc." To add to the amazement, they could find no reason for the paper to be there. "No one knew about it, no one claimed it." On a lawn in Delaware a piece of paper had appeared out of nowhere with the information they were seeking. Just coincidence? Steve Lealos, www.ldschurchnews.com/archives. 19 January 2008, p. 16.

CHAPTER 6

Best of the Internet
KEY FAMILY HISTORY WEB SITES

The internet contains a wealth of information and makes it easy to contact and stay in touch with others who might be working on your family roots. Whether you are experienced or a novice in tracing your family roots using the Internet, these personally-reviewed and singled-out-for-excellence web sites will empower you in your search for your treasured family heritage. A virtual *treasure trove* of empowering, irreplaceable knowledge and information—much of which had been essentially "lost" to mankind in dusty archives around the world—is now instantly available to you at your fingertips at any time.

Web sites come in all degrees of value, efficiency, and friendliness. And since everyone has different needs, not all are equally useful for every family historian, but each may have something of immense value to offer you and perhaps add an important piece to your family history puzzle.

This collection of key web sites is not meant to be a comprehensive listing of family history web sites available, as there are well-known web directories, such as *Cyndi's List,* that do this very well. Searching the various online genealogy databases can be time-consuming and even difficult. Rather, this is a valuable, easy-to-use selection of personally pre-screened, key web sites to save you valuable time, help you get started and get organized, and help you add new branches to your family tree, thus empowering you with the *Best of the Internet. (See also the Best LDS Family History Web Sites in Chapter 7.)* These sites and resources are free unless marked with an **$$$** to signify that access to some or all of the content requires a fee.

Opportunity in Difficulties

Winston Churchill

"A pessimist sees the difficulty in every opportunity; an optimist sees the opportunity in every difficulty." – Winston Churchill (1874-1965)

6 Best of the Internet

Family History Insights - 6

Spencer W. Kimball
© by Intellectual Reserve, Inc.

Help From the Other Side

"...my grandfather...searched all his life to get together his genealogical records; and when he died... he had been unsuccessful in establishing his line back more than the second generation beyond him. I am sure that most of my family members feel the same as I do–that there was a thin veil between him and the earth, after he had gone to the other side, and that which he was unable to do as a mortal he perhaps was able to do after he had gone into eternity. After he passed away, the spirit of research took hold of...two distant relatives. ... The family feels definitely that the spirit of Elijah was at work on the other side and that our grandfather had been able to inspire men on this side to search out these records; and as a result, two large volumes are in our possession with about seventeen thousand names." Spencer W. Kimball, *The Teachings of Spencer W. Kimball*, p. 543

The Miracle of the Chinese Bamboo Tree

After the seed for this amazing tree is planted, watered, and fertilized regularly every year you see NOTHING for four years except for a tiny shoot coming out of a bulb. During those four years, all the growth is underground in a massive, fibrous root structure that spreads deep and wide in the earth. But sometime during the fifth year the Chinese Bamboo tree grows to EIGHTY FEET IN SIX WEEKS! Family history is much akin to the growing process of the Chinese bamboo tree. It is often discouraging. We seemingly do things right, and nothing happens. But for those who do things right and are not discouraged and are persistent things will happen. Through patience, perseverance, diligence, work and nurturing, that "fifth year" will come, and all will be astonished at the growth and change which takes place. Finally we begin to receive the rewards. To paraphrase Winston Churchill, we must "never, never, NEVER give up!"

Oliver Wendell Holmes

Where Are You Headed?

"The greatest thing in this world is not so much where we are, but in what direction we are moving." Oliver Wendell Holmes (1809-1894), Physician & professor

Henry David Thoreau

What Are You Doing?

"It is not enough to be busy; so are the ants. The question is: What are we busy about?" Henry David Thoreau (1817-1862), Author, poet & naturalist

Thomas A. Edison

Close to Success

"Many of life's failures are people who did not realize how close they were to success when they gave up." Thomas A. Edison (1847-1931), Inventor & businessman

Maya Angelou

Know Where You're Going

"No man can know where he is going unless he knows exactly where he has been and exactly how he arrived at his present place." Maya Angelou (1928-)

David E. Rencher

Promptings of the Spirit

"In this day and age of computer technology and computer wizardry there are things which do and do not work. We cannot overcome the promptings of the spirit and expect to find our ancestors. If we ignore that, above all else, we will not have the experiences which we continue to have if we listen to the promptings and go when and where we are told to go." David E. Rencher, AG, FUGA, http://familyhistory.byu.edu/resources/firesides/2004-11-12.pdf

Best of the Internet

KEY FAMILY HISTORY WEB SITES

Top Ten U.S. Web Sites to Search for Your Ancestors

There are literally thousands of Web sites available on the Internet to help you trace your family roots and stories which can become overwhelming if you don't know where to start. But some sites really stand out at providing the best information and records to get you headed in the right direction. Here's my list of the top sites.

These *Best of the Internet* web sites can help you trace your family roots, connect to your ancestor's lives, and locate information about your ancestor's culture, traditions, homeland, and history.

Best of the Internet Hotlinks at Easyfamilyhistory.com -

Everything you need to make your genealogy easy.™

The Internet is the place– the place where some of the most exciting family history resource advances are taking place. So it's important that you not only have information about these resources, but be able to conveniently and readily access the hundreds of websites listed in this guidebook/ resource book. To assist you, we have created a companion website so you can conveniently access all of these (and other) web sites with just a keystroke or two. No more typing in those lengthy website addresses.

This new companion site allows you to easily connect to the hundreds of key family history web sites worldwide which contain billions of database records and resources. You also get website reviews, software reviews, how-to and historical articles, and pertinent announcements. You can easily locate the referenced web sites, and for your convenience, every link to a website is LIVE, so that you can simply click on the link and go to the website or send an email. You just point and click to access the site instantly.

And since *new* web sites become available constantly, and web addresses often change, we constantly scour the Internet and review all the new information and web sites to keep the hotlinks current. We work hard to try to keep you up-to-date on changes and the latest news and tips. So this web site is a friendly, easy-to-use, up-to-date Internet directory of the *best* family history web sites just for you. Enjoy!

6 Best of the Internet

1. FamilySearch.org -

www.familysearch.org

FamilySearch™ is one of the comprehensive, preeminent family history web sites on the Internet. It provides access to the Family History Library and the largest collection of *free* family history, family tree and genealogy records in the world. You can do significant research online and also discover what records you need to search to find your ancestors in record-breaking time. It provides easy access for the gathering and sharing of family history information. Due to the free access to billions of records, their recent and ongoing projects to: improve their infrastructure, digitize and index their extensive collection of genealogical records held in the Granite Mountain Records Vault, partnerships with others in digitizing

FamilySearch is in the early stages of designing the new replacement home page for the esteemed FamilySearch.org website.

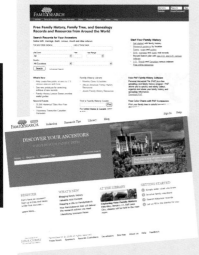

At print time, here is what FamilySearch looks like now, and the current concept design (Alpha) for the new home page. The expected release date for the new site design has not been made public.

New FamilySearch home page (alpha)

their records, expanding their new extensive collection of published family histories, upgrading their new Family History Library Catalog, adding new searchable maps, a digital image viewer, and their new wiki site, I've selected this as the number one overall site.

"New FamilySearch" Preview

A major project to improve *FamilySearch* has been in process for the past few years to upgrade the software and infrastructure. They have been developing ways to make organizing, viewing and sharing personal family histories online easier, faster and more accurate for more people. It is temporarily called "New FamilySearch" and it is temporarily located at http://new.familysearch.org. But soon it will be called *FamilySearch FamilyTree* and will be relocated to the regular website.

FamilyTree is a single family tree that all of us share and work on in common. It provides a free, multi-language, internet-based environment for everyone to collaborate, and will eventually include capabilities to link scanned images of proof documents with each record. It has the option to dispute and provide alternative lineages with notes and proof documents. The links to images of documents is a key component to compiling accurate lineages. This ability to combine our genealogy data with online proof documents (for free) will revolutionize family history research collaboration and be a boon to tracing and sharing your family roots and stories.

FamilySearch has begun to implement the new system worldwide in gradual phases, and at press time have issued a very limited release to LDS Church members only—which is a great way to work out all of the bugs with a small user group before the major world roll-out. Hopefully this means that we will be spared the disappointment of slow access and the usual major problems of a gigantic new release, and that we'll be able to find support from experienced local Family History Center volunteers when FamilyTree is available to everyone. Right now, it lacks many niceties considered standard in a genealogy product, but many exciting new features are coming.

Most of us are not be able to access FamilyTree right now until the full roll-out, but as it becomes available and their new products and services are fully developed, they will be added to their Web site and announcements made. No release dates have been announced at this time; however, here is more information on FamilySearch and a preview of FamilySearch FamilyTree.

What the New FamilySearch Does

See What Information FamilyTree Has about You and Your Ancestors

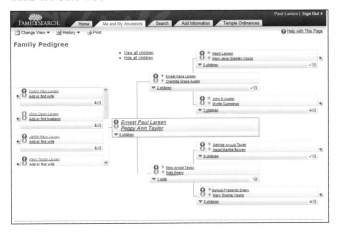

In addition to names, dates, places, and relationships, you will also see very comprehensive source citations, including links to source images, if the original contributors provided them. FamilySearch contains hundreds of millions of records about individuals. It will also include a mapping utility which maps locations where an individual has resided. By clicking on the link a pop up displays the events that took place at that location, i.e.: birth, marriage, death, etc.

Work with Others on Shared Family Lines

FamilySearch helps you work with others to make sure your family history is as accurate and complete as possible. To make this possible,

FamilyTree keeps track of who contributes which information. Depending on how much contact information a contributor chooses to display, you may be able to contact him or her by e-mail, standard mail, or telephone. As you look at your family history in FamilySearch, you will find places where an ancestor is missing or has incomplete information. When this happens, you first want to see if someone else has added that individual. Before you add a new individual or family, search FamilySearch to see if someone else has already added that information. If you find it, you can just connect it to your family line. There is no need to enter it again. Another way to see if someone else has already entered information about an individual is to see if FamilyTree can find any possible duplicates. If it finds a possible duplicate, you decide if the information is about the same individual. If so, you can combine the information. All of the information will be preserved.

After an individual's information is combined into one record, everyone can see and work on it together to:

- Evaluate the accuracy of the information
- Make corrections if needed
- Add notes and sources
- Dispute incorrect information

Add New Information and Make Corrections

In FamilyTree you will find yourself in an environment where you can work with others to identify the correct information and preserve the most accurate information that can be found about your family. FamilySearch protects your information. When you contribute information, only you can change or delete it. If other users contribute different information about the same ancestor, FamilyTree keeps this new information in addition to your information. You can easily add new information. You can also correct the information that you added previously. Information about deceased individuals is available instantly to other users. If you contribute information about individuals who may still be living, only you will be able to see it.

Instead of providing other information, some users may indicate disagreement with a piece of information. This is called "disputing." A user who enters a dispute should include a detailed explanation so that everyone can see why he or she believes the information is incorrect. The dispute can then start a discussion among contributors, which will ideally lead to the most correct information being identified and preserved and incorrect information being removed.

Specific for LDS Members. Several features are specific to the membership of the LDS Church which simplifies the process required to prepare family names for temple ordinances. LDS Church members will be able to: Easily see ordinance information and status of work in progress, significantly reduce duplication of research and ordinance work, and prepare temple names from home over the Internet.

Protecting Privacy Rights

To protect the privacy rights of living people, FamilyTree limits the amount of information that you can see about individuals who may still be living. If you contribute an individual who might be living, only you can see him or her. Other users cannot, even close relatives and the individuals themselves.

How FamilySearch Determines If an Individual May Still Be Living

FamilySearch considers that an individual may be living if both of the following situations apply:

- He or she was born at least 110 years ago or married at least 100 years ago.
- The record contains no death information.

How FamilySearch Displays Living People

In FamilyTree, you can easily identify individuals who may be living. In the details and on the family pedigree, the individual's name is displayed in italics. The text is lighter than the names of deceased people. In the details, the word "Living" appears next to the individual's name.

Registering to Use FamilySearch FamilyTree

Before you can use FamilyTree, you need to register. Registration is required so that they can protect your privacy and the information that you contribute to FamilyTree. Even if you have already registered to use the existing www.family search.org Internet site, you still need to register to use FamilyTree. No one else can use the same user name as your sign-in name for the FamilyTree. You can use the same password in both places as long as it meets the security requirements for both places.

Contact Information

By providing contact information, other people who are doing research on lines that connect with yours can contact you and share information they have gathered. You can use contact information to get in touch with others who might be related to you. FamilySearch automatically displays your contact name with every piece of information that you contribute. You can choose to have

FamilySearch FamilyTree List of Certified Affiliates (at press time)

WHERE GENERATIONS MEET

FamilySearch's free computer software program, Personal Ancestral File (PAF) does not synchronize with Family Tree and will not be upgraded. Therefore, PAF users are required to purchase another software program or use a PAF add-on product if they want to be able to work offline in a desktop application and update their records online in the FamilySearch Family Tree from PAF. If a user wants to work and save their family history only online, then no desktop software is needed. In order for all major family history computer software to work correctly (or synchronize) with new FamilySearch, they need to make some enhancements or adaptations. FamilySearch has chosen to certify minimum requirements for product features, processes, or vendor services to make it easier for consumers to understand what a vendor may or may not be offering for you to synchronize your records with Family Tree. At the present time, here is the list of certified affiliates.

Affiliate/Product	Access	Print	Update	Sync	Mult-Lang.	PAF Add-In
GENERATION MAPS GenMaps Client (WEB) www.generationmaps.com	X	X				
INCLINE SOFTWARE Ancestral Quest (WIN) www.ancquest.com	X	X	X	X	X	X
OHANA SOFTWARE FamilyInsight (WIN)	X		X	X	X	X
FamilyInsight (MAC)	X		X	X	X	
Get My Ancestors (WIN/MAC) www.ohanasoftware.com	X				X	
MILLENNIA Legacy FamilyTree (WIN) www.legacyfamilytree.com	X	X	X	X	X	
PROGENY SOFTWARE Charting Companion (WIN) www.progency.com	X	X				
ROOTS MAGIC Roots Magic(WIN) www.rootsmagic.com	X	X	X	X		
USFAMILYTREE Grow Branch (WEB) www.usfamilytree..com	X		X			

ACCESS – Search, read   UPDATE – Person publish   SYNC – Person-sync process
PAF ADD-IN – Adds Access, Update, Sync, Match/Combine to PAF

Vendors of certified features will be licensed to use the FamilySearch Certified Logo on the product packaging, website, and marketing literature.

FamilyTree also display the following information: Your full name, telephone number, mailing address, and E-mail address.

Signing in to Use the New FamilyTree

Each time you use FamilySearch, you will need to sign in. Signing in allows FamilyTree to give you the following benefits:

- It can show you the information that it has about you and your ancestors.
- It can list you as the contributor of all changes that you make to information in the system.
- It can protect the information that you contribute to the system from change by others. Since it knows what information you contribute while you are signed in, it can prevent anyone else from changing it.

FamilySearch Labs - http://labs.familysearch.org

Take a look at some of the new things FamilySearch is working on. They are testing a variety of products such as Records Search, Family Tree, Standard Finder and Research Wiki. You can sign up as a beta tester and help them develop even better products for future use.

FamilySearch Records Search -
http://pilot.familysearch.org

You can search millions of *new indexed records* for your ancestors. More records are being added every month by volunteer indexers online. If you are interested in helping or want to see what projects they are currently transcribing, go to www.familysearch indexing.org.

FamilySearch Wiki - http://wiki.familysearch.org

Free family history research advice for the community, by the community. A large, on-line library where you can find thousands of articles

and how-to instructions about doing family history or even ask a personal family history question. It assists you in finding your ancestors, and offers information on how to find, use, and analyze records of genealogical value for beginners, intermediate and expert researchers. Since this is a wiki Web site, you can add to existing articles or write new articles.

FamilySearch Community - http://forums.familysearchsupport.org/index.php

Unofficial discussion forums for new FamilySearch.org

Unlocking the Granite Vault

FamilySearch is also in the process of a new massive project called the *Scanstone Project.* They are scanning, digitizing and indexing their extensive collection of genealogical records held in the Granite Mountain Vault, and seeking volunteer help for the project (see *Enlisting Your Help* below). This is a climate-controlled, underground storage facility to safeguard master copies of all their microfilm records. The storage facility, built literally into a mountainside, is located about 25 miles from downtown Salt Lake City, Utah.

Records contained in the Family History Library (which are safeguarded in the mountain vault) and in FamilySearch databases have been gathered from a wide variety of sources worldwide in an ongoing collection effort that has been under way for more than a century. Most of the microfilm collection has been produced by microfilming original sources worldwide. There are more than 5 billion documents (with untold billions of names) on 2 1/2 million rolls of microfilm and 1 1/2 million microfiche. The U.S. Library of Congress contains 29 million books, and the FamilySearch records hold 132 times that much data. In cooperation with legal custodians of

FamilySearch granite vault

records worldwide, FamilySearch has now replaced its microfilm cameras with digital cameras, and has over 200 cameras currently digitizing records in 47 countries.

As part of this digital conversion and capture project, they are currently producing over 60 million images per month or approximately 370,000 rolls of microfilm per year, the equivalent of about 6 million 300-page volumes. Volunteers extract family history information from digital images of historical documents to create indexes that assist everyone in finding their ancestors. With electronic help, each and every name and word in every record will be indexed so that we can find particular ancestors quickly. Names become the primary focus of the databases; localities and jurisdictions become identifiers. The microfilm conversion project is expected to be completed within the next 5-7 years. The process to create free online indexes to all of the digital images will take longer and be an ongoing initiative, and an index to these "records in process" is available online. The eventual result will give you the ability to search and have billions of indexed genealogy records, linked to digital images of the originals, at your finger tips.

Published Family Histories - www.family search.org > *Search Records* > *Historical Books*

The Family History Library has an extensive collection of published family histories and is digitizing more everyday—even faster. The effort targets published family, society, county, and town histories, as well as numerous other historical publications that are digitally preserved and made

Enlisting Your Help -
http://familysearchindexing.org

FamilySearch is enlisting the help of thousands to index all those newly digitized records. *FamilySearch Indexing* is a worldwide, non-profit community effort to harness volunteers to gather, transcribe, and index records of genealogical significance. You can help create free public access to the U.S. census indexes and other records. The key life events of billions of people are being preserved and shared through the efforts of people like you. Using their online indexing system, volunteers from around the world are able to quickly and easily transcribe the records—all from the convenience of your home. The indexes are then posted for FREE at FamilySearch.org. Millions of rolls of microfilm provide census, vital, probate, and church records from over 100 countries for indexing projects.

Governments, churches, societies, and commercial companies are also working to make more records available. YOU CAN HELP by volunteering to index one of the current U.S. census projects or the upcoming England and Wales census projects. To participate as a volunteer (currently 170,000 volunteers), you simply sign up at www.familysearch indexing.org, click through a tutorial provided in both English and Spanish and then select the project you want to work on. There's an online help desk if you have questions, or you could go to a local family history center and get individual instruction. Once you are online, you recognize that the work of one person makes a contribution, no matter how much time you have to give.

accessible for free online. FamilySearch has nearly a million publications in its famous Family History Library, and there are millions of similar publications elsewhere in the United States. Working with volunteers and select affiliate libraries, it plans to create the largest digital collection of published histories on the Web. It is helping to digitize and publish collections from the Allen County Public Library, Brigham Young's Harold B. Lee Library, Houston Public Library, and Mid-Continent Public Library Midwest Genealogy Center in Independence, Missouri. When all is said and done, there will be over a million publications in the digital collection online. It will be the largest free resource of its kind.

Searchable Maps

FamilySearch will also be expanded with searchable maps. Partnering with the University of Austria Map Department, the maps of the Austro-Hungarian Empire (central Europe) were selected to add first. Jurisdictions overlap, several localities appear to have the same name, countries have been destroyed and wiped off the map, others have been created and added to the map, territory assigned to a new country carries a different name in each country—one place has two or more different names. FamilySearch is indexing ancestor's names, the places where your ancestors are found, and the map reference. So with a click you can view and print the actual locality where your ancestors lived. This one feature alone will save you hours of research time. Then you can retrieve a copy of the record images to document your genealogy at a fraction of the time we spend today.

The Family History Library Catalog

The primary resources offered right now are numerous searchable online databases, research guidance, and the library catalog. The online

catalog describes the books, microfilms, and microfiche in the Family History Library in Salt Lake City, Utah. The library houses a collection of genealogical records that includes the names of more than 3 billion deceased people. It is the largest collection of its kind in the world, including: vital records (birth, marriage, and death records from both government and church sources), census returns, court, property, and probate records, cemetery records, emigration and immigration lists, printed genealogies, and family and county histories.

When you want to look at actual records of the people you are researching, you can visit a Family History Center nearest you (there are over 4,500 branches of the Family History Library worldwide) and order copies of the records from the main library in Salt Lake City for a nominal fee. To locate the nearest Family History Center, simply click on *Find a Family History Center* on the front web site page, or you may call 1-800-346-6044 in the United States and Canada.

To use the catalog, search for your surname and various places that your ancestors lived, looking for information that might be relevant to your research. Choose from the various searches including:

> **Place:** used to locate records for a certain place such as city, county, state, etc. Each jurisdiction

has different records available, so it is important to search all jurisdictions for your area (i.e. both the city and county records).

Surname: used to locate family histories which include that surname or last name.

Author: used to search for a record by author.

Subject: used to search for a certain topic (based on Library of Congress subject headings).

Keyword: To find entries that contains a certain word or combination of words.

Enhanced New Catalog in Process

FamilySearch is currently collaborating with www.FamilyLink.com to publish the Family History Library Catalog using new technology. The new technology will enhance and extend the value of the catalog that currently has more than four million entries. Users will be able to add new sources that are currently in the library catalog, and extend its scope of coverage. They will be able to improve the source descriptions and even rate and review sources as to their usefulness. The user feedback combined with the intelligent search algorithm being developed will make the catalog better and easier to use. *(See GenSeek.com info below under FamilyLink for more details.)*

The International Genealogical Index™

(IGI) lists the dates and places of births, christenings, and marriages for more than 285 million deceased people. The index includes people who lived at any time after the early 1500s up through the early 1900s. These names have been researched and extracted from thousands of original records. Most of these records are compiled from public domain sources. The IGI database makes otherwise difficult-to-access information readily available to the public at no cost.

The Pedigree Resource File™ (PRF) is a large

collection of family histories submitted by individuals via the internet to help you identify and link your ancestors. There are over 225 million names in the database, and approximately 1.2 million names are submitted to this file every month. It is also a publicly-available method of preserving your genealogy on a computer database. The comprehensive index to PRF is available free on-line but the actual database files (which would include a submitter's sources and notes) are currently only available on compact disc which you can either use *free* in Family History Centers worldwide, or purchase at a nominal cost. (If you wish to purchase, go to www.ldscatalog.com, click on *family history / software & databases* in the left column.) Each disc contains about 1.1 million names. Results from searching the index online will tell you what disc the respective information can be found on. Information is organized in family groups and pedigrees, and is printed exactly as submitted and not combined with information from other submitters as is done in Ancestral File.

Ancestral File™ is a collection of approximately 37 million lineage-linked names of people throughout the world that are organized into pedigrees and family group record forms. The information includes dates and places of birth, marriages, and deaths. It also contains names and addresses of the individuals who contributed the information. You can print copies of the records or copy them to your computer hard drive for use in your family history database by creating a GEDCOM file *(see Chapter 2 for more details)*. The site does not verify the accuracy of the information. It is simply a pool of information donated by thousands of people. The Ancestral File has not been updated since 2000 because of the major FamilySearch overhaul in process.

Vital Records Index is a partial index of vital records–collections of official birth, marriage, and death records–from around the world, including Mexico, Scandinavia, North America, the British Isles, and Western Europe. The official governmental records of births, marriages, and deaths in the United States and every Canadian province except Québec are called vital records. In other countries and Québec, official government records are called *civil registration.*

Research Assistance/Helps

FamilySearch offers two types of research assistance. The *Research Guidance* service is an online wizard that offers detailed research advice to a user based on his or her answers to a series of questions. *Research Helps* are research guides that can be read online or downloaded as a PDF.

There are many guides' available covering geographic areas and most types of genealogical records.

U.S. Social Security Death Index - Contains information about persons whose deaths were reported to the Social Security Administration from about 1937 through September 30, 2000. The majority of the death records are from 1962 and later. This file provides birth and death dates and identifies the person's last place of residence and the place the death payment was sent. The Social Security number and the state of residence when the Social Security number was issued are also provided. This index contains vital statistics for over 70 million deceased individuals.

Free Computer Software - FamilySearch

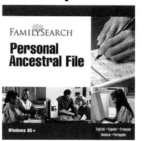

also offers a free copy of *Personal Ancestral File (PAF),* a popular family history computer program that allows you to record and publish your family history. *(See Chapter 5 for more details.)*

Other Resources - *FamilySearch* is also an index to other key web sites around the world. It searches numerous family history web sites according to category, surname or place, and has become a portal to thousands of other genealogical web sites. It also searches the following records:

Census Records

Including the 1880 United States (approximately 50 million individuals), 1881 British Isles (about 25 million people; Scottish records not included), and the 1881 Canadian Census (4.3 million people). These indexed censuses, searchable by name, birth date, or birthplace represent a treasure trove of easily accessible information. The 1880 U.S. Census work took 17 years and over 11.5 million hours to complete bringing the total number of census names available to 85 million. *(See more details in the Census Charts in Chapter 3.)*

At the time of this writing, some of these vital record indexes are not online, but are available in Family History Centers worldwide or can be purchased for your personal use.

The *Scottish Church Records* database is available in Family History Centers around the world and online at: www.nas.gov.uk/recordkeeping/churchrecords.asp and at www.scotlandspeople.gov.uk.

Searching Scottish Records

This database includes an index of approximately 10,000,000 names extracted from records of the Church of Scotland. Most records come from the late 1500s to 1854. Birth, christening, and marriage information is included and can be searched by looking for an individual, a marriage record, or parents of an individual.

2. Ancestry.com -

www.ancestry.com $$$

With more than 7 billion names and 27,000 searchable databases, Ancestry.com is a premium online source for family history information, including more than 26,000 historical records collections. Even though Ancestry has relatively high subscription fees, users have access to hundreds of millions of fully searchable individual records, including all available US Census records (1790–1930), vast military records, immeasurable passenger arrivals records at major U.S. ports, city directories, vital records, and family histories making the fees well worth your investment. Users can search by record type, locality, or simply view scanned images of original historical documents. Access to these records is available through both free and premium subscription models, with nearly half of the content available on the site offered free to all visitors. With a paid subscription base of over

850,000 Ancestry.com is among the largest paid subscription sites on the Internet and a premier resource to learn about your family history. Ancestry.com also has local websites in nine countries, including U.K., Canada, Germany, Italy, France, Sweden, and Australia, among others. 14-Day Free trial. U.S. Membership $19.95/month, $16.95/month for 3 months, $12.95/month for 12 months.

Ancestry WorldTree -
www.ancestry.com/trees/awt

Rootsweb WorldConnect -
http://wc.rootsweb.ancestry.com

Ancestry WorldTree—and Rootsweb WorldConnect—is a free collection of user-submitted GEDCOMs (family trees). You can access WorldTree and World Connect from two different websites, but either way, it is the same program and the same set of trees. The database contains more than 480 million names in family trees submitted by users. To search only WorldTrees or WorldConnect use the URL addresses above. Ancestry.com *general tree searches* include other family trees not in WorldTree, but general searches also include WorldTree only when searching for "EXACT matches only".

Ancestry.com is part of *The Generations Network, Inc.,* a private provider of a preeminent network of web sites for connecting families with their histories and with one another. The company's tools, content, and community help empower individuals to find the people most important to them and to share their unique family stories. By offering a variety of family websites, they give families all over the world a unique venue for keeping in touch and strengthening relationships. Ancestry.com and Rootsweb.com are two of the research sites that you will use the most. The network includes:

RootsWeb.com - www.rootsweb.com *See Web site no. 3 below for details.*

Genealogy.com - www.genealogy.com

Provides the tools, resources (about 90,000 links to sites to help do research), and community that

empowers you to uncover and share your unique family stories, and to research, organize and document your heritage. It produces the best-selling family tree software, *Family Tree Maker (see Chapter 5 for more details).*

MyFamily.com - www.myfamily.com

In a secure, password-protected environment, users can hold family discussions, create online family photo albums, maintain a calendar of family events and share family history information quickly and easily. Since 1998, myfamily.com has helped millions of people keep in touch with their family and friends by sharing photos, stories, news, family trees and more on their very own private web site.

DNA.Ancestry.com - http://dna.ancestry.com

Expand your family tree, and discover ancient ancestry just by swapping your cheek. Learn about cheek-swab collection, DNA science and how to choose a test, order a DNA test, and see sample results.

Ancestry.co.uk - www.ancestry.co.uk maintains an extensive archive of records from England, Ireland, Scotland and Wales, including census records along with civil, ecclesiastical and immigration records.

Ancestry.ca - www.ancestry.ca - Over 410 million Canadian family history records are available online. In addition to the fully indexed Censuses of Canada for 1851, 1891, 1901, 1906 and 1911, key Canadian collections include the Canadian Passenger Lists - 1865 to 1935 and U.S. / Canada Border Crossings from 1895 to 1956, Quebec

Church & Vital Records (Drouin Collection) - 1621 to 1967, Ontario and British Columbia Church & Vital records from as early as 1747 and military records from WWI. Ancestry.ca offers an extensive learning center and robust online tree-building tools.

Ancestry.de - www.ancestry.de is a German website offering a significant collection of historic records, including exclusive census and passenger documents. It also offers the German family researcher an extensive learning center, and the latest robust online Ancestry tree-building tools.

Ancestry.com.au - www.ancestry.com.au offers access to over 5 billion family history records worldwide, including more than 570 million UK and Irish records as well as a growing set of Australian family history records dating from the arrival of the first immigrants in 1788 onwards.

3. RootsWeb.com -

www.rootsweb.com

A thriving, *free* genealogy community on the web providing a robust worldwide environment for learning, collaborating and sharing for the expert and novice alike. The site provides access to huge transcribed records from volunteer researchers, and contains extensive interactive guides and numerous research tools for tracing family histories. The site's *WorldConnect Project* contains more than 480 million ancestor names. Besides helpful advice such as the *RootsWeb Guide to Tracing Family Trees,* it boasts over 31,000 mailing lists, over 132,000 message boards, and the RootsWeb Surname List of more than 1.2 million surname entries. It also hosts many major websites and sources of free data, such as: Cyndi's List, USGenWeb Project, the Obituary Daily Times

(an index to published obituaries), National Genealogical Society, FreeBMD (the Civil Registration index of births, marriages and deaths for England and Wales); and Genealogy.org. RootsWeb is part of *The Generations Network*.

4. FamilyLink.com/ WorldVitalRecords.com -

www.familylink.com $$$

FamilyLink.com, Inc. is a family of services that includes WorldVitalRecords.com, FamilyHistory Link.com, WebTree.com, WorldHistory.com, GenSeek.com and the We're Related and My Family (http://tinyurl.com/7m9cty) applications on Facebook. The focus of the company is to provide innovative tools to connect families. FamilyLink currently has more than 12 million unique global visitors who generate 31.2 million page views per month.

WorldVitalRecords.com -
www.worldvitalrecords.com $$$

Provides affordable access to genealogy databases and family history tools used by more than 258,000 monthly visitors and tens of thousands of paying subscribers. With

thousands of databases—including birth, death, military, census, and parish records—WorldVitalRecords.com makes it easy to fill in missing information in your family tree. Some of its partners include Everton Publishers, Quintin Publications, Archive CD Books Australia, Gould Genealogy, Immigrant Ships Transcribers Guild, Archive CD Books Canada, The Statue of Liberty-Ellis Island Foundation, Inc., SmallTownPapers®, Accessible Archives, Genealogical Publishing Company, Find My Past, Godfrey Memorial Library, Find A Grave, and FamilySearch. U.S. Collection - $5.95/month, $39.95/year; World Collection - $14.95/month, $119.40/year.

We're Related -
http://apps.facebook.com/we_r_related

The fastest growing social network for families and genealogists and the most popular Facebook application for families. With more than 19 million users, We're Related is one of the five most popular applications on Facebook. We're Related allows individuals to find relatives, connect with friends and family members, build family trees, and share news and photos. Free.

FamilyHistoryLink.com -
www.familyhistorylink.com

A free destination and platform for family social networking. This new service (beta) connects families from around the world and across social networking platforms and mobile devices. This is the hub to view everything that is happening with your family members, including status updates, news, blog posts, photos, videos and more. You can organize your family and find and connect with other family members, upload and organize all your family photos and view photos from the rest of your family, build or upload your family tree and share

it with your family, email your entire family and stay updated with everyone. Free.

WorldHistory.com - www.worldhistory.com

A site dedicated to providing historical context around places, people, and events. The site allows you to access local and global historical events by time and location. Perfect tool to help with travel plans or to better understand the historical context of your genealogy. Free.

GenSeek.com - www.genseek.com

The new gateway to family history that combines genealogy research with social networking to expose the world's largest catalog of genealogy sources in a new, more accessible way. Built around the Family History Library Catalog published at FamilySearch.org in an exclusive commercial arrangement, GenSeek.com aims to provide access to all of the world's known genealogy collections and databases, both online and offline. Free.

WebTree.com - www.webtree.com

An online service for publishing family trees in GEDCOM format for sharing and easy access. The millions of names found in family trees at WebTree.com are searchable from WebTree.com and WorldVital Records.com. Free.

5. Footnote.com -

www.footnote.com $$$

Through partnerships with some of the most prominent archives in America including the National Archives, Footnote digitizes millions of documents, records and photos that paint a picture of our shared past that few have seen before. The collections include records relating to the Revolutionary War, Civil War, WWI, WWII, the Vietnam War, the Great Depression, interactive 1860 and 1930 census images, African American History, Native Americans, historical newspapers, naturalization documents, and city directories. Many of the collections are free and all indexed information for every collection is freely accessible, then viewed with a paid subscription. Attracting over a million people to the site every month, Footnote goes beyond just making valuable documents available on the Internet. Tools on the site make it easy to engage with history. You can upload your photos and documents, make comments on documents and create your own web pages to display and share your discoveries. $11.95/month, $69.95/year.

6. U.S.GenWeb.org -

www.usgenweb.org

This free, sprawling, all-volunteer site is packed with how-to tips, queries and records such as censuses, tombstones, family group sheets, cemetery surveys and marriage indexes for every U.S. state and virtually every county. Organization is by county and state, so they provide links to all the state genealogy websites (which includes historical information on the county and geographical boundaries) which, in turn, provide gateways to the counties. They often provide abstracts of actual records on file (such as cemetery, marriage, birth, death, census, tax, probate, or military records). They also sponsor important special projects at the national level and links to all those pages, as well.

7. GenealogyBank.com -

www.genealogybank.com $$$

Follow your family through America's history. Climb beyond the names and dates on your family tree to the recorded details of their daily lives.

Find the facts in four centuries of fragile, rare newspapers, books and documents. Contains over 29 million obituaries appearing in American newspapers from 1977 to the present. A unique source that provides you with complete text of more than 11,700 books, pamphlets and printed items including: U.S. genealogies, biographies, funeral sermons, local histories, cards, charts and more published prior to 1900. Find military records, casualty lists, Revolutionary and Civil War pension requests, widow's claims, orphan petitions, land grants and much more including all of the American State Papers (1789-1838) and all genealogical content carefully selected from the U.S. Serial Set (1817-1980). More than 229,700 reports, lists and documents. New content added monthly. $19.95/month, $69.95/year.

8. U.S. National Archives -

www.archives.gov

The National Archives and Records Administration is the nation's record keeper. It's a treasure trove of records and documents to trace your family roots. This site increasingly lets you tap its treasures from home, e.g. see Footnote. Access to Archival Databases encompasses more than 85 million historical records, including extracts from WWII Army enlistment papers and 19th-century arrivals of German, Italian, Irish and Russian immigrants. For historical photos and maps and American Indian records, try the *Archival Research Catalog.* The records that are most commonly used by genealogists include:. The actual census, military, immigration (Ship Passenger Lists), naturalization, and land records are not online, but there are finding aids, such as microfilm indexes, and information on how to conduct research in the different types of records.

9. Godfrey Memorial Library -

www.godfrey.org $$$

The Godfrey Memorial Library has long been a valuable resource for genealogists. This private library houses over 200,000 books and periodicals in its collection including: state and local histories, international resources, family histories, biographies, records by religious organizations, church records, funeral records, cemetery records, military records, maps, and an extensive collection of hand-written material, much of which is not available elsewhere. In addition, the Godfrey Library produces the *American Genealogical-Biographical Index*, which is the equivalent of more than 200 printed volumes. This database contains millions of records of people whose names have appeared in printed genealogical records and family histories. It's an especially good resource for historic newspapers, including the London Times, 19th century U.S. newspapers, and early American newspapers. $35/year (without the newspaper databases)

10. Family Tree Connection.com -

www.familytreeconnection.com $$$

A growing collection of unique data indexed from a variety of secondary sources such as high school and college yearbooks, Masonic rosters, club and society member lists, insurance claims data, church directories, orphanage and soldiers' home residents, prisoner logs and much, much more. This data is very useful for connecting with your ancestors, and isn't available elsewhere. The records are compiled from rare documents, pamphlets and unique out-of-print books that contain genealogical tidbits about people from around the world. The database resides at Genealogy Today and is integrated into the search engine on that site. $29.95/year.

Existing Family Trees

FamilySearch.org - www.familysearch.org

One of the comprehensive, preeminent family history web sites on the Internet. It provides access

to the Family History Library and the largest collection of *free* family history, family tree and genealogy records in the world. The *International Genealogical Index* contains more than 285 million people researched and extracted from original records. The *Pedigree Resource File* contains over 225 million names in family trees with about 1.2 million new names submitted to this database every month. *Ancestral File* contains about 37 million lineage-linked names of people throughout the world. FamilySearch provides easy access for the gathering and sharing of family history information. Free.

Ancestry World Tree - www.ancestry.com/trees/awt

Rootsweb WorldConnect - http://wc.rootsweb.ancestry.com

Ancestry World Tree (and Rootsweb WorldConnect) is a free collection of user-submitted GEDCOMs (family trees). You can access World Tree and World Connect from two different websites, but either way, it is the same program and the same set of trees. The database contains more than 480 million names in family trees submitted by users. If you wish to search only World Trees or WorldConnect alone use the URL addresses above. However, an Ancestry.com *general tree search* also includes other family trees not in World Tree. A general search may also include World Tree but only when you click the *"Exact matches only"* button. Free.

MyTrees.com - www.mytrees.com $$$

Contains a pedigree-linked database with over 370 million names, share your family tree worldwide, build your own family tree on-line, and store family history pictures online for display with

your family tree. You can search through millions of names in a family pedigree linked format. You can preview the site before becoming a member by searching their Ancestry Archive Index to determine if you have potential names of interest. You can also connect with researchers and other resources through this site. $7/10-days, $15/month, $35/quarter, $100/year with an one-time free month when you submit a GEDCOM of your family history with at least 15 families and 60 individuals.

One Great Family.com -
www.onegreatfamily.com $$$

A family history program that allows everyone to combine their knowledge and data to build one huge, shared database. Using sophisticated, patented technology, they are linking all of the family trees together into one shared, worldwide database with shared multimedia, notes, research, biographies and citations. The idea is to leverage the effort and research of all users rather than duplicating research that others have already done. Contains about 200 million submitted pedigree-linked names in their family tree database. A significant, groundbreaking new enhancement to its unique, powerful automated searching tools allows the system to precisely merge entire branches of a common family tree, yet preserve a unique version of the family history and highlight any differing information as a "Conflict" so submitters can collaborate and resolve the conflicting information together. 7-Day free trial, $9.95/month, $19.95/quarter, $59.95/year.

GenCircles Global Tree -
www.GenCircles.com/globaltree $$$

Global Tree contains over 90 million names which you can search

for free. If you are a submitter to GT you can use their technology (called SmartMatch) to pair names in your pedigree with those in GT. Free.

Web Directories/Portals

AcademicGenealogy.com -
www.academic-genealogy.com

A mega portal of key worldwide educational genealogical databases and resources. Professional, worldwide humanities and social sciences mega portal, connected directly to numerously related sub-sets, with billions of primary or secondary database family history and genealogy records.

Cyndi's List.com - www.cyndislist.com

Perhaps the best known of the comprehensive web directories that serve as a list or catalog to the entire Internet to help you find other family history web sites. It contains a categorized and cross-referenced index of over 265,000 genealogical online resources; a list of links listed in over 180 different categories that point you to genealogical research sites. It receives more than 3 million visits each month.

Linkpendium.com - www.linkpendium.com

A huge directory of over 7 million genealogy web links categorized by U.S. localities and worldwide surnames.

GenealogyToolbox.com -
www.genealogytoolbox.com

A searchable, categorized (by people, places, and topics) collection of tools to help you research your genealogy or family history. Provides links to

hundreds of thousands of family history Web sites, as well as linking to content and digitized images of original documents.

GenealogySleuth -

www.progenealogists.com/genealogysleuthb.htm

A list of web sites that professional genealogists use daily when conducting U.S. genealogy research. You can also link to the International Genealogy Sleuth.

AccessGenealogy - www.accessgenealogy.com

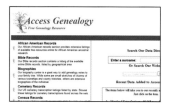

A free search center that offers searching of many different types of records, such as census reports, newspapers, periodicals, emigration and immigration forms, vital records, voting records, military records, Native American genealogy, library archives, cemeteries, churches, and courts; plus Native American and African American essentials. It includes tons of links to other web sites.

Many web sites are directories of where you can go to try and locate more information, or an addresses to write for vital records. They do not contain actual records, but direct you where to find them.

GenealogyHomePage.com -
www.genhomepage.com

Links to genealogy tutorials, resources, newsgroups, online resources, maps and software.

RootsSearch.net - www.rootssearch.net

A genealogy portal where you can post queries, download software, find websites by surname and more.

AncestorHunt.com - www.ancestorhunt.com

Convenient genealogy search engines for Ellis Island, Census online, RootsWeb, Social Security Death Index, LDS Church records, Ancestry.com, United Kingdom Records, CensusDiggins, Genealogy.com and more.

OliveTreeGenealogy.com -
www.olivetreegenealogy.com

Here you will find links to obscure genealogy databases, genealogy resources you can use offline to find ancestors, nuggets of information about a variety of subjects, explanations of genealogical terms, genealogy repositories, address and phone numbers of places and organizations you will need in your family tree search, and much more.

FamilyHistory101.com -
http://familyhistory101.com

This site is an introduction to the wide and rich variety of materials that you can use to build a bridge

for your personal journey back in time. Contains numerous web links to database records.

Other Valuable Databases

NewEnglandAncestors.org - www.newenglandancestors.org $$$

The New England Historical Genealogical Society research library provides access to some of the most important and valuable genealogical resources available anywhere in the world that are not available anywhere else. It is home to more than 2,400 searchable databases containing over 110 million names, over 12 million original documents, artifacts, records, manuscripts, books, family papers, bibles, and photographs dating back more than four centuries. And every week, they add at least one new database on-line. Although their name says New England, they also offer an extensive collection of resources for New York, Canada and Europe as well. $75.00/year

Tribal Pages.com - www.tribalpages.com $$$

This innovative collaboration site hosts more than 175,000 pedigree files, a database of more than 80 million

names and 2 million photos. Plus, you can store your own family tree data here and generate charts and reports right from the site.

HeritageQuest Online.com -
www.heritagequestonline.com

You can't subscribe to this website yourself, but your local library can. If your library subscribes, you can use your library card at home to access the complete U.S. Census (1790-1930), over 24,000 family and local histories, Revolutionary War Pension and Bounty-Land Applications, Freedman's Bank records (1865-1874), the PERSI index to 2.1 million genealogy articles, and the U.S. Serial Set of Memorials, Petitions and Private Relief Actions of Congress.

New England Early Connections -
www.genealogyne.com $$$

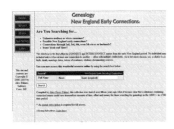

A 73,000+ name database containing connected names for those searching for ancestors from the early New England period of 1600-1700+/-

. No individual name is included unless it has at least one connection to another, through father, mother, son, daughter, spouse, sister, brother with accompanying basic data when available: birth, death, marriage dates, towns of residence, citations documenting sources. An annual subscription is required for full access. $34.95

FamilyHistory Online.net –
www.familyhistoryonline.net

The Federation of Family History Societies publishes records compiled by over 210 family history societies – quality data from experienced researchers

Best of the Internet 6

with local knowledge providing more accurate details. You can now search over 67 million records including parish registers, memorial inscriptions, censuses, poor law documents and others. Search the name index for free, and pay a small fee to view the details if desired.

American Memory Library -
www.memory.loc.gov

The Library of Congress' friendly web site to a wealth of digitized historical documents and photos – more than 9 million items in all, organized into more than 100 thematic collections. The library's regular catalog is also an excellent place to look up pretty much any book in existence.

Canadian Genealogy Centre -
www.collectionscanada.gc.ca/genealogy

Library and Archives Canada collects and preserves Canada's documentary heritage including publications, archival records, sound and audio-visual materials, photographs, artworks, and electronic documents

such as websites. It offers genealogical content, services, advice, research tools and searchable databases for vital, census, immigration and naturalization, military, land and people records, all in both official languages.

UK NationalArchives -
www.nationalarchives.gov.uk

The official archive for England, Wales and the central UK government, containing 1,000 years of history. Provides searchable databases for vital, census, passenger lists, military, citizenship and naturalization, wills records, and more

WorldCat - www.oclc.org > US English Site > *WorldCat*

Tap into the treasures of more than 69,000 libraries worldwide with this one-click search of more than 1.3 billion holdings in 112 countries.

FindMyPast.com - www.findmypast.com

A family history website based in London containing over 550 million family history records, with more being added all the time. They were the first to put the birth, marriage and death records of England and Wales online. You will find links to many resources as well as useful tips and advice on researching your family tree. It helps you organize and illustrate your family tree, adding pictures, stories, dates and events. You can also communicate with other members who are researching their family trees. Searching and building an online family tree with the innovative *Family Tree Explorer* software is free. However, to view records you will need to purchase credits, either by buying pay-per-view units or one of three subscription options. £14.95/30 days, £64.95/year.

Genealogy.com Library -

www.genealogy.com/cgi-bin/odl_browse.cgi?SUBDB=GLC $$$

One of the largest online genealogy collections in the world with over 100 million records spanning five centuries. Requires subscription.

$9.99/month $49.99/year

WorldGenWeb.org - www.worldgenweb.org

This is the global counterpart of US GenWeb dedicated to providing family history and historical records and resources for world-wide access. Most countries have their own sites and many, especially for European ancestries, are packed with advice for beginners.

SearchSystems.net -

www.searchsystems.net $$$

A directory of public records and a resource for background checks and criminal records on the Internet. A good resource of business information, corporate filings, property records, deeds, mortgages, criminal and civil court filings, inmates, offenders, births, deaths, marriages, unclaimed property, professional licenses, and much more. Offers a database of over 300 million state, national, and international criminal records, and a database of over 100 million bankruptcies, judgments, and tax liens. Easy access to billions of records. $9.95/month $29.95/year

Genealogy Today.com -

www.genealogytoday.com

They track new and exciting resources for family historians, and host some features and unique databases themselves. It utilizes *Genealogist's Index to the World Wide Web* which is a combined index for family history research that contains over 10 million names across 5,000 sites. You'll find hundreds of articles on a variety of family history topics, a community of amateur and professional genealogists, plus a store filled with unique items.

Tools to Make It Easier

About Family History.com -

http://familyhistory.about.com -and- http://genealogy.about.com

The "About" network consists of an online neighborhood of hundreds of helpful experts, eager to share their wealth of

knowledge with you. It's organized into categories that cover more than 50,000 subjects with over 1 million links to the best resources on the Net. Each category includes the best new content, relevant links, How-To's, Forums, and answers to just about any question. The family history pages–hosted by Kimberly Powell, a professional genealogist, Web developer, author of *Everything Family Tree, 2nd Edition by Adams Media* (2006), and Webmaster for the Western Pennsylvania Genealogical Society– authentically covers many subjects, such as: Ways to celebrate your family heritage, family history projects, find your family history, American family immigration center, genealogy databases, coat of arms, family history resources on the internet, family history software, and much more. Every month, over 60 million people visit this site for help. It offers solutions with over 2 million original articles, product reviews, videos, tutorials and more.

Roots Television.com - http://rootstelevision.com

A new kind of web site that features Internet TV (or short videos) for all family history lovers available at any time you wish to view it. They even have some training programs to teach you how to do better Family History research. And now you can view the numerous videos on your TV and other devices. They're working hard to find those hidden gems that are scattered everywhere and bring them under one umbrella so you can find everything roots-related you could possibly imagine–all in one place. You can also access links to family history blogs, vlogs (video blogs), and online shopping.

One-Step Search Tools – www.stevemorse.org

Offers dozens of unique software tools for searching passenger records, census and vital records, and natu-ralization records. There

are tools for DNA genealogy, relationship calculator, calendar, zip codes, characters in foreign alphabets, and more.

Dear MYRTLE.com - www.dearmyrtle.com

Pat Richley's *Dear Myrtle* free website, your friend in genealogy, is a fun, helpful family history site with a blog of genealogy news and tips, beginning online lessons, and information about getting organized, family history for kids, using Family History Centers, and writing your personal history. She is the author of *Joy of Genealogy,* and you can also listen to her Family History Hour podcast via your computer or transferred to any .mp3 player.

Shared Tree.com - www.sharedtree.com

A free online family history and genealogy application. There's nothing to download, it's GEDCOM compatible, files have no size limit, and you can collaborate with family and friends instantly.

WeRelate.org - www.werelate.org

A free genealogy wiki where users generate and update the content; sponsored by the Foundation for On-Line Genealogy in partnership with the Allen County Public Library with pages for over 2,000,000 people and families and growing. You can upload GEDCOM files, your documents and photos, share family stories and biographies, and generate maps of ancestors' life events.

Random Acts of Genealogical Kindness -
http://raogk.org

A global volunteer organization with over 4000 volunteers in every U.S. state and many international locations have helped thousands of researchers. Their volunteers take time to do everything from looking up courthouse records to taking pictures of tombstones. All they ask in return is reimbursement for their expenses (never their time) and a thank you.

U.S. Government Made Easy -
www.usa.gov/Citizen/Topics/History_Family.shtml

Official information and services from the U.S. government for genealogists and family historians: Learn how you and your ancestors interacted with the government.

Bible Records.com - www.biblerecords.com

Home to over 1100 Bibles online representing about 3,400 surnames. You can search the collection or browse by Bible or by surname.

Generation Maps.com -
www.generationmaps.com $$$

An easy to use, very affordable, genealogy chart design and printing service. They offer personalized working charts, beautiful decorative charts, custom heirloom charts, and a printing service for charts you've created. Now you don't have to fill in a chart yourself – just send your genealogy computer file and/or your digital photos, tell them how you want it to look, and it arrives on your doorstep for a very reasonable price. They can help you get your research out where you can see it and surround your family with a sense of their heritage. It's also a wonderful, easy way to explain to your family members the research that has been accomplished.

How to Obtain Birth, Death, Marriage, and Divorce Certificates - www.cdc.gov/ nchswww/howto/w2w/w2welcom.htm

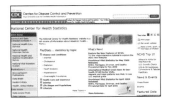

Where to write for vital records from the National Center for Health Statistics.

Geneabios.com - www.geneabios.com

Free genealogy database of biographies. Search for ancestors by entering a name or location, or see a list of all genealogy biographies in the database.

Genealogy Search Advice - www.genealogy-search-advice.com

Get free genealogy search advice that builds on what you already know about your ancestry. Simply answer a series of questions to get specific suggestions on how to best use online genealogy records for researching your ancestors.

FamilyForest.com - www.familyforest.com $$$

A fully sourced lineage-linked database that digitally connects people with each other and with the history they created. Search, browse and print family group sheets, kinship charts, ancestor charts, fan charts, ahnentafel charts, and descendant charts. $9.95

Cousin Calculator - www.iroots.net/tools/cusncalc

Calculates the relationship between two people.

This Day in History -

www.progenealogists.com/dayinhistory.asp

Find out what happened on the day that you or your ancestor was born.

Internet Archive - www.archive.org

A non-profit digital library of Internet sites and other cultural artifacts in digital form: music, movies, audio records, text, software, and web pages. You can search their database and download certain documents.

Current Value of Old Money -

http://projects.exeter.ac.uk/RDavies/ arian/current/howmuch.html

How much would a specified amount of money at a certain period of time be worth today?

Inflation Calculator - www.westegg.com/inflation

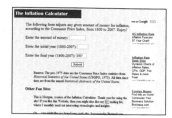

Adjusts any given amount of money for inflation, according to the Consumer Price Index, from 1800 to 2007.

Family Histories That have Been Published

FamilySearch Published Histories - www.family search.org > Search Records > Historical Books

The Family History Library has an extensive collection of published family histories and is digitizing more everyday—even faster. The effort targets published family, society, county, and town histories, as well as numerous other historical publications that are digitally preserved and made accessible for free online. FamilySearch has nearly a million publications in its famous library, and there are millions of similar publications elsewhere in the United States. Working with volunteers and select affiliate libraries, it plans to create the largest digital collection of published histories on the Web. It is helping to digitize and publish collections from the Allen County Public Library, Houston Public Library, and Mid-Continent Public Library Midwest Genealogy Center in Independence, Missouri. When all is said and done, there will be over a million publications in the digital collection online. It will be the largest free resource of its kind. Go to www.familysearch.org > Search Records > Historical Books. You can also search the library catalog for histories by clicking on Library > Library Catalog. First, do a Surname

Search in the catalog, then search for records from the place where your ancestor lived.

Ancestry.com - www.ancestry.com > *Search* > *Stories, Memories, Histories*

Selected histories that profile families from all fifty U.S. states, Canada, and the British Isles going back to the 1700s.

Library of Congress - www.loc.gov/rr/genealogy

One of the world's premier collections of U.S. and foreign genealogical and local historical publications.

WorldCat - www.oclc.org > *WorldCat*

Online Computer Library Center (OCLC) hosts WorldCat, the window to the world's libraries. WorldCat is a global network of library content and services that uses the Web to let you be more connected.

Cyndi's List.com - www.cyndislist.com/lib-state.htm

Extensive Web links to state libraries, archives, genealogical and historical societies.

HeritageQuestOnline.com - www.heritagequestonline.com > *Search Books*

Find information on people and places in over 23,000 family and local histories. You can't

access this website yourself, but you can through your local library. If your library subscribes, you can use your library card at home to access the Web site.

BYU Published Family Histories - www.lib.byu.edu/fslab

The BYU Family History Archive is a collection of published genealogy and family history books. The archive includes histories of families, county and local histories, how-to books on genealogy, genealogy magazines and periodicals (including some international), medieval books (including histories and pedigrees), and gazetteers. It also includes some specialized collections.

Google.com Books - www.books.google.com

Right now, you can search the *full text of some 7 million books,* including genealogy and family history books, through Google Book Search. The books come from two sources. *The Library Project:* they've partnered with renowned libraries around the world to include their collections. For books that are out of copyright, you can read and download the entire book.

For books that are still in copyright, however, the results are like a card catalog; they show you info about the book and, generally, a few snippets of text showing your search term in context. *The Partner Program:* they've partnered with over 20,000 publishers and authors to make their books discoverable on Google. Right now, you can flip through a few preview pages of these books, just like you'd browse them at a bookstore or library. You'll also see links to libraries and bookstores where you can borrow or buy the book.

However, as soon as the new groundbreaking agreement with authors and publishers has been approved (by the court), you'll be able to purchase full online access to millions of books, the vast majority of which are out of print. This means you will be able to read an entire book from any Internet-connected computer, simply by logging in to your account, and it will remain on your electronic bookshelf, so you can come back and access it whenever you want in the future. The tremendous wealth of knowledge that lies within the books of the world will soon be even more at your fingertips.

Libraries and Archives

Rich Sources of New, Unique Information

The following web sites have directories of genealogy libraries and archives.

Library Directories

Cyndi's List - www.cyndislist.com/lib-b.htm

Directory of Genealogy Libraries in the U.S. - www.gwest.org/gen_libs.htm

The Family History Library - www.familysearch.org

The library houses a collection of genealogical records that includes the names of more than 3 billion deceased people. It is the largest collection of its kind in the world

National Archives & Records - www.nara.gov

NARA is America's national record keeper. It is the archives of the Government of the United States.

Library of Congress - www.loc.gov

One of the world's leading cultural institutions. You should look at American Memory which offers more than 7 million digital items from more than 100 historical collections, America's Story, and American Treasures, an unprecedented permanent exhibition of the rarest, most interesting or significant items relating to America's past.

Godfrey Memorial Library - www.godfrey.org $$$

The Library offers access to many premium databases at a reasonable rate. It's an especially good resource for historic newspapers, including the London Times, 19th century US newspapers, and early American newspapers. $15/year

Vital Records

Records of births, marriages, deaths, divorces and adoptions kept by most countries are one of the best resources for helping you to build your family tree.

About.com - http://genealogy.about.com/od/vital_records/a/research.htm

Introduction to vital records.

Cyndi'sList - www.cyndislist.com

Hotlinks for general resource web sites and by state.

National Center for Health Statistics - www.cdc.gov/nchs/howto/w2w/w2welcom.htm

Where to write for vital records.

Vital Records Assistant - www.vitalrec.com

A comprehensive resource for locating vital records: U.S. birth certificates, death records and marriage licenses.

WorldVitalRecords - www.worldvitalrecords.com
> *Record Types > Birth & Marriage Records*

Browse all birth, marriage and death records databases.

BirthDatabase.com - www.birthdatabase.com

A database of 120 million names and birth dates.

Social Security Death Index - http://ssdi.rootsweb.ancestry.com/cgi-bin/ssdi.cgi

Over 83 million records.

Bible Records Online - www.biblerecords.com

A site dedicated to transcribing and digitizing the contents of family records that were written inside family Bibles and in other important

documents from as early as the 1500s through today. Often, these were the only written records of births, marriages and deaths of a family and these remain solid components to proving a family genealogy.

Western States Marriages Index -
http://abish.byui.edu/specialCollections/westernStates/search.cfm

Early marriage records from counties in the western part of the United States. It is not comprehensive for the time period and/or localities described.

However, their goal for is to have marriages from all 12 western states.

Death Indexes.com - www.deathindexes.com

A directory of links to websites with online death indexes, listed by state and county.

Funeral Cards - www.genealogytoday.com/guide/funeral_cards-a.html

While not a traditional "vital record", they often provide great clues like death and birth dates, name of the cemetery where the deceased was interred, name of the funeral home, and sometimes even a photo of the ancestor.

GenealogySleuth - www.progenealogists.com > Genealogy Sleuth

Links to vital records for each state.

USGenWeb Archives - www.usgwarchives.net

The USGenWeb Digital Library offers actual transcriptions of public domain records on the Internet. A cooperative effort of volunteers containing electronically formatted files on census records, marriage bonds, wills, and other public documents.

American History & Genealogy Project - www.ahgp.org

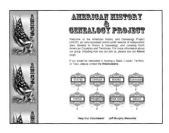

A not-for-profit network of independent sites devoted to history and genealogy, and covering North American countries and territories.

State and County QuickFacts - http://quickfacts.census.gov/qfd

The U.S. Census Bureau's quick, easy access to facts about people, business, and geography.

Census Records
A Snapshot of History

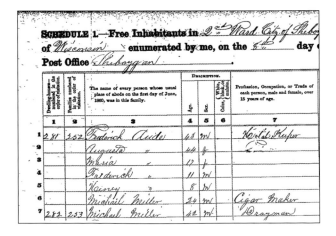

Ancestry.com - www.ancestry.com > *U.S. Census Collection* (scroll down) $$$

This site offers the most U.S. and UK census information available online. Their companion website www.ancestry.ca contains many Canada census records.

FamilySearch.org - www.familysearch.org

In addition to the completed U.S. and UK schedules, many new and updated census records are becoming available as they are indexed. You can search these new records and track their progress at www.familysearch.org > *Search Records > Records Search pilot.*

Heritage Quest.com -
www.heritagequestonline.com

Contains U.S. Census indexes and images; only indexes "Head of Household". It is available online free (at home) through your local library with your library card, and at some 1400 Family History Centers in No. America.

World Vital Records.com -
www.worldvitalrecords.com $$$

Various census images and transcriptions from 1790-1930. Free at Family History Centers.

Find My Past.com - www.findmypast.com $$$

1841, 1851, 1861, 1871, 1881, 1891, 1901 and 1911 UK Censuses. It's free to search but to view the original images requires you to be a paying member. 1841 and 1861 Censuses are free at FamilySearch.org.

Footnote Census.com - www.footnote.com $$$

Explore and search the interactive 1860 and 1930 US Federal Censuses, and leave a comment, photograph, story, or a document on a person's record.

Census Online.com - www.census-online.com

Guide to online census records with over 45,000 web links.

Immigration Records

Tracking Your Ancestors Voyage

American Family Immigration History Center -
www.ellisislandrecords.org

The Ellis Island site contains the immigrant arrival records stored in the Ellis Island Archives containing some 22 million immigration records from 1892-1924 available for free searching.

CastleGarden.org - www.castlegarden.org

Free access to an extraordinary database of information on 10 million immigrants from 1830 through 1892. Over 73 million Americans can trace their ancestors to this early immigration period.

Immigrant Ships.net – www.immigrantships.net

A free searchable directory by volunteers who have transcribed over 9,000 passenger lists. It also offers a directory of sites to research emigration, immigration and naturalization, 100+ passenger list sites, ethnic research, libraries and archives, passenger ship types, descriptions and images, and additional worldwide maritime information.

Ancestry's U.S. Immigrant Collection –
www.ancestry.com $$$

Ship passenger lists, naturalization records, ship photos and much more.

Canadian Genealogy Centre -
www.collectionscanada.gc.ca/genealogy

Canada's documentary web site offers immigration and naturalization databases in both official languages, as well as vital, census, military, and land record databases.

One-Step Search Tools - http://stevemorse.org

Some people have been frustrated at not being able to locate a particular ancestor in the Ellis Island Archives, Castle Garden, and other censuses and vital records sites.

Transcribing millions of foreign-sounding names and places written in often difficult-to-decipher handwriting on pages that were frequently faded, smeared, or otherwise damaged was difficult. And many of the names were perhaps faithful replications of misspellings in the original records. Dr. Stephen Morse developed his own specialized search engine that enables you to search these databases in more ways that are faster and in some cases more useful: by passenger, "sounds-like" using the last name, town search, Jewish passengers, ancestor's village, date, and damaged images which are not indexed. If at first you don't succeed, try using different names (or spellings) your ancestor may have used, last-name only searches, switching the first and last names in your search, and by approximating their arrival date.

Military Records

Track Your Ancestors Footsteps through History

Revolutionary War Pension Files -
www.heritagequestonline.com

Index and supporting file images to participation in Revolutionary War. It is available free through

your local library with your library card, and at some Family History Centers.

Footnote Military Records -
www.footnote.com $$$

An online repository for original historical documents relating to the Revolutionary War, Civil War, WWI, WWII, the Vietnam War, historical newspapers, and many more. The documents are made possible by their unique partnership with The National Archives and other archives from around the U.S. They recently released the first ever interactive World War II collection, which includes an interactive version of the USS Arizona Memorial, WWII Hero Pages, and WWII photos and documents previously unavailable on the internet. Their Hero Pages is a tribute or memorial to war heroes. It features an interactive timeline and map, a place to upload photos, documents and letters, and a place to share stories about individuals who fought in WWII. They also feature the largest image of the Vietnam War Memorial where visitors can view the service records and member contributions for each name on the wall. All the indexes are free to search which includes names, places, topics, a list of documents and a

small image of the document, but a membership is required to view the full image. Free at Family History Centers. $11.95/month, $69.95/year.

Ancestry Military Collection -
www.ancestry.com $$$

Discover the heroes in your family tree in their U.S. Military Collection - the largest online assortment of U.S. military records, covering more than three centuries of American wars and conflicts. With more than 100 million names and 700 titles and databases in military records from all 50 U.S. states, there are countless opportunities to learn the stories of courage and sacrifice in your family tree.

Cemeteries, Gravesites, Obituaries

Distant Cousin.com - www.distantcousin.com

A grab bag of newspaper obituaries, city directories, census records, ship lists, school yearbooks, military records and other resources. They provide access to more than 6 million records from 1,500-plus sources.

Find a Grave.com - www.findagrave.com

Who needs to go tromping around graveyards when you have this easy-to-search site, which makes it easy to, well, dig into graves? You can make quick progress finding not only ancestors' final resting places but also their birth and death dates, transcribed from tombstones, among the 22 million records here.

Interment.net - www.interment.net

Provides free access to thousands of cemetery records, tombstone inscriptions and veteran burials, from cemeteries in the USA, Canada,

England, Ireland, Australia, New Zealand, and other countries. There are currently 3.9 million cemetery records across 8,375 cemeteries available for searching on this site.

MortalitySchedules.com - www.mortalityschedules.com

If your ancestor died within the 12 months preceding the 1850, 1860, 1870 or 1880 census enumeration, you won't find them in the regular census, but you will find them in lists know as Mortality Schedules available on this site.

Veterans Gravesite Locator - http://gravelocator.cem.va.gov

Search for burial locations of veterans and their family members in VA National Cemeteries, state veterans cemeteries, various other military and Department of Interior cemeteries, and for veterans buried in private cemeteries when the grave is marked with a government grave marker.

Historical Data

GenealogyBank.com - www.genealogybank.com $$$

With millions of records added monthly, GenealogyBank now has over 253 million family history records and an estimated 1

billion names found in: Historical Newspapers (1690-1980) 2,500 titles, America's Obituaries (1977-Today) – over 29 million obits from more than 1,100 newspapers, Historical Books & Documents (1789-1980), Social Security Death Index (1937-Today) – more than 83 million death records. Most comprehensive SSDI site online! You can search for free, but you need to subscribe ($9.95) to view the details.

Making of America - http://moa.umdl.umich.edu and http://moa.cit.cornell.edu/moa

This is a joint project between the University of Michigan and Cornell University which provides free access to a large collection of 19th century books, journal articles, and imprints on two websites.

Library of Congress - www.americaslibrary.org

The largest library in the world which has millions of amazing things that will surprise you.

World History.com - www.worldhistory.com

A new free social history web site that offers interactive maps, timelines, videos,

geocoded photos, museum artifacts, genealogy and much more.

eHistory.com - www.ehistory.com

Serves up more than 130,000 pages of historical content, 5,300 timeline events, 800 battle outlines, 350 biographies and thousands of images and maps.

HyperHistory.com - www.hyperhistory.com

An interactive combination of lifelines, timelines, and maps covering over 3,000 years of world history, plus numerous web links to other sites.

Best of History Web Sites.net -
www.besthistorysites.net

Web links to the best sites for Prehistory, Ancient/Biblical History, Medieval History, American History, Early Modern Europe, World War II, Art History, Oral History, and maps.

European History -
http://eudocs.lib.byu.edu/index.php/Main_Page

These free links from BYU library connect to European primary historical documents – ancient, medieval, renaissance, and modern times – that shed light on *key historical happenings* within the respective countries and within the broadest sense of political, economic, social and cultural history.

Maps & Geographical Information

Mapping Your Ancestry; Discover the Place Your Ancestors Called Home

Google Maps - www.maps.google.com

A popular, free web mapping service that offers street maps (U.S., Australia, Canada, Japan, New Zealand, and Western Europe), satellite maps for the whole world, and a hybrid map (a combination of satellite imagery with an overlay of streets, city names, and landmarks).

USGS Gazetteer -
http://geonames.usgs.gov/pls/gnis/web_query.gnis_web_query_form

Enter a place name to find out where it is located. Also has other uses, such as finding the location of every church, school, or cemetery in a particular county.

Color U.S. Landform Atlas -
http://fermi.jhuapl.edu/states/states.html

You can view new maps and imagery that have never before been posted to the internet. You will see 3-

D maps, high resolution maps, registered maps, as well as maps of Mars, Europe, Asia, all of the continents, and more.

USGenWeb.org - www.usgenweb.org

Contains resources and queries for a specific state or county in the USA.

Bureau of Land Management - www.glorecords.blm.gov

This is the place to start exploring land records, including more than 3 million federal land title records for Eastern public-land states (1820 to 1908) and images of serial patents issued from 1908 to the mid-1960s. Land east of the Mississippi that wasn't in one of the original colonies belonged to the U.S. government and was sold originally to the first settlers. Images of field notes and survey plats, dating to 1810, are being added on a state-by-state basis. Searching is fast and powerful, and you'll find plenty of help for understanding the records you locate.

Worldwide GenWeb - http://worldgenweb.org

Resources and read/post queries that relate to a specific country.

Perry-Castañeda Library Map Collection - www.lib.utexas.edu/maps

This site brings historical and current interest maps from around the world straight to your computer screen.

U.S. General Land Office Records - http://content.ancestry.com/iexec/?htx=List&dbid=1246 $$$

This database contains land patents from 1796-1907 for 13 U.S. states. Information recorded in land patents includes: name of patentee, issue date, state of patent, acres of land, legal land description, authority under which the land was acquired, and other details relating to the land given.

Ethnic Resources

African American Roots

Cyndi's List.com - www.cyndislist.com

Perhaps the best known index website; lists over 265,000 links to sites to help you with research; over 180 different categories. Contains hundreds of links to websites for doing African American research.

AfriGeneas.com - www.afrigeneas.com

A searchable database of surnames for researching families of African ancestry. They offer a guide to family history resources around the world, and a mailing list of information about families of African ancestry. They also have impressive links to other websites to do research.

Slave Voyages.org -

www.slavevoyages.org/tast/index.faces

The Trans-Atlantic Slave Trade Database has information on almost 35,000 slaving voyages that forcibly embarked over 10 million Africans for transport to the Americas between the sixteenth and nineteenth centuries. It offers a chance to rediscover the reality of one of the largest forced movements of peoples in world history. It documents the slave trade from Africa to the New World from the 1500s to the 1800s. The names of 70,000 human cargo are also documented (slaves' African names).

National Archive Resources -

www.archives.gov/genealogy/ heritage/index.html

Directory of web links to African-American resources.

Christine's Genealogy Website -

www.ccharity.com

An excellent site about African-American history and genealogy.

Freedman's Bank Records -

www.familysearch.org > *Search Records* > *Record Search* > *USA*

A searchable database documenting several generations of African Americans immediately following the Civil War.

The records cover the time period from about 1864 to 1871 and document the names and family relationships of those who used the bank. There are approximately 480,000 names in the file, which have been entered in a pedigree-linked GEDCOM format. (*See Chapter 2 for details.*) You can also purchase the CD for a nominal fee at www.ldscatalog.com > (do a quick search for *Freedman*) - $6.50

Hispanic / Latino Americans

Mexico Research Guide - www.familysearch.org > Research Helps > Articles

The LDS Church has also developed a comprehensive 68-page Research Outline about Mexican family history records to search.

Cyndi's List of Hispanic Sites -

www.cyndislist.com/hispanic.htm

Catalog of genealogical sites arranged by topic and country. Includes web links to Internet sites; mailing lists; people and families; news groups; publications, and transcriptions of records; societies; and villages, and colonies.

Hispanic Roots Television -

www.rootstelevision.com >*Hispanic Genealogy*

An online television network featuring on-demand videos absolutely free. The Hispanic Roots Channel features free genealogy family history videos focused on Hispanic, Latino, South American, and Mexican research.

Native Americans

How to Trace Indian Ancestry -
www.doi.gov/ancestry.html

U.S. Department of Interior's website on tracing your Indian ancestry.

Cyndi's List.com - www.cyndislist.com > Native American

Numerous links to web sites for tracing your Native American family roots.

Footnote.com Native American -
www.footnote.com $$$

Footnote is an online repository for original historical documents. Some areas are free, while others can be freely searched and then viewed with a paid subscription. They have nearly 900,000 Native American records currently.

Access Genealogy - www.accessgenealogy.com

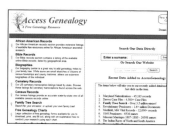

A free genealogy resource with tons of links, this portal also offers census, vital, immigration, cemetery and military records; plus Native American and African American essentials.

Other Ethnic Resources

National Archive Resources -
www.archives.gov/genealogy/ heritage/index.html

Directory of web links to various ethnic resources. Includes: United Kingdom and Ireland; Australia and New Zealand; Canadian and French-Canadian; Eastern European and Russian; Hispanic: Central and South America, Mexico, Caribbean, West Indies; Jewish; Western European; and more.

Cyndi's List.com - www.cyndislist.com > Topical Index > Ethnic Groups and People

Numerous links to web sites for tracing many Ethnic heritages.

Newspapers and Periodicals
What Was Their Life Like?

Google Historical News Search -
http://news.google.com/archivesearch

Google enables you to search through more than 200 years of historical newspaper archives for free.

GenealogyBank.com -
www.genealogybank.com $$$

Search over 127 million historical newspaper articles and find obituaries, marriage notices and often surprising facts about your ancestors.

NewspaperArchive.com -
www.newspaperarchive.com $$$

Access to more than 93 million historical newspaper pages.

Newspaper Abstracts.com -
www.newspaperabstracts.com

A good resource for family history research using newspapers. It currently contains about 62,000 pages of abstracts and extracts from historical newspapers, and growing. Newspapers contain much information that may not be found elsewhere such as births, marriages, deaths, court notices, land sales, tax notices, businesses, etc. They also hold many glimpses of information in their community news and provide us with fascinating details about the lives of our ancestors. There are well over 100 million pages of newspapers preserved on microfilm in the United States alone.

WorldVitalRecords.com -
www.worldvitalrecords.com $$$

Exclusive access to the Small Town Newspaper Collection.

U.S. Newspaper Program -
www.neh.gov/projects/usnp.html

A cooperative national effort among the states and the federal government to locate, catalog, and preserve on microfilm newspapers published in the United States from the eighteenth century to the present. You can access the database through participating libraries across the country.

Library of Congress - www.loc.gov/rr/news

An extensive newspaper collection of over 9,000 U.S. newspaper titles, 25,000 non-US newspaper titles, 7,000 current periodicals, 6,000 comic books, and 1 million government publications.

FamilySearch.org - www.familysearch.org > *Library*

This site offers thousands of microfilmed newspapers from around the world which can be ordered through your local Family History Center for free. Use the Place Search button in the Family

History Library Catalog for your ancestor's location to find what newspapers and other records have been microfilmed.

Ancestry's Newspaper Collection -
www.ancestry.com/newspapers $$$

 You can search a large collection of large and small newspapers beginning in the early 1800s and some extending into the 2000s.

Photographs

Preserving the Past for Future Generations

Google's Photo Organizer -
http://picasa.google.com

 Find, organize and share your photos. Picasa is a *free* software download from Google that helps you: Locate and organize all the photos on your computer, edit and add effects to your photos with a few simple clicks, find, organize and share your photos.

Dead Fred.com - www.deadfred.com

 This original online photo-reunion site has grown to more than 40,000 old pictures, some 16,000 surnames, and over 89,000 records. Your ancestors might be waiting for you here.

Ancient Faces.com - www.ancientfaces.com

 A visual genealogy website that has thousands of old photos that adds a face to your lists of names and dates.

Western History Photography Collection -
www.photoswest.org

 This searchable selection of 95,000 images from the collections of the Denver Public Library and the Colorado Historical Society documents the history of Colorado and the American West. Bring your Old West family history to life with scenes of American Indians, pioneers, railroads, mining, frontier towns, ranch life, scenery, news events and more.

Ancestor Photo Archive.com -
http://ancestorarchive.com

 Free collection of vintage family photos, for sharing, or reuniting with their families.

Family Photoloom.com - www.photoloom.com
$$$

 A dynamic web application that connects your photos, genealogy, stories, and documents to create truly seamless family history. You can organize your pictures around your family history (and into albums), index family relationships, and tag faces and resource documents. Free trial. $39/year.

CHAPTER 7

The Best LDS Web Sites

KEY LDS FAMILY HISTORY WEB SITES AND THE STORY BEHIND THEIR ENORMOUS CONTRIBUTIONS TO FAMILY HISTORY

© by Intellectual Reserve, Inc.

Millions of people who are interested in genealogy and family history around the world owe a great deal to the LDS Church due to its unique, invaluable collection and preservation of billions of family history records worldwide for over a century, and then making the records available to everyone for free, regardless of religious affiliation. They created and operate the largest Family History Library in the world and the preeminent www.family-search.org web site which has become one of the most popular sites on the Internet ever. A major, exciting project to improve *FamilySearch* has been in process for the past few years to improve ways to make organizing, viewing and sharing family histories online easier, faster and better for everyone. At press time, they have issued a limited, phased-beta release and will begin rolling it out worldwide as soon as it's ready.

© by Intellectual Reserve, Inc.

Comprehensive Resource Site with Live Web Links

Step-by-Step Colorfully Illustrated Guidebooks

Since new family history databases and web sites become available regularly (and web addresses often change), we constantly review all the new information and keep you up-to-date on changes and the latest news and trends on the *EasyFamilyHistory.com* companion Web site. It's a user-friendly, easy-to-use Internet directory of the *Best of the Internet* family history web sites. It provides a brief overview of each site and active *hotlinks* to easily connect to the key family history web sites worldwide containing billions of database records and valuable resources. Enjoy!

EasyFamily History.com

Family History Insights - 7

What Does "Third Cousin Once Removed" Mean?

Most of the time family relationships are simple. We know our father and mother, our brothers and sisters, aunts, uncles, grandparents, etc. In our society, *cousinhood* is our way of expressing how closely two people are related to each other. We do this by counting generations back to our common ancestor, and subtracting one. For example, two people who share the same grandparents count two generations to their common ancestors. Two minus one equals one, so they are "first" cousins. If their closest common ancestors were their great great grandparents, they would be "third" cousins (four generations, minus one, equals three). We say *removed* when the number of generations is unequal. If you count three generations to a common ancestor (your great grandfather), and your cousin counts four generations to that same ancestor (her great great grandfather), your *cousinhood* is expressed first in terms of the closest relationship (second cousins), with an amendment showing the difference of one generation (once removed). Determining relationships can sound complex, but if you remember that you're simply counting generations, it's easier.

Genuine History

"A morsel of genuine history is a thing so rare as to be always valuable." – Thomas Jefferson (1743-1826), Founding Father, 3rd President

Thomas Jefferson

Standing on Ancestors Shoulders

The only way to look into the future is by standing on the shoulders of the past. – unknown

A Tree Without Roots

"To forget one's ancestors is to be a brook without a source, a tree without a root." – Chinese Proverb

Digging in Dirt/Facts

The difference between a geologist and a genealogist is that one digs in the dirt and sometimes finds artifacts, while the other digs in facts and sometimes finds dirt. – Unknown

Benefits From Ancestors

"What task could be more agreeable than to tell of the benefits conferred on us by our ancestors, so that you may get to know the achievements of those from whom you have received both the basis of your beliefs and the inspiration to conduct your life properly?" – William Malmesbury, 1125 A.D.

Spiritually Refining

"No work is more of a protection to [us] than... genealogical research. ... No work is more spiritually refining. No work we do gives us more power. Our labors... cover us with a shield and a protection." Boyd K. Packer

Boyd K. Packer
© by Intellectual Reserve, Inc.

An Historian

"An historian is a prophet in retrospect." August von Schlegel (1767-1845), German poet

August von Schlegel

Ancestors Wisdom

"We have hardly any land-marks from the wisdom of our ancestors, to guide us. At best we can only follow the spirit of their proceeding in other cases." Edmund Burke, (1729-1797), Irish statesman & author

Edmund Burke

Why are Latter-day Saints so Interested in Family History?

AND HOW DOES THAT BENEFIT ALL OF US?

Mormon Temple, Salt Lake City, Utah

Most people have little knowledge of the LDS Church or the reasons why they collect family history records which benefit all of us so greatly. In this section I attempt to provide some answers to these questions. In addition, it's amazing how many new and exciting digital record collections are being made available on the Internet in recent years at an ever-increasing rate. However, Latter-day Saint (LDS) web sites are not as easy to find but can be very helpful in your research. This chapter, therefore, also spotlights many of these lesser known but very valuable resources.

This collection of *The Best LDS Family History Web Sites* is not meant to be a complete listing of all

LDS web sites available. There are more comprehensive sources available. Rather, this is a user-friendly selection of pre-screened, *key* LDS Web sites to save you valuable time and empower you with this information.

Who Are the Mormons?

"Jesus Christ"
by Harry Anderson
© by Intellectual Reserve, Inc.

The Church of Jesus Christ of Latter-day Saints (casually known as the LDS or Mormon Church) is one of the world's fastest-growing Christian religions. The worldwide headquarters are in Salt Lake City, Utah, but the Church was founded in a log cabin in upstate New York in 1830 with a mere six members. Church membership is now over 13 million in 177 nations worldwide with hundreds of thousands of new members joining each year in many parts of the world. It currently has the fourth-largest membership of any church within the United States.

Latter-day Saints, it seems, have always had a peculiar hold on the American imagination. Few know who they really are, and their story is still one of the great neglected American narratives. In the early years, Mormons were feared, ridiculed, and persecuted by eminent religious figures, politicians, and others, and calumny and lies about the Mormons were spread by their enemies. Mormons claim that the LDS Church is a restoration of New Testament Christianity as taught by Jesus and His apostles. It is not Protestant, Evangelical, Catholic or Orthodox. *Further information is available on their website www.mormon.org.*

The LDS Church remains mysterious to many today because some central tenets of Mormonism seem confusing to those outside the faith, and unfortunately, many myths and falsehoods about

the LDS faith still exist. Yet, in the past several decades, the LDS Church has transformed itself from a perceived fringe religion into a thriving dynamic one that embraces mainstream American values. The basic values of morality, civility and family espoused by the LDS Church are similar to those of other highly regarded faiths. Its members include prominent and powerful politicians, university presidents and corporate leaders. They are found at every level of society – in business and agriculture, education and the sciences, political parties and government, the entertainment industry and news media.

Unique Beliefs Drive Search for Ancestors and Ancestral Benefits

Latter-day Saints are actively involved in family history work, but they are involved for unique reasons. They believe that life does not end at death, that the marriage relationship and the family unit can continue beyond the grave, and that their deceased ancestors can also receive the blessing of being eternally united with their families.

Most people want to believe that they will be re-united with their spouse and family after death. When husband and wife tenderly love each other, they are comforted with the hope of its continuance after death and are taught to

Why Mormons Build Temples

Mormon Temple, San Diego, California

About 130 Mormon temples (with another 16 in process) adorn sites in North, South, and Central America, Europe, Asia, Africa, and numerous islands of the sea. Mormon temples differ from a church meetinghouse used for weekly worship services. They believe that their temples are holy places of worship where they make sacred covenants with God, that temple worship played a prominent role in the Bible's Old Testament, and that temple work today is a restoration of practices that have been lost in a great apostasy from the original gospel of Jesus Christ. In the temple, priesthood ordinances for the living and the dead are preformed, and sacred covenants are made. According to the LDS faith, the primary purpose of the temple is to "seal" or unite families together for eternity. For this reason, LDS Church members actively search out information about their ancestors.

Mormon Temple, Bountiful, Utah

hold steadfastly to the ideal of the eternity of marriage and family.

Elizabeth Barrett Browning

To illustrate this yearning for an eternal family, in the famous sonnet entitled "How do I love thee?" Elizabeth Barrett Browning ponders the profundity of her love for Robert, and then concludes: *"If God chooses, I shall but love thee better after death."* Usually when someone's loving spouse dies, the survivor is comforted by the thought that eventually they will be together again in heaven, and their relationship will continue as before.

Marriages in the LDS faith are distinct and different from marriages in other denominations. Latter-day Saints not only believe that the marital and family bond can continue in the post-earth life, but indeed is *necessary* for eternal life. Therefore, they make special covenants in their temples because they believe that these covenants, when faithfully kept, can unite families together for eternity.

One of the ordinances performed in the LDS temples is *celestial marriage* which they believe is far more than the common marriage covenant "until death do we part". In this ordinance husband and wife are *"sealed"* to one another for all eternity, along with their family. They believe that a sealing performed in the temple continues forever if the husband and wife are faithful to each other and keep the promises they make. Thus, one of the highest religious goals for Latter-day Saints is to be married for eternity, and to have their children sealed to them in an LDS temple and to strive continually to strengthen the bonds of love and righteousness in marriage. Civil marriages are recognized as lawful and beneficial, but they believe that they do not continue after death. Mormon marriages solemnized in the temple enjoy a divorce rate significantly lower than the U.S. national average.

They also believe that their ancestors who have died without this essential gospel ordinance may receive this ordinance and be united with their spouse and family for eternity through the work done in temples. They believe it is their privilege and duty to perform these sacred ordinances vicariously for their deceased progenitors. So acting in behalf of their ancestors who have died, LDS members participate in the *sealings* of husband-to-wife and children-to-parents all of whom may accept these covenants, if they so choose, in the afterlife spirit world where they reside.

Controversy About a Mormon Belief

Another ordinance performed in their temples is *baptism for the dead* – vicarious or "proxy" baptism –

A special baptismal font resting upon the backs of 12 oxen to perform proxy baptisms for deceased ancestors.

for their deceased ancestors – those who died without the opportunity to receive the gospel of Jesus Christ. These baptisms are performed by a living person acting on behalf of one who is dead, as practiced in New Testament times, as they say. According to the LDS faith, members are motivated by love and compassion and they believe that this will help bring happiness and peace to those ancestors who have passed on.

Apostle Paul

Though *baptism for the dead* is briefly mentioned but not explained in the Bible by the Apostle Paul (1 Corinthians 15:29), the LDS Church says that this is a reference to an accepted practice in the original Church established by Jesus which has long since been forgotten or ignored by mainstream Christianity today. A restoration of this ancient Christian practice has uniquely become a foundational doctrine of the Latter-day Saint faith.

Summary

These unique beliefs drive their collection and preservation of billions of records worldwide to better be able to search for their Ancestors – which benefits everyone. To help members in tracing their genealogies, the LDS Church has photographed vital records throughout the world for about 100 years that identify billions of persons who have died. Now that new technology is available, they are unlocking the Granite Mountain Vault where these records have been safely stored for many decades. There are more than 5 billion documents stored (with untold billions of names) – 132 times more data than the U.S. Library of Congress.

FamilySearch is currently scanning, digitizing and indexing this extensive collection of genealogical records held in the Granite Vault. They are scanning over 32 million

> Members of the LDS Church gather family history records and construct temples in which "eternal marriage", sealing (or uniting) of families together forever, and baptisms for their ancestors can be performed which they believe provides blessings to their ancestors.

Ancestors Personal Choice

The LDS Church notes, however, that any rite performed in a Latter-day Saint temple on behalf of a deceased person (who yet lives as a spirit being) is a rite of *offering* only, exacting no forced compliance nor acceptance of the rite. There is no imposed change of identity, heritage or religious belief, nor is the individual's name added to the membership rolls of the LDS Church.

While members of the LDS Church consider it a great loving service to perform vicarious ordinances for their deceased, some members of other faiths have taken offense. Apparently, the Mormons have done this Christian act of service with nothing but good intentions, but they did not understand their gesture might offend others, for example Jews.

To be sensitive to the issue of proxy baptizing for non-Mormons that are not related to Church members, the LDS Church in recent years has published a general policy of only performing temple ordinances for direct ancestors of Church members. In addition, the Church has removed (or is still in the process of removing) sensitive names, such as Jewish Holocaust victims, from its *International Genealogical Index.*

The LDS Church says that vicarious baptism does not mean that the decedent is forced to accept the ordinance performed for him or her. The deceased person does NOT become a member of the LDS Church. It merely means that the decedent has the option to accept the ordinance and the benefits which baptism provides.

images per month, the equivalent of about 6 million 300-page volumes per year. They are requesting your help to index these records which will be freely available to everyone on FamilySearch.org. There are currently about 170,000 worldwide volunteers indexing these records, but they are seeking 1.5 million volunteers. It's easy, you can work on your own time, and they train you. You can get more info on their web site http://family-searchindexing.org.

The LDS Church provides free access to these records to everyone through FamilySearch, the Family History Library in Salt Lake City and in over 4,500 local Family History Centers worldwide. *Further information about these resources is available in Chapter 6, and at www.FamilySearch.org.*

So for Latter-day Saints, family history is more than a hobby. They believe that they have a religious obligation to trace their genealogies, and that LDS temple work is for the redemption of the dead, more specifically their own deceased relatives. So within Mormon temples, members perform the ordinances necessary for their ancestors who have died, and are sealed together as families forever to be able to enjoy the blessings of eternal life. For this reason the LDS Church has collected and continues to collect billions of records worldwide. And fortunately for us, they make the records available to everyone for free.

Typical Family History Center

The Best LDS Web Sites

Online Directories of LDS Web Sites

Here are some online Web site directories (and a book) that provide web links specifically for LDS family history.

EasyFamilyHistory.com -
www.easyfamilyhistory.com

My free reviewed list (with summaries) of the *Best LDS Family History Web Sites* including active, up-to-date web hotlinks. It also is a valuable resource site for getting started and provides unique tools for teaching family history classes. *Everything you need to make your genealogy easy.*™

Cyndi's List of LDS Records -
www.cyndislist.com/lds

A comprehensive list of LDS related websites organized by the following topics: Family History Centers,

Family History Library, FamilySearch, history of the LDS Church, Mailing Lists, Miscellaneous Genealogy Resources, Professional Researchers, Publications/Software, Queries and Lists.

FamilySearch.org Web Links - www.family-search.org > *Free Online Resources* (Listed under *Start Your Family History*)

Web links to Census records, Vital records, Immigration records, Military records, and Other Key Web Resources.

Genealogy Links.org -
http://genealogy-links.org

US & Canada census indexes, immigration, birth, marriage, death, cemetery, obituary, maps, colonial ancestors, LDS info, Paf, Legacy. Contains many LDS/Utah references including information on history, genealogy, and immigration.

Allen's Mormon Site.org -
www.mormonsite.org > *Links*

LDS Web links created by Allen Leigh on a wide variety of different topics, including some genealogy links.

LDS and Utah Records -
http://uvpafug.org/classes/dons/dons-lds&utahrecords.html

Web links and notes by Donald Snow, family history instructor, categorized under the following

headings: Major web sites, Utah and Arizona Vital Records, LDS Church records, LDS family history CD, and Miscellaneous.

My LDS Links.com - www.myldslinks.com

Another web portal of LDS Web Links organized by specific topics, including some family history and genealogy.

Book: *A Guide to Mormon Family History Sources* - www.kipsperry.com $16.95

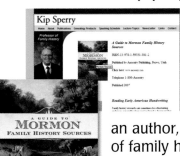

A comprehensive list of LDS family history websites, databases, and much more in one book by Kip Sperry, an author, lecturer, and Professor of family history at BYU. Available to purchase online from www.AncestryStore.com.

LDS Rankings.com - www.ldsrankings.com

Directory of a wide variety of LDS Websites including some genealogy sites.

LDS Index.org - www.ldsindex.org

Another directory of LDS related web sites.

LDS Internet Resource - www.ldsfiles.com

Ideas, activities, talks, lessons, clipart and more for many LDS subjects, including family history.

Members of the LDS Church can also go to **EasyFamilyHistory.com** to access up-to-date information, specific tips, quotes, and guidelines to help you do family history and temple work.

Help for LDS Church Members

The web site also contains specific information for Latter-day Saints (as well as for everyone) interested in family history, and will specifically guide you in your quest to complete your family history. LDS Church members can find the following articles:

- Family History Insights from Church Leaders
- Prophets Speak on Family History
- Help From the Other Side of the Veil
- Turning Our Heart to our Fathers
- What are the Promises Made to the Fathers?
- Who is the Prophet Elijah and Why is it Important?
- What Should Latter-day Saints be Doing?
- Redemption of the Dead
- Who Needs Temple Ordinances?
- How to Submit a Name to the Temple
- *"New"* FamilySearch Family Tree Guidelines
- Simple Guidelines For Submitting Names

Where Do I Start?

FamilySearch.org - www.familysearch.org

You need to register as a member of the LDS Church to access the temple ordinance info. Then click on the *International Genealogical Index (IGI)* and search for your ancestor and determine if they need temple ordinances. (*See more details about "Submitting a Family Ordinance Request in New FamilySearch" at www.easyfamilyhistory.com.*) If *new FamilySearch* Family Tree is available in your area, you need to register separately (in addition to regular FamilySearch).

LDS Members Guide to Temple and Family History Work - https://new.familysearch.org/en/static/help/pdf/membersguide.pdf

Newly updated guide with the following 7 chapters:

1 The Purpose of Temple and Family History Work

2 Getting Started

3 Gathering Information from Home

4 Recording Family History Information

5 Gathering Information from Family

6 Gathering Information from Public Records

7 Providing Temple Ordinances

Appendix: Forms, Questions for Interviewing Family Members, Record Selection Table.

Tracing LDS Families - http://wiki.family-search.org > Search for *'Tracing LDS Families'*

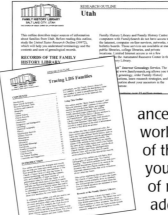

A Research Outline detailing the strategies and records that can help you learn more about your ancestors from around the world who were members of the LDS Church. It helps you decide which types of records to search. In addition to this outline, you will also need to use the research outlines available for the state, province, and nation where your ancestor lived. For example, the *Utah Research Outline* and the *United States Research Outline* would help locate many records about Church members in those places. Go to www.FamilySearch.org > *Research Helps > Articles,* and click on 'PDF' under each article.

Early Latter-day Saints.com - www.earlylds.com

This site provides information about the lives and families of pioneer Latter-day Saints (over 61,000 names) who lived in the more than 90 settlements of Latter-day Saints in the Missouri Valley, across the state of Iowa, and Winter Quarters in Nebraska from 1830–1868. You will find individual and family information in family group, pedigree and descendant reports some with photographs as well as biographies, settlement histories, maps, cemeteries, and timelines that will help you understand their lives and times. It also contains an index of over 100 books found in the Pioneer Research Library at the Mormon Trail Center at Historic Winter Quarters, and links to Census records and other research sites. Click *'Help'* to view the introductory information.

Early LDS Church Membership -

www.worldvitalrecords.com > *Record Types* >
Popular Collections > *LDS Collection* $$$ -or-
http://www.worldvitalrecords.com/indexinfo.as
px?ix=usa_il_nauvoo_early_lds_members

A database of birth, marriage, and death records comprised of a 50-volume list (about 113,000 names) of people who were members of the LDS Church from 1830 to 1848 and who lived in the United States, Canada or Great Britain. The database created by Susan Black was compiled using more than 300 primary and secondary sources on early Latter-day Saints, but it does not necessarily include every member of the Church who lived during the time period. This site includes other LDS databases of value and allows you to *browse* the list for free. But at Family History Centers you can also browse and view the actual databases for free.

Early Church Information File -

https://wiki.familysearch.org >
(Perform a search for this title)

An alphabetical index of individuals on 75 rolls of microfilm. It contains about 1,500,000 entries from over 1,200 sources about Latter-day Saints and their neighbors. The index is international in scope and should be among the first sources checked when searching for Latter-day Saint ancestors or persons living in areas heavily populated by Latter-day Saints. It mainly covers sources from 1830 to the mid-1900s; includes LDS Church records, LDS immigration records, cemetery records, biographies, journals, and some published books. Microfilm numbers for each individual are listed in the Family History Library Catalog.

Tracing Mormon Pioneers -

www.xmission.com/~nelsonb/pioneer

Tips for tracing Mormon Pioneer ancestry from Europe, Scandinavia, Australia, and South Africa to Salt Lake City, Utah. Includes an index of thousands of references of those who migrated to Utah during 1847-1868, plus an index search tool for *Utah Census Records.*

PBS Ancestors TV Series -

www.byub.org/ancestors

The companion web site to the PBS family history and genealogy television series featuring: beginning your research, helpful resources, online tools, inspiring video clips about personal stories, and recommended links.

123 Genealogy.com - www.123genealogy.com $$$

Family history tutorial videos focusing on methodology, software, internet and research topics. The best genealogy experts become your personal tutors as you learn step-by-step the ins and outs of family history.

Adding New Branches to Your Family Tree

Mormon Pioneer Overland Travel -

www.lds.org > *About the Church* > *Church History* > *Library* > *Resources Available Online*

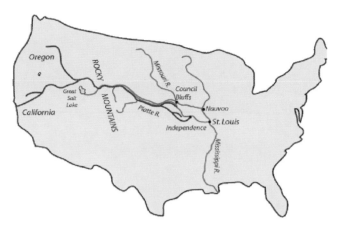

Or try: www.lds.org/churchhistory/library/pioneercompanysearch/1,15773,3966-1,00.html

The most complete index of individuals and companies that crossed the plains to Utah between 1847 and 1868. Includes transcribed excerpts from trail diaries, letters, and newspaper reports.

BYU Immigrant Ancestors Project -
http://immigrants.byu.edu

An ongoing project sponsored by BYU's *Center for Family History and Genealogy* uses emigration registers to locate information about the birthplaces of immigrants in their native countries, which is not found in the port registers and naturalization documents in the destination countries.

Membership Card Index -
www.xmission.com/~nelsonb/minnie

This unique card index (also known as the "Minnie Margetts File") indexes selected LDS Church membership records, primarily in the United States and England from 1839-1915.

Nauvoo Records of Baptisms - http://family history.byu.edu/publications/baptisms.html

A valuable seven-volume set of over 15,000 baptisms, not found elsewhere, that have been extracted, edited, and alphabetized from faded holographic baptismal records, including information on work done in the Mississippi River.

Mormon Immigration Index -
www.ldscatalog.com > *(do a quick search)*

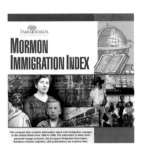

The newly-released Index on compact disk documents the journeys of over 94,000 LDS Church converts who crossed the Atlantic or Pacific oceans to gather in Nauvoo, Illinois, or other frontier outposts, between 1840 and 1890. Includes the name, age, and country of origin of each passenger, ports of departure and arrival, approximate number of passengers on each ship, the assigned company leaders, often a brief history of the voyage, plus autobiographies, journals, diaries and letters of approximately 1,000 immigrant converts. These accounts provide a compelling view of those who crossed the oceans and then by land, rivers, and rails gathered in Salt Lake City, and will be available online in the future at www.lds.org.

Danish and Scandinavian Immigration -
www.ida.net/users/really

Contains web links for a Research Outline for Denmark, emigration from Scandinavia, listing of Parishes, Census and Probates, place lists, maps, surnames lists, helps and tips.

Web Links for Specific Utah Resources

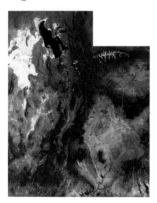

Linkpendium.com - www.linkpendium.com > Utah Genealogy (listed under Localities: USA)

A good statewide directory of about 4,500 family history web links.

Cyndi's List.com / Utah - www.cyndislist.com/ut.htm

Another good directory of about 1,500 web links.

Death and Marriage Notices - www.rootsweb.ancestry.com/~utsaltla/obit_DeseretNews_1850s.html

Abstracts of Deaths and Marriages Notices in the *Deseret News Weekly* of Salt Lake City, Utah (1852-1900) made available by UtahGenWeb.

Utah Digital Newspapers - http://digitalnewspapers.org

Contains over 600,000 pages of Utah historical newspapers and other digital collections.

Utah Research Center - http://historyresearch.utah.gov

Research **Utah Death Certificates** from 1904-1956; research historic state and local government records from 1850 to today; and research manuscripts, photographs, books, maps, and online resources about Utah and the West.

Utah State History / Cemeteries - http://history.utah.gov/apps/burials/execute/searchburials

Explore Utah's history and its place in the West, search thousands of photographs, and find many of Utah's cemetery records online.

Utah Census Search - www.xmission.com/%7Enelsonb/census_search.htm

An index for Utah Census records from 1850-1880.

Utah Census Search

Western States Marriage Index -
http://abish.byui.edu/specialCollections/
westernStates/search.cfm

A current ongoing project that contains about 700,000 marriage records to date from selected counties in California, western Colorado, Montana, Oregon, Utah, eastern Washington, Wyoming and New Mexico.

Washington County Pioneer Index -
www.lofthouse.com/USA/Utah/washington/
pioneers/main.html

An index of the names and vital information of Utah Pioneers who entered Washington County, Utah up to 1870. The resources include: U.S. 1860 and 1870 Censes, early LDS Ward membership records, cemetery records, local histories, family group sheets, and indexes of land deeds.

Washington County Early Marriage Index -
www.lofthouse.com/USA/Utah/washington/
marriage/index.html

Contains over 2,000 marriages in Washington County, Utah from 1862-1919.

Salt Lake City Directories -
www.rootsweb.com/~utsaltla/
Directories/index.html

Links to early residential directories.

Utah Digital Collections and Indexes -
http://historyresearch.utah.gov/indexes/index.html

Salt Lake County death certificate images, 1905-1956

Daughters of Utah Pioneers -
www.dupinternational.org

The members of the Daughters of the Utah Pioneers (DUP) have prepared and collected thousands of biographies of early pioneers (1847-1869). A pioneer is an ancestor who came to the Utah Territory/State of Deseret; died crossing the plains; or was born in the Utah Territory/State of Deseret before May 10, 1869, the coming of the railroad. Also available are photographs of many of the early LDS church members.

You can search for a pioneer on their website and then request a copy of their biography.

Finding Your Family Stories, Traditions and Photos

Adding Historical Context

BYU Family History Archive -
www.lib.byu.edu/fhc

One of the greatest online genealogy resources available that is still relatively unknown. It currently includes a collection of about 20,000 diaries, biographies, family histories, Elders journals, oral histories, gazetteers, and a medieval section. However, they continue to add new volumes each week, and they are targeting over 100,000 published family histories and thousands of local histories, city directories and other related records all of which can be easily searched by surname, geographic area, book title, or author. You can simply browse all the family histories or view the full text of each. The best way to quickly find the histories most likely to be of use to you is to use the Keyword searches. This promises to become the most comprehensive collection of city and county histories on the Web. And it's free!

Trails of Hope: Overland Diaries and Letters - http://overlandtrails.lib.byu.edu

A collection of the original writings of 49 voyagers on the Mormon, California, Oregon, and Montana pioneer trails who wrote while traveling on the trail; includes maps, trail guides, photographs, watercolors and art sketches between 1846-1869.

JosephSmithPapers.org - http://josephsmithpapers.org

This is a scholarly, comprehensive *"papers"* project that will publish all documents created by Joseph Smith and by those whose work he directed. It will eventually constitute about 30 volumes, organized into six series with about two volumes published each year until the project is complete. This first volume is available at press time and is a part of the *Journals Series.* Other series include: Documents, Revelations and Translations, History, Legal and Business, and Administrative. In the works for several decades, it provides new information and insights about Joseph Smith, early Mormonism, nineteenth-century American religion, and the people, places, and times in which he lived. Each volume will provide biographical descriptions, and this website will ultimately provide a comprehensive biographical directory for all the volumes.

Endorsed by the U.S. National Archives' National Historical Publication and Records Commission.

Mormon Missionary Diaries -
www.lib.byu.edu/dlib/mmd

A superb collection of over 63,000 pages of missionary diaries including some individuals fairly prominent in the LDS Church.

It provides an opportunity to read and understand the missionary experiences, the joys, the sorrows, the struggles that can change lives. The earliest missionary diary in the collection is a one–volume diary penned in 1832 by Hyrum Smith.

Journals of Early Members of the Church -
www.boap.org/LDS/Early-Saints

Journals, diaries, biographies and autobiographies of some early Mormons and others who knew Joseph Smith, Jr. and/or his contemporaries.

Biography and Journal Excerpts -
www.signaturebookslibrary.org

Some biography and journal excerpts and resources on different topics about Utah, Mormonism and the West including the full text of some out-of-print books.

Mormon Biographical Registers -
http://byustudies.byu.edu/Indexes/ BioAlpha/MBRegisterA.aspx

A list of people in selected Mormon biographical registers.

Mormon Biographical Sketches -
www.saintswithouthalos.com

A website devoted to the life and times of Joseph Smith from 1831 to 1839 (the Ohio/ Missouri period); includes biographical sketches of his contemporaries.

LDS Biographical Encyclopedia -
www.lib.byu.edu/online.html > *All Collections > Misc. Books > Encyclopedic History of Church*

A compilation of over 5000 biographical sketches and more than 2000 photographs of prominent men and women in the LDS Church, authored by Andrew Jenson, Assistant Church Historian. It comprises 4-volumes from 1901-1936 available on line in the special books collection at BYU. It includes accounts of all the general authorities and many of the presidents and bishops of the stakes and wards. This work is particularly valuable in providing brief histories of Church units from their beginnings up to 1930.

Joseph Smith.net Resource Center -
www.josephsmith.net

Contains historical digitized documents from the life and times of Joseph Smith, photographs of many of the sites of the Restoration, and the Joseph Smith Papers.

Mormons and Their Neighbors -
www.lib.byu.edu/Ancestry

An index compiled by Marvin E. Wiggins in the 1970s (which took more than a decade to compile) of over 100,000 biographical sketches appearing in 236 published volumes; includes people living between 1820 and 1981 in northern Mexico, New Mexico, Arizona, southern California, Nevada, Utah, Idaho, Wyoming, and southwestern Canada. It is not a name index, only published works containing actual biographical information were indexed. Most of the titles are housed in the BYU Library. Copies of the biographies can be requested from your own public or university library via Interlibrary Loan.

Welsh Mormon History.org -
www.welshmormonhistory.org

Contains journal excerpts, vital information, biographies, and photos. This site seeks to preserve and share information about the early converts to Mormonism in Wales, and is the product of Dr. Ronald Dennis' research.

Mormon Publications -
www.lib.byu.edu/online.html Or try <http://contentdm.lib.byu.edu/cdm4/browse.php?CISOROOT=%2FNCMP1820-1846>

A digital collection in the BYU Library of early Mormon publications which includes books, missionary tracts,

doctrinal treatises, hymnals and periodicals which helped define the doctrinal development and historical movements of the Mormon people in the 19th and 20th centuries.

Studies in Mormon History -
http://mormonhistory.byu.edu

An online indexed bibliography that is being updated constantly. It includes articles, books, theses, dissertations, and diaries dealing with the history of the Church written from the time of its inception in 1830 to the present.

Encyclopedia of Mormonism -
www.lib.byu.edu/Macmillan

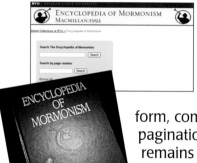

A digital collection in the BYU Library of the out-of-print Macmillan's 1992 publication in full, searchable form, complete with original pagination and illustrations. It remains the most encyclopedic coverage of Mormonism ever produced. It broadly covers the basic elements and enduring features of Mormon history, doctrine, scripture, organization, and culture.

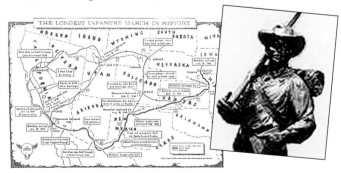

Mormon Battalion.com -
www.mormonbattalion.com

Contains a brief history of the U.S. Mormon

Battalion along with a documented, researched roster, photographs, and maps.

LDS Families Info - www.sedgwickresearch.com > *Family Website Links*

Biographical information on many well-known LDS families.

Historical Documents of the LDS Church - www.centerplace.org/history

From the Evening and Morning Star, Messenger Advocate, and Times and Seasons.

FarWestHistory.com - www.farwesthistory.com

Interactive map and history of Far West.

Mormon Frontier Foundation - www.jwha.info/mmff/mmffhp.htm

History of early settlements in Missouri.

BYU Winter Quarters Project - http://winterquarters.byu.edu

Searchable pioneer database and information on the settlements in Nebraska.

Mountain West Digital Library - http://155.97.12.155/mwdl

An aggregation of digital collections from universities, colleges, public libraries, museums, and historical societies in Utah, Nevada, and Idaho.

Early Mormon History Articles - www.sidneyrigdon.com/dbroadhu/artindex.htm

Old newspaper articles on the Mormons indexed by region.

- *Working files:* copies of pedigree charts, family group sheets
- *Other documents* and quick-reference aids
- *To do list*

You can then carry these binders easily with you to the library or family history center for doing research as needed. Once your research is completed, you can enter the information into your computer family history database, document your findings in the *Sources* section, and make necessary explanations in the *Notes* section.

When writing for information, you should enclose a self-addressed, stamped envelope.

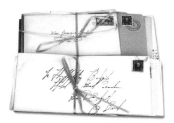

Always keep your originals safe and protected.

You can keep valuable original documents, family histories, and photographs stored in archival quality sheet protectors in binders filed in folders in your file cabinet.

Organizing Your e-Mails and Letters

Family history is a collaborative effort. You often write many emails or letters.

Keep copies of all your letters and emails in a letter file folder or organized on your computer, and when you receive an answer to a letter, pull your original letter from the file, attach it to the reply, and file both in the appropriate family file folder. Or you can keep your inquiry in the document folder of that particular family where you can refer to it as you are researching that family.

Research Notes

As you do research, keep notes about each family (or surname).

Record the new information on your family group sheets and pedigree charts in your computer database, and record the source for all new information. File each document and all of your notes in the appropriate file folders. *(See documenting your information in Chapter 2.)*

Archiving Your Family Photos, Documents and Heirlooms

You may want to digitize or scan your photographs and documents to preserve them for posterity and be able to readily share them with other family members. This converts them to a more permanent and usable format in today's world. You can then add your valuable photos to your family history software program, a family Web page, family blog, or family online photo album you've created, or just e-mail the pictures to others.

You should plan now to protect your photographs and documents; don't wait until a disaster happens to them.

Using today's technology you can readily archive all of your heirloom photos, slides, negatives, home movies, letters, journals, maps, newspaper articles, etc. But you need to have a computer, a scanner, and graphics software.

You should consider saving your images in TIF format for archiving purposes, and then you may want to re-save them as a JPG file for e-mailing, Web pages, and other uses.

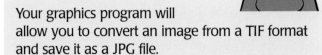

Your graphics program will allow you to convert an image from a TIF format and save it as a JPG file.

If you want to archive your family **photographs,** a good scanner and a graphics software program will allow you to scan your photos and save them on your hard drive or a disk. The scanner doesn't have to be expensive. Most scanners today will scan at a minimum of 300 dpi (dots per inch) or higher. The higher the dpi, the higher the resolution of your image, and also the more disk space it takes to store them on your computer.

Graphic File Formats

Whether you're downloading a picture from the Internet or scanning in a family photograph, the graphic file format you use will determine how good or poor the final result is. In today's computer world there are many different graphic file formats to choose from. Each format has its own unique advantages, disadvantages, and quirks. Here's a brief summary of the different key formats:

BMP - This is the native Microsoft Windows file format which means it will work with all Microsoft programs (Word, Excel, PowerPoint, Publisher, etc.), but not necessarily other non-Microsoft applications. It's effective for graphics, but **not as effective for photographs.**

JPG - or JPEG (pronounced "jay-peg") stands for *Joint Photographic Experts Group* and is good for emailing photographs to friends, and for web page or blog use, because it's one of the smallest. But JPG uses compression on every save which means that **some quality is lost each time the file is**

saved, and it cannot be recovered. This is similar to copying a cassette tape to another cassette tape. The quality is degraded with each copy.

GIF - *Graphics Interchange Format* have historically been the best for use with line art. This includes clip art, logos, and drawings, but is limited to only 256 colors, which makes it **poorly suited for pho- tographic purposes.** GIF also allows a transparent background which is important for creating logos and icons.

PNG - *Portable Network Graphics* is a bitmapped image format that employs lossless data compression. It was **created to improve upon and replace GIF** as an image-file format not requiring a patent license.

TIF - *Tagged Image File Format* is widely used for **master copies of scanned data.** As images are scanned in they are saved in tif format, then manipulated and saved in other formats, but are very large which means it takes up more space on your computer.

Slides and Negatives

Slides and negatives are a little more complicated, and will require a scanner with a *'slide adapter'* that allows you to scan slides, and a tool to scan negatives. Most scanners come with graphics software to help you obtain the sharpest images possible. You can review scanners (and other hardware and software) at www.itreviews.co.uk/hardware.

Depending on what you want and the quality of your photos, you may want to crop, add a caption, re-size, or adjust colors and contrast to improve the quality. If you have negatives, you may want to make a print of your photo. To do this, you will need a graphics software program and printer, although your flatbed scanner will allow you to do some editing of your photos.

There are free and inexpensive programs such as:

■ **Picasa -** http://picasa.google.com which is free from Google

■ **TuCows.com -** www.tucows.com (currently hosts more than 40,000 software titles)

■ **Download.com -** www.download.com offers content in four major categories: Software (over 100,000 freeware, shareware, and try-first downloads),

Music, Games, and Videos.

But if you want or need to manipulate and edit your photos even more, you may want

to purchase better software, such as:

■ **PhotoShop Elements -** www.adobe.com $139.99 Free trial.

■ **PhotoImpact X3 -** www.corel.com $49.99

Where Do I Store My Photos and Documents?

You can also consider storing all your computer information with a secure online automatic backup company, such as:

Mozy.com - www.mozy.com (2 GB free, $4.95/month unlimited capacity),

You will need to decide where you want to permanently store your photos and documents.

At first, you may simply want to save them to your "C" drive in assorted folders you create under *My Pictures*. Later, you may want to consider storing them also on a CD or DVD as a backup. There are many recordable CD-ROM and DVD drives, which allow you to record (or burn) data onto them.

Carbonite.com - www.carbonite.com ($49.95/year unlimited capacity).

© by Intellectual Reserve, Inc.

Transporting Data

Flash Drives (jump drives, thumb drives, USB flash drives, flash memory) have become wildly popular in the last few years and for good reasons. A USB flash drive is a memory data storage device with a USB (universal serial bus) interface to connect directly with your PC computer or laptop. They are removable and rewritable, smaller than a tube of lipstick and easily fit into your pocket or purse. Storage capacities typically range from 64 MB (megabyte) to 64 GB (gigabyte), allow 1 million write or erase cycles, and have 10-year data retention. They are cheap, rugged, very convenient and are now the standard for transporting your data from one computer to another, or temporary storage of information that you are transporting.

Nothing actually moves in a flash drive. It consists of a small printed circuit board protected inside a plastic, metal, or rubberized case, and is robust enough for carrying in your pocket or on a key chain with no additional protection. They provide a lot of capability and allow you to find and retrieve information almost instantly. They are the convenient equivalent of thousands of floppy disks, hundreds of CDs, or even dozens of DVD disks. You can easily store your entire address book (with thousands of names, addresses, and e-mail addresses), calendar, thousands of photos, etc. You can purchase a 32 MB for as little as $3.99, or up to a 64 GB for about $60.

Home Movies

Your family's home movies add another dimension to your family history archives. You may want to consider having your home movies converted to DVD which is less fragile, more permanent, and easier to watch and share. But you will probably need a professional who has the equipment to convert them. Different types of home movies include: Recent VHS video tapes, and movies on reels of film – 8mm, Super 8, or 16mm. No one makes film movies any longer, and the projector accessories are only available through specialty camera stores. A basic service will convert them into DVD files, but some may offer editing or restoration as well. Call your local camera stores to inquire.

VHS movies are usually priced by the minute to convert them, whereas reels of film are usually priced by the foot. Another option to consider is to refilm an old movie yourself. If you have the proper equipment, play your old home movies, and while they are playing record it with your digital video recorder. The quality is usually reasonable and you can then burn DVDs with the digital files. A DVD is not a permanent solution either, but it will last much longer than VHS or film.

Check out this Library of Congress site for advice on the care, handling and storage of your valuable photos, videos, books, CDs, tapes, newspapers, and other historical items.

Caring for Your Photos –
ww.loc.gov/preserv/careothr.html

computer diskettes we used just a few years ago, and the magnetic tape reels 20 years ago? Remember when CD drives cost hundreds of dollars and were slow as molasses? When media changes, we can no longer read the data. No doubt the flash drives, CD-ROMs, DVDs, Blu-Ray (the next-generation optical disc format that is considered cutting-edge today), and flash drives we use to digitally store our data today will also become obsolete in the future. We will probably need to transfer our photographs and data to newer storage media in the future to keep pace as technology changes.

It turns out that technological innovations take a while to seep into the collective conscious-ness and become widely accepted, and that gives us a chance to properly digest them. Don't get frustrated about not keeping up. We're all in the same boat, so let's all paddle together. Relax, don't get discouraged, and be confident in the pursuit of slow and steady progress in your family history journey.

Keeping Up With Technology

Technology is a wonderful thing. It's essential to everything around us today, even those things that aren't considered technological. You deal with technology daily in your home, office, all forms of travel, security systems, air conditioning, computers, networks, software, phone systems, and much, much more. A wise man said:

"The role of technology in [genealogy] work has been accelerated by the Lord himself, who has had a guiding hand in its developments and will continue to do so." (Howard W. Hunter, Fireside, Nov. 13, 1994)

Howard Hunter
© by Intellectual Reserve, Inc.

Keep in mind that computer storage media changes over time. Remember the 5.25"

Technology has enabled us to trace our own family roots and stories today that wouldn't have been possible a short time ago. And it's fun and much easier today because of technology.

Portable Scanners

In computing, a scanner is a device that optically scans images of any kind – printed text, charts, maps, photographs, handwriting, an object, etc. – and converts it to a digital image. A scanner is a good alternative to using a photocopier and can help capture data for your family history research. Scanners come in portable hand-held, feed-in, and flatbed (which produces the highest quality). A portable scanner can save the digital images of up to 50 letter-size documents at once.

The scanned result is a non-compressed digital image, which can be either downloaded to a printer, transferred to a

computer's memory (hard disk) for further processing and storage, or attached to an e-mail message. Pictures are normally stored in image formats such as uncompressed Bitmap, *losslessly* compressed TIFF and PNG (allows the exact original data to be reconstructed from the compressed data), and *lossily* compressed JPEG (allows an approximation of the original data to be reconstructed, in exchange for better compression rates). Documents are best stored in TIFF or PDF format; JPEG is good for pictures, but particularly unsuitable for text. PDF (Portable Document Format) files have become a generally accepted standard for electronic document distribution and they can be viewed by anyone with free Adobe® Acrobat Reader software (go to www.adobe.com).

Digital Cameras

Due to increasing resolution and new features (such as anti-shake), digital cameras have become an attractive alternative to scanners. You can copy more information quicker than scanning or by hand, and easily manage a large number of files (rather than a large amount of paper). It's fast, portable, and you can digitize thick books without damaging the book spine. Some disadvantages may include distortion, reflections, shadows, and low contrast. Here are some tips for using your digital camera.

Move in and focus. It is important to use a macro (close-up) setting so that the page or paragraph-sized information will fill the page. You don't need to record the page margins; you want an image of the information on the page. Lay the book on the desk and stand above it, getting your camera shooting as per-pendicular to the book as possible. Don't forget to physically turn the camera to a vertical view as most pages are taller than they are wide and you can get closer that way.

Always copy the title page and the publication information. Make sure that the page number can be read, even if that means you must take a separate shot of just the page number. Check your image. Always immediately review your shots. Sometimes you might find that the camera didn't focus properly or that you copied only part of the information you wanted. You can erase and immediately shoot a better image. Try to hold the camera steady, squeezing the shutter button, trying not to jerk the camera.

You may want to consider some photo editing software. Many photos will need to be taken at an angle to avoid reflections or with different camera rotations to match the subject. Pretty much any software can handle the rotation, but other software can remove the distortions caused by strange camera angles as well as apply many types of correction to bring out hard to read images. Check out side-by-side comparisons review at http://photo-editing-software-review.toptenreviews.com.

Once captured as digital images by your scanner or camera, printed documents such as wills, biographies, and obituaries can be converted from image files into text files by downloading the images to your PC. You can then copy it into your family history software program to add to your family web site, blog, or other information.

Of course, with a digital camera you can also take pictures of memorabilia and heirlooms, e.g. Grandpa's old rocking chair, grandma's treasured family photos from the wall or that special piece of china that she always used for Sunday dinners, the family Bible inscriptions that are in your Aunt's safekeeping especially if she won't let those treasured family keepsakes out of her sight. Then get the story of the memorabilia or heirloom from those that remember.

Handheld Computers

A handheld computer or PDA (personal digital assistant) is a small computer that can fit in your shirt pocket or purse, and is a very useful device today. It was originally used to maintain and manage personal information like To Do Lists, calendars, and contacts. However, like everything else, the computing power has increased dramatically and now PDAs can be used like portable PCs to run word processing, spreadsheets, presentations and you can also browse the web if it has wireless capabilities. *Smartphones,* such as Apple iPhone and Blackberry phones, are popular devices because they combine the functionality of PDAs and phones to handle phone calls, e-mail and mobile-office functions.

This means that now with genealogy software programs for handheld computers you can conveniently take your family history with you when you travel. You no longer have to carry a bunch of three-ring binders or even a laptop PC with you to the library or Family History Center. A large, complete family history database can be carried in your pocket or a purse, and can save you time and increase your efficiency.

Sometime in the future, even census enumerators will use handheld computers to collect data. The handhelds will replace the millions of costly paper forms and maps that enumerators must carry when going door to door to visit people who did not mail in their census forms.

Handheld Software

Pocket Genealogist -
www.northernhillssoftware.com $$$

Genealogy software for Windows mobile-based devices, including the PocketPC, Smartphones, and Handheld PC. Supports most data types including events, facts, notes, sources, repositories, addresses, to do lists, latitude/longitude, DNA, multimedia (images) and LDS ordinances. Basic version $20, Advanced $35.

My Roots - www.tapperware.com/MyRoots $$$

A full-featured shareware genealogy program for Palm OS handhelds, can display ancestor and descendant trees for any person. It also offers searching, sorting, filtering, and many other features. It lets you take your genealogy data with you wherever you go. Since handheld computers can fit in your shirt pocket or purse, they are much more convenient than a laptop or a 3-ring binder. With My Roots, you can stay organized and work more efficiently whether you're at a courthouse, library, or family reunion. A free conversion utility, for PC or Mac, lets you import data from or export data to standard GED files. Free trial version available. $24.95

PAF (Personal Ancestral File) -
www.familysearch.org Free

Works only on Palm OS handhelds and only allows you to view the data on your Palm, not enter new data.

Organizing Your Personal Library

In today's world, Internet sites are probably the fastest, easiest-accessible, and most-used reference sources by most people who use the Internet. Your favorite places on the internet really become your own self-made personal Internet library.

If you are a user of Microsoft's *Internet Explorer*™ browser, you mark your sites as "favorite places". (A Web browser is a software application which enables you to display and interact with text, images, videos, music, games and other information typically located on a Web site.) In the *Firefox, Google Chrome,* and *Safari* browsers, you are familiar with the term "bookmark."

Firefox features one-click bookmarking to bookmark, search and organize Web sites quickly and easily.

Google Chrome, the new web browser developed by Google, claims to make the web faster, safer, and easier with sophisticated technology.

They both allow you to bookmark a web page by just clicking the star icon at the left edge of the address bar and you're done.

Apple's *Safari* claims to be the fastest and easiest-to-use web browser. One click opens the single-window interface, where you can browse, search, and organize bookmarks.

The bookmarked collections of Web sites that you have compiled provide you with personal resources and can be organized into categories to fit your needs. Organize your internet library into major subject areas with sub-categories. Major categories might include: art, church, family history, health, investments, music, news, travel, etc., any subject you want for which you create a folder in your bookmark file. Then you can create sub-folders under the main folders if you wish. It's easy to do. Refer to your browser's *Help* file for details of how to do this if you need.

Is your collection of printed books starting to take over your home? If desired, create a database or document detailing your collection of books that helps you organize them. A couple of web sites – www.library thing.com and www.goodreads.com – allows you to

maintain a database of your own book collection, enables you to share your collection electronically on a personal website, and connects you with people who read the same things.

Free Home Library Software -
www.pilibrary.com

This software allows you to create as many libraries as you need: Books, journals, magazines, CDs, videos, photographs, digital graphic files (JPGs, GIFs, etc.), audio files (Podcasts, Music), HTML (Internet information), PDF/Textual documents, web sites, etc.

Do What Works For You

No one filing system works for everyone. Your family history is a personal thing, and the options for organizing your information are endless. But by developing and using a system to organize all your information and documents, you will have the data you need, where you need it, when you need it. Establish a method for how you handle new information. Find the system that works best for you. Once you've established a system, it becomes easier to stay organized. Stay with your system, and all your records will stay organized, making them more valuable to you, and allowing you to use your limited family history time more efficiently.

Get started today to digitize and archive your precious photographs and documents to preserve them for posterity and share them with other family members. Don't wait until a disaster happens to them.

Preserve Your Journal for Posterity

"By now, in my own personal history, I have managed to fill seventy-eight large volumes, which are my personal journal. There have been times when I have been so tired at the end of a day that the effort could hardly be managed, but I am so grateful that I have not let slip away from me and my posterity those things which needed to be recorded." Spencer W. Kimball, *Ensign,* Oct. 1980, 72.

Spencer Kimball
© by Intellectual Reserve, Inc.

Journaling Helps Us Get Past Difficult Times

"...important in journal writing is the recording of both our failures and successes. If we can look back and see where we failed in the past and

Gawain and Gayle J. Wells

why, we are better able to chart a course for success in the future. Likewise, recounting triumphs and accomplishments can be a great source of strength in periods of discouragement and frustration and can help us get past other difficult times." Gawain and Gayle J. Wells, *Ensign,* July 1986, 47

J. Fielding Smith
© by Intellectual Reserve, Inc.

We Profit by Our Ancestors Mistakes and Achievements

"The importance of written records in the lives of men and the activities of nations is apparent to everyone because through them we have advance in knowledge and power. We profit by the thoughts and actions of those who have gone before because their experiences become ours as we put them into action. We profit by their mistakes and by their successful achievements. We accept the actions of the ages past, and thus, using our judgement, we gather out from that which has been recorded that which will be of benefit to us, and so we incorporate it in our lives."   J. Fielding Smith

Johann von Goethe

Pride in Ancestors

"Happy the man who thinks of his ancestors with pride, who likes to tell of their deeds and greatness, and rejoices to feel himself linked to their goodly chain." Johann von Goethe (1749-1832), German writer

George Mackay Brown

Ancestors Treasury

"We cannot live fully without the treasury our ancestors have left to us." George Mackay Brown (1921-1996), Scottish poet & author

CHAPTER 9

Leaving an Enduring Legacy

SHARING YOUR FAMILY'S STORY, WRITING YOUR FAMILY HISTORY, ORAL INTERVIEWS

© by Intellectual Reserve, Inc.

Everyone has a story to tell.

Some people may mistakenly believe they have nothing of importance to pass on to others...no legacy they can leave. But you need to know that you don't have to be wealthy, famous, or talented to leave a meaningful legacy for your descendants. Some of the most inspirational, enduring legacies are from people outside of history books and newspaper headlines. Everyday, plain ordinary people are creating and passing down inspirational, historical legacies. And you can be one of them.

9 Leaving a Legacy

Suggested Activities

1. Conduct an oral interview with a parent, grandparent, aunt, etc.

2. Make a commitment to start keeping your personal history. Record your thoughts and feelings as well as the events of your day-to-day life.

3. Begin to write your own life story. Which ancestors on your pedigree chart do you identify with the most? If you could talk to them about their lives, what questions would you ask? What would you like to know about them that you haven't been able to find through your research? With that in mind, begin to write your own life story.

4. Record some personal, biographical information about yourself, including a physical description, the places you've lived, and your professional training and experience.

5. Compile a list of other topics that you would like to include in your personal history, keeping in mind the things you wish you knew about your ancestors, and schedule a regular time for working on it. If writing it down seems difficult, talk into a tape recorder or video camera and then find someone who can do a written transcription for you.

Theodore M. Burton
© by Intellectual Reserve, Inc.

Provide Uplifting, Faith-Promoting Strength

"Much of what we now regard as scripture was not anything more or less than men writing of their own spiritual experiences for the benefit of their posterity.... we ought to write of our own lives and our own experiences to form a sacred record for our descendants. We must provide for them the same uplifting, faith-promoting strength that the ancient scriptures now give us." Theodore M. Burton, *Ensign*, Jan. 1977, 13

"Old Testament Prophet" by Judith Mehr
© by Intellectual Reserve, Inc.

Resources For Writing Your History

Writing our personal and family histories may sometimes seem discouraging. We may not know where to begin, or what to say or how to organize our thoughts. Here are some ideas and excellent resources to help you get started and organize your work.

Getting Started
Keeping A Journal

Keeping a journal is not necessarily difficult. But does take some discipline. Here are some suggestions:

Choose a Convenient Method - Select either a book to handwrite your journal or a computer. By choosing a method that is convenient, you will be more likely to follow through. Specialized computer software is available (see below), or you can use just your word-processing software if you choose. You could consider turning the writing into a ritual. Choose the *right* book to write in, and with a pen that feels good to you and looks good on the page.

Establish a Schedule - Like any new habit, keeping a journal is something that you must work at, especially at first. You will discover more about what you are experiencing if you write in your journal at the same time in the same place every day or every time. Decide how often you will make entries: daily, weekly, monthly, etc. When will you make the entries—early in the morning, at bedtime, on Sundays? With todays busy schedules, we often find ourselves rushing from one task to the next. By scheduling a little time to record your personal history, you are allowing time for yourself to reflect on the day and on your life as a whole. This may be very therapeutic for you. When you have decided, stay with it.

Decide What to Record - A journal is a record of your day-to-day life, but it is more than just a diary. It deals with your experiences and how you handled them. It deals with the values and principles you have learned and how you applied them in your life. It should also record events in your life, such as education, employment, marriage, and children. It should be something you can reflect back on...and learn from. Allow your mind to roam freely through the present, the distant past, and the shifting future. Don't deny whatever comes up as you are writing, no matter how silly it seems. You remembered it for some reason.

Be inspired by others. Check out your local library for other people's family histories. Reading the works of others may inspire you in your own writing.

Hidden Benefits of Keeping A History

Gawain & Gayle Wells

Gawain and Gayle J. Wells provide us with excellent insight on the many hidden blessings that come from these record-keeping activities: 1) gathering and reading histories of our progenitors, 2) writing our own personal history, and 3) keeping a journal. Here are some excerpts from a wonderful magazine article they wrote:

"Many unanticipated joys and blessings come from keeping a history. The blessings come not only from *completing* the records, but also from the process of *writing* them. What are some of these unexpected blessings?"

We Are Strengthened

"It can be a great thrill to discover a diary or journal written by a grandparent or loved one. For example, the record of a great-grandmother's experiences as a bride and young mother can touch the heart of a granddaughter and cause deep love, even though the two are generations apart. ...We greatly benefit from the testimonies of our own ancestors as they recount for us their trials and sacrifices. But many of our parents and grandparents left no written account of their lives for us to read. Even so, it is possible – and important – to obtain a record about them. ... Discovering our family and our heritage can help us discover ourselves."

Reliving Each Experience

"As I began recording my earliest recollections for chapter one of my personal history," Gayle recalls. "I found myself reliving each experience. Details and images came into my mind that I hadn't remembered before. I became so absorbed that I found myself weeping–and laughing–as I recorded certain incidents. It was as if I were actually stepping back in time. ... I was experiencing my own past, but observing it now with the advantage of maturity and perspective. ... We can also gain a greater appreciation for our parents as we write about them in our personal histories. Recalling our lives' formative events from an adult point of view helps us recognize how often we depended upon our parents for emotional support as well as physical help."

Touching the Lives of Others

"Writing in a journal is the best way to keep our personal history current. But a journal can best play its important role in our lives if we use it consistently. We might consider our journal as a map of our past, present, and future. We can look back to see where we have been, and then, with greater understanding and perspective, go forward, strengthened by our own experiences. ... We are and must continue to be a history-keeping people. As we are blessed in reading records kept by ancient prophets as well as our own ancestors, we...may touch the lives of those who follow us. And...we will experience greater joy and meaning in our lives." Hidden Benefits of Keeping a History, *Ensign*, July 1986, 47-48

Take It Easy - Writing your personal history may seem overwhelming at first, but if you do it a little at a time, it's much less intimidating. If you focus on short periods of your life, it will seem much more manageable. And you don't have to write in chronological order. You can write about any event or period of your life as your memories are stirred.

Ideas Help Stimulate - Include news events that were happening at that time in your life which not only help set it against the circumstances of the times, but also make your story more interesting. You may also find that by remembering historical events, you will be stimulating more of your personal memories. Memorabilia can also help bring back memories, such as: music, photos, letters, talking with family or friends, even familiar smells and sounds.

Be Personable - Record your triumphs over adversity, your recovery after a fall, your progress when all seemed black, your rejoicing when you had finally achieved. Share your thoughts and feelings; give your descendants a glimpse into the real you.

Be Creative - Have fun creating your memoirs and most likely others will enjoy reading it. You can include interesting things like photos, maps, news articles, receipts, favorite quotations and jokes, cards, etc.

> Let your memories be a reflection of you and your devotion to writing your family history. But do it!

Your journals and records will be a great source of inspiration to your children, your grandchildren, and others through many generations.

Helpful Software and Websites for Writing Your Story

Personal Historian.com - www.personalhistorian.com $$$

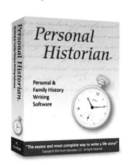

Software which assists you in writing personal histories about yourself and other individuals. It breaks this seemingly monumental task into small, manageable pieces and then reconstructs it into a complete, publishable document. It includes an extensive library of timelines, historical facts, cultural trivia, and memory triggers which give color and context to the history. You can publish your completed history to your printer, word processor or PDF file. $29.95

Write Your Life Story! - http://home.netcom.com/ ~genealogy/life_story.htm $$$

This is a software program that was created after talking to a group of writers. When asked "how do you even begin..." they all replied, "Make an outline of each year of your life." With this program you are guided through creating your basic outline right through to the finished manuscript. It can be difficult to organize the various data you have collected and generate a life story. The software can help you organize the details of an ancestor's life or your own. $19.95

Writing the Journey - www.writingthejourney.com

This is an online writing website that includes ideas, information about

journal-keeping software, a free newsletter, an online workshop, exercises to improve your journal-writing skills, and more. The heart of this website is their online journal writing workshop. You can explore some of the concepts important to journal writing, and complete exercises designed to teach you new journal writing techniques. They believe that journal writing is one of the great tools for listening to your heart. They developed this website to share information about how to get the most from your journal. With your heart to guide you, your life is a spiritual adventure!

Genwriters - www.genwriters.com

Writing for Future Generations. A source to find ideas and resources to bring your family history to life.

Association of Personal Historians.org -
www.personalhistorians.org

The Association is an organization dedicated to helping others preserve their personal histories and life stories. Here you can search out a professional to help you record your own (or a loved one's) life stories. You can also find tips on the many different ways you can capture your own memories. Discover the joys of preserving personal history. Producing life story legacies through books, oral histories or videos - with thoughts, feelings and memories - this site helps enrich lives for generations to come.

Life Story Center -
http://usm.maine.edu/olli/national/
lifestorycenter > *Center for Life Stories*

Can you remember what's happened in your lifetime? Here's a nostalgia website which has great

pages for triggering memories and historical events and dates. It has lots of entertaining and useful links.

Cyndi's List.com -
www.cyndislist.com/writing.htm

Start with the collection of websites under the "Writing Your Family's History" section.

Librarians' Internet Index - www.lii.org

A publicly-funded website and weekly newsletter with a searchable database for the best of the Web organized into 14 main topics and nearly 300 related topics.

Internet Public Library - www.ipl.org

A convenient service called *Ask an IPL Librarian* in which their dedicated online volunteer staff answers reference questions. Do a search for "writing family history".

Lifestory Writing -
http://heartandcraft.blogspot.com $$$

Paperback book by Sharon M. Lippincott contains tips, guidelines and observations to help ordinary people learn to write extraordinary stories defining their own lives in their own voices and their own terms. $16.95

Keeping a Journal - www.wofford.edu > *Search "Keeping a Journal"*

Articles and a workshop on keeping a journal from Wofford College.

Writing Resources on the Web -
http://web.mit.edu/uaa/www/writing/links

MIT online web link resources for general and technical writing.

Writing.org - www.writing.org

This non-commercial site offers how-to articles for writers (and especially for new writers). The goal is to help you break into the writing business and avoid being victimized by scam artists.

Books to Consider

You need some reference books at your fingertips. They'll save you lots of time in your pursuit of creating an enduring legacy.

Producing a Quality Family History $$$

This is one of the best-written guide books for anyone looking to create a useful, lasting history of their family. Patricia Law Hatcher guides you through the steps required to create an attractive, functional family history report, and have made understanding the organization and creative process simple. It covers every aspect for the beginner and focuses the attention of even the advanced family historian and experienced writer on what is needed to generate a high quality publication. $19.95

Joan R. Neubauer Books $$$

Award winning author and acclaimed speaker has written several books about writing and journaling.

Dear Diary: The Art and Craft of Writing a Creative Journal - How to use a journal to accomplish goals, achieve spiritual growth, and keep a great family record. $5.95

From Memories to Manuscript: The Five-Step Method of Writing Your Life Story - Steps to create your autobiography and teaches you the full process of publication. $5.95

The Complete Idiot's Guide to Journaling - How to get started, the benefits of journaling, elements of a good journal, and helps you decide what to write about. $16.95

Writing Family History Made Very Easy $$$

Noeline Kyle offers practical and innovative suggestions to writing family histories and beautifully preserving your legacy for centuries to come. Features varied samples and styles of writing to effectively capture family traditions and memories. All aspects of the writing and researching process are explained, from choosing a format to publishing a family history. $14.95

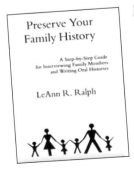

Preserve Your Family History: A Step-by-Step Guide for Interviewing Family Members and Writing Oral Histories $$$

To preserve your family stories, all you need is a list of people to interview, a tape recorder

and a copy of this book by LeAnn Ralph which contains more than 400 questions on 30 different topics. $11.95

You Can Write Your Family History $$$

How to record the fascinating tales of your ancestors by Sharon Carmack. The best methods for: Conducting historical and thematic research, organizing materials, outlining and plotting a story, illustrating with pictures and charts, and making money writing the histories of other families. $19.95

George Morgan's Web Articles

George G. Morgan is the internationally renowned author of the "*Along Those Lines ...*" weekly genealogy column at Eastman's Genealogy Newsletter, www.eogn.com, (previously at www.Ancestry.com), president of the International Society of Family History Writers and Editors (www.rootsweb.com/~cgc), and author of scores of articles for magazines, journals and newsletters across the U.S., Canada, and in the U.K.

Among the scores of magazine and journal articles, George wrote articles about connecting with your ancestors. Here's a brief review and the web links to a few of his *Along Those Lines...* articles.

Picturing Your Ancestors -
www.ancestry.com/ library/view/columns/george/6574.asp

What family history would be complete without descriptions of your ancestors? George Morgan discusses photo options: when great photographs are available, when photographs

Books by George Morgan

http://ahaseminars.com

The Official Guide to Ancestry.com

How to Do Everything with Your Genealogy

Celebrating the Family

Your Family Reunion: How to Plan It, Organize It, and Enjoy It

English Genealogical Research in the Major London Repositories

The Genealogy Forum on America Online: The Official User's Guide

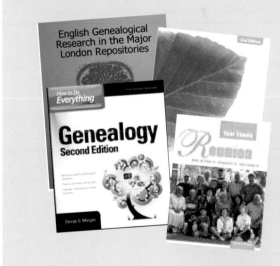

cannot be reproduced, and when there are no photos. What do you do? After you develop your family history, and having researched history, geography, social conditions, environment, personal images, etc., now weave it all together into a compelling story.

Picturing their Environment - www.ancestry.com /library/view/columns/george/6553.asp

It's important to place your ancestors into the context of the times, places, and events in which they lived. We all are influenced by the environment in which we live. One way to add details to your written family history is to paint a picture of the environment in which they lived. He examines the details that can be developed to add "color" to your family's history, as well as some resources that may help. Our ancestors had nothing more than quills and ink to write with, and they traveled by horse and wagon, steamer ship, sailing ship, handcart, etc. It's hard to imagine what that must have been like. Study the places where your ancestors lived and the conditions at the time: transportation, food, medicine, agriculture, industry, home life, clothing, religion, politics, government, weather, etc. We can weave those details into the descriptions of our ancestor's environment and better understand them.

Defining Local Context - www.ancestry.com/ library/view/columns/george/6533.asp

In this article, George examines some of the resources which may be available to add accuracy, depth, and a greater interest to

your written family history. He said that although it's useful to know details of their life, it's more important to know any stories and details of the influences in their life. Our ancestors may have lived in dramatic and historic places and times, and placing them into a global or national context is essential to understanding and writing their stories. Delve into the place they lived and gather the most concise picture you can in order to paint an accurate biographical, historical and social picture.

A Contextual Timeline - www.ancestry.com/ library/view/columns/george/6511.asp

It's essential to build a historical and social

context for your ancestors. In order to unravel mysteries and flesh out their stories, research the times and places your ancestors lived. Everyone's life is influenced by where they live and the events occurring around them. You must delve into the everyday lives of your ancestors if you are to understand who they were and why they made the decisions they made. The ordinary day-to-day activities help define who they are and are a reflection of their lives and times. George discusses the *WHO, WHAT, WHERE, WHEN,* and *HOW* of a story. "Researching the time period is essential so that you know what historical events were transpiring and what everyday life was like: food, clothing, transportation, communication, socialization, etc."

Collecting Your Family Stories

Every person has a story to tell. Family stories are tales about people, places, and events related to your family and your ancestors. The memorable stories of our lives and of others in our family take on special importance, even if everyone tells different versions of the same event. These tales are family heirlooms held close to the heart. They are a gift to each generation that preserves them by remembering them and passing them on to future generations, and will become some of the most valuable and exciting information you can document about your family history. We call these family stories *oral history,* which is history the way our parents and grandparents remember it.

There is some urgency in collecting these precious family stories because older people will obviously not be around forever. Often, a parent, grandparent or great aunt is the last living person who knows these stories, and if they pass on before their story is recorded, it is lost forever and may never be known. By gathering your family stories, and learning more about the personalities and heritage of your ancestors, they become more than just names and dates. They become real people with real struggles and dreams and triumphs in their lives just like you.

It doesn't matter if your family was famous or just regular people like most of us, there is great value in getting to know them. Start with older people who you believe might not be able to wait for you to get around to gathering their story. Decide what you would like to learn about from each family member, and don't delay in interviewing them. And don't limit yourself to one person, collect several perspectives on the same subject by getting lots of stories from different family members. One thing you can count on, your family stories are guaranteed to become absolutely priceless possessions in your family for many generations to come.

Conducting an Oral Interview

Whether your interview is in person, by phone, or by mail, there are some important steps which will encourage a more open and thorough interview.

Older relatives can be very helpful in piecing together your family's history. Often there is at least one person in a family who has assumed

Here's an excellent article about how to prepare and conduct an oral history interview.

Capturing the Past - www.byubroadcasting.org/capturingpast

In the article, they provide four main steps in conducting an oral interview with family members:

Planning the Interview
Preparing for the Interview
Conducting an Interview
Preserving the Interview

the role of family historian – *the keeper of the flame* – and may already have accumulated and organized a great deal of genealogical information. Get reacquainted with family members through family history interviews.

Some of the things you will need to conduct an interview are: digital recorder or video camera, digital tapes, and a list of questions to help you remember what things you want to know about this person. You can *listen* better if

you don't have to be thinking about your next question.

Usually, the *less talking* you do, the better the interview. So don't interrupt when they're telling their story. And usually limit your interview to 1½ hours so they don't get worn out. Store the tapes in a safe place and make a transcription as soon as convenient.

Use your pedigree chart to help determine what you want to learn from your interview with a family member.

Interview Tips

- Prepare your questions in advance (see interview questions).

- Check to make sure your recording equipment is working properly and that you have enough tape, batteries, and other accessories for the interview.

- Give the person you are interviewing time to prepare for the interview, at least a week if possible.

- Ask the person you are interviewing to start gathering family photographs, documents, letters, or any other items that will help them share their memories with you.

- Bring someone with you to the interview if possible to handle the camera or tape recorder so that you can keep your attention focused on the person you are interviewing.

- Store the tapes in a safe place and transcribe the interview to help preserve it.

- Enter the information you gather in the interview on your pedigree chart, family group record, and research log.

Suggested Activities

Identify your oldest living relatives and decide which one you would like to interview first. Schedule a time for a personal visit. Look at the information you have recorded on your pedigree chart and make a list of questions to ask your relative that will help you fill in the blank spaces on your chart. When you have completed the interview, record the new family history information on your pedigree chart, family group record and research log.

Interview Questions

Here's a list of possible questions for your interview, but don't feel bound by them. Write down other ideas and questions you can ask at an appropriate time.

Tell me about or what do you remember about?...

- Your early home life
- The home you were raised in
- Special items in the house/favorite possessions/toy
- How it was heated and lighted?
- How you got water/when you got indoor plumbing, electricity or gas, phone, TV
- Household chores
- Favorite pets
- Area/neighborhood where you lived/was there a railroad/post office/stores or shops?
- Your memories of your parents
- Father's work/occupation
- Mother's work
- Physical characteristics that run in your family/serious illnesses
- Any memorable traditions your family practiced

- Any stories that you can remember you were told as a child
- Close friends of the family
- How the family obtained food
- From the farm/garden

- From a general store (prices?)
- Family's favorite meals/special family recipes
- Special foods eaten on certain occasions
- How the family did laundry
- First automatic washer
- Washboards/clothes lines/soaps
- Bathing/grooming
- Saturday night bath
- barbershops
- your clothing as a child
- long underwear/button shoes/hats
- different from today's fashions?
- Your family's religious affiliation
- Where you went to church
- What religious ceremonies you took part in
- Did you have godparents or sponsors?
- School days
- Where you went to school/how you got to school
- Studies and homework/favorite subject-discipline
- Your friends when you were growing up
- What you did for fun
- Favorite games or sports/hobbies
- Favorite toys
- Family entertainment at home
- Musical instruments/favorite songs
- Radio programs
- Movie theaters
- Prices
- Favorite movies and film stars
- Family outings/vacations
- Family reunions

- Amusement parks and swimming spots
- Holidays/community celebrations
- Picnics/camping
- Road trips
- Transportation
- Horse and buggy/wagon
- First automobile/specific make, model, color
- Street cars and trolleys
- Trains/ships
- Any other inventions or developments that changed your life, and how
- Excursions to the "city"
- Favorite department stores/five and dime stores
- Favorite restaurants
- Your dating, courtship, and marriage/how did you meet?
- Wedding reception/invitation/music
- Favorite dating/dancing spots
- Popular music/dances

- World War I
- Relatives who fought
- Patriotic events
- Life during the Roaring Twenties/Depression
- World War II
- Where were you for Pearl Harbor/D-Day?
- Effect on your family
- Other historical people and events/events that stand out in the memory of your childhood (historical, personal, familial, storms or disasters, fire, etc.)
- Sinking of the Titanic
- Assassination of John F. Kennedy/Martin Luther King
- Changes that have occurred during your lifetime
- Technology
- Roles of men and women
- Family life

More personal questions

You can ask more personal questions about the person's life if you think they're comfortable about it. Such questions might include:

- Your most important achievements.
- Your biggest disappointments.
- What you wish you had learned before it was too late?
- What values and principles you consider most important?
- What advice you would give to future generations?

- Most important lessons in life.
- The most wonderful thing that has happened to you in your life / the worst?
- The most adventuresome thing you have ever done?
- Your personal secret for happiness?
- What brings you the most joy and peace?
- Faith-promoting stories in your life?
- What would you like to be remembered for?

Get started in creating your legacy today! Do It!

CHAPTER 10

Other Rewarding Opportunities

10 Other Rewarding Opportunities

There are many rewarding opportunities in family history other than building your family tree and connecting with the lives of your ancestors. Technology has made other family history activities – such as, creating your own family web site, family blog, online photo album, or just holding a family reunion – very fun, easy, and exciting. I hope you explore all of these other rewarding opportunities. You don't have to be a genius or computer guru to accomplish great things, even if you never considered them previously. Just have a little courage to jump in and start paddling and you will discover miraculous things happen to you and your family as a result.

Suggested Activities

1. Hold a family reunion.
2. Start a family newsletter or blog.
3. Create a family web site.
4. Create a list of all the descendants of your grandparents and share it with all of your cousins.
5. Protect and preserve irreplaceable family records and heirlooms.
6. Publish a family history of your ancestors.
7. Look for ways to express your family history through painting, needlework, music or other creative channels.
8. Link into your ancestral homelands through traditional foods, festivals, and customs.

Family History Insights - 10

Richard G. Scott
© by Intellectual Reserve, Inc.

You Will Find a Way

"I don't need to tell you the details of where to go and who to see. When you determine you are going to succeed, you will find a way. You will discover those who can help you. I promise you the Lord will bless you in your efforts...and He will guide your... efforts to [find] your ancestors." Richard G. Scott (1928-), *Ensign*, Oct. 1990

Horace Mann

Do As Our Ancestors

"It would be more honorable to our distinguished ancestors to praise them in words less, but in deeds to imitate them more." Horace Mann (1796-1859), Education reformer, politician

Mark Twain

Good in Every Heart

"God has put something noble and good into every heart His hand created." Mark Twain (Samuel Clemens) (1835-1910), Author and humorist

Ardeth Kapp

Everyone is a Somebody

"No one is a nobody! Everyone is a somebody….! We are all [sons and] daughters of God." Ardeth Kapp (1931-)

Marvin J. Ashton

Nobody is a Nobody

"In God's eyes, nobody is a nobody. We should never lose sight of what we may become and who we are." Marvin J. Ashton (1915-1994), *Ensign*, May 1988, 63.

Melvin J. Ballard

You Will Find It

"The spirit and influence of your dead will guide those who are interested in finding those records. If there is anywhere on the earth anything concerning them, you will find it." Melvin J. Ballard (1873-1939), *Sermons of Melvin Joseph Ballard,* p. 230

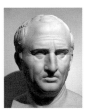

Marcus Cicero

Knowing Our Ancestors

"To be ignorant of what occurred before you were born is to remain always a child. For what is the worth of human life, unless it is woven into the life of our ancestors by the records of history?" Marcus Cicero (106-43 BC), Roman philosopher, stateman

Backwards Progress

Only a genealogist regards a step backwards as progress. Unknown

Cassiodorus

Invited to Great Things

"He is invited to great things who receives small things greatly." Cassiodorus (c. 485 - c. 585), Roman statesman, writer

Ralph Waldo Emerson

The Best Day

"Write it on your heart that every day is the best day in the year." Ralph Waldo Emerson (1803-1882), Philosopher and poet

I Hope You'll Remember Me

My Christian friends, both old and young,
I hope, in Christ, you'll all be strong. …
I hope you'll all remember me,
If no more my face you'll see.
And in trust, in prayers, I crave
That we shall meet beyond the grave.
Oh glorious day, Oh blessed hope.
My heart leaps forward at the thought!
When in that happy land we'll meet.
We'll no more take the parting hand,
But with our holy blessed Lord,
We'll shout and sing with one accord.

John Brown, 1830, *Ensign,* Mar. 2002, 70

Sharing Your Family History

There are more really good, easy and fun ways to share your family history today than ever before.

Easy Ways to Share Your Family History

■ Submit your info to large family tree databases

■ Create your own family web site (either hosted by your Internet Service Provider or by a social networking site)

■ Create your own family blog

■ Create your own online family photo album

■ Email information and documents or send simple GedCom's to other family members *(see Chapter 2 for information about how to create and send a GedCom file).*

Once you have dug up your family history records and organized them into a computer database file, you may want to share your information and stories with others. It's important to share them for many different reasons.

It's more meaningful to you personally when you share with your dear relatives, plus sharing helps preserve your history for future generations. Sharing your family tree on the Internet is a great way to connect with your extended family and collaborate on your shared family history, and it helps them get involved. It allows other relatives to view your information and add their own, thus making it more complete. It's also a great way to exchange family photos, recipes and stories. By sharing your information you can help others in their research and reduce the duplication of effort.

Publishing Your Family Tree on the Web

The Best Places to Put Your Family History Online

You can easily publish your compiled family tree online simply by uploading a GedCom to an existing family tree database. Some are free and some require a membership fee. Your GedCom can contain your entire family history or just one or more family lines. It can also exclude personal information about living people. There are several websites that allow you to deposit your information, index your family names, view the data, and download a GedCom to interested parties. *See Chapters 2 and 3 for more details on these websites.*

10 Other Rewarding Opportunities

Free Existing Family Trees

See Chapter 3 for more information on huge online family trees.

Ancestry World Tree (and RootsWeb WorldConnect) - www.ancestry.com/trees/awt

Contains more than 480 million ancestor names.

FamilySearch Pedigree Resource File - www.FamilySearch.org

The Index for millions of family trees is online but the detailed data is currently on CDs available for free at Family History Centers or you can purchase your own for a small fee.

Subscription Family Trees $$$

OneGreatFamily.com - www.OneGreatFamily.com

Contains over 180 million submitted pedigree-linked names in their family tree database.

GlobalTree - www.GenCircles.com/globaltree

Contains over 90 million names which you can search for free.

MyTrees.com - www.MyTrees.com

A pedigree-linked database with over 370 million names

GeneaNet.org - www.Geneanet.org

Build your online family tree and share it.

GenServ.com - www.Genserv.com

A collection of GEDCOM data files; free trial if you submit your info.

How to Submit Your Family Tree Online

First, save your genealogy as a GedCom file. See the instructions provided with your family history software for more information on how to do this, but most programs are simple. For example, if you are using PAF, click on *file > export and then* indicate where you want to export to, i.e. which folder to save your GedCom file. When you are ready to submit the file, go to the internet site you want to submit your family tree to, after logging-in (or registering) select the *Share Your Information* or *Submit your Family Tree* button. Then select the GedCom file you wish to submit (or upload). It's that easy!

Creating Your Own Family Web Site

Social Networking Web Sites

Social networking refers to web sites and services that allow you to connect with friends, family, and colleagues online, as well as meet people with similar interests or hobbies. At these web sites you can connect with your family, swap stories and recipes, share family photos, and build collaborative family trees. You and your extended family can collaborate and share information on your shared family tree.

Some of the sites use advanced technologies like wikis (a type of website that allows the visitors to add, remove, and sometimes edit the available content), RSS (subscribed to timely updates or web feeds from favored websites), mapping, and online family tree building to help you connect with your family and ancestors. All of these family history social networking sites have great appeal, wonderful capabilities, and are private and secure. Here are the most popular social networking sites to explore. *(See Chapter 3 for more information on each of these networking sites.)*

Geni.com - www.geni.com

FamilyLink.com - www.familylink.com

MyFamily.com - www.myfamily.com

MyHeritage.com - www.myheritage.com

GeneTree.com - www.genetree.com

Genes Reunited.com -
www.genesreunited.com

Amiglia.com - www.amiglia.com

Our Story.com - www.ourstory.com

WeRelate.org - www.werelate.org

KinCafe.com - www.kincafe.com

Famiva.com - www.famiva.com

How to Create Your Own Family Web Pages

1. Use a Family History Computer Program to convert your family information to web pages. Essentially all family history software programs today will provide for publishing your information on the Web (i.e. turn your database into HTML). When you create web pages, the program usually saves them on your hard disk in a folder specified by you. *(See Chapter 5 for more information.)*

Using Word Processors - You can also use a word processor like Corel WordPerfect or Microsoft Word to design the page layouts. Just do a "save as" an HTML (HyperText Markup Language used by web pages). You can include pictures, histories, tables, and decorate the pages with interesting clip-art if you want.

Using PDFs in Your Website - You can create beautiful pages in your website by using PDF (Portable Document File) documents using the free Adobe Acrobat Reader program at www.adobe.com. To create a PDF document from a family history program or a word processor, simply select the PDF button as your printer (or *Publish* to PDF under the file menu).

Hosting Your Own Family Site

Creating Web publishing for hosting your own family web site is simple, inexpensive, and widely available. Many family history software programs will create an attractive, well-indexed home page displaying your family tree. All you need to do is get an Internet Service Provider (ISP) to post it for you. In addition to your family tree, you can also share photos, post news, chat online, publish a family calendar, create a mailing address, preserve family history memories, email, etc. for your extended family to share and download. You can decide to allow people to update information on the website or just access it. Most sites provide this service for usually a modest subscription fee. Usually you need to let people know about the website and give them a password to access the information. These popular websites include:

http://tribalpages.com

www.KindredKonnections.com

www.Genealogy.com

www.familylobby.com

www.thefamilypost.com

http://familyinhistory.com

http://www.myevent.com

www.famster.com

http://getmyfamilysite.com

A free shareware program that creates great PDF files is called PDF995 at www.pdf995.com.

Creating Hyperlinks - You can help viewers navigate from one place to another on your website by creating hyperlinks in your document that point to other destinations. For example, each name in an index or history can hyperlink to a family group sheet with that family name. Or you can embed website hyperlinks to other websites.

2. Select a Place to Store Your Web Pages on the Internet (a host or Internet Service Provider (ISP)). You can publish your family history in many places. Many ISPs allot some disk space on their computers for their users. Dozens of companies offer free web space up to about ten megabytes (10MB) as long as you allow them to display an ad on the visitor's screen. This may be sufficient for smaller sites, but you will not have much opportunity for growth.

Good Free Hosts Are Hard to Find

The following free web hosts have been around long enough to establish longevity, a track record of reasonable customer support, accessability to beginners, and a basic level of free hosting offerings. Some excel more in one area than another, and they are not equally adept in all areas. Bear in mind that none of the free hosts offer the same level of service and support provided by many budget hosts.

www.freeservers.com

Solid free web hosting. (Ad-free plans as low as $3.95/month.)

www.webhero.com

No monthly fee banner-less hosting is available with paid domain registration.

www.rootsweb.com

Free website space for genealogy users. No commercial use, personal photo albums, games, video or music files, or adult-oriented material.

Great Low-cost Hosting Alternatives

You may decide to choose a paid web hosting service. Take a look at these top 4 low-cost hosts. They have solid reputations for good service at affordable prices.

www.myfamily.com

In a secure, password-protected environment, you can create online family photo albums, share family news, maintain a calendar of family events, and more. There's also a toll-free phone number to record your family stories and memories. The basic site is free which includes uploading 100 MB per member per month (with unlimited storage space) and complete backup protection. You can upgrade for extra features such as: Ad-free, professionally-designed and customizable themes, your custom domain, and 1 GB per member of monthly uploads (10x more than basic) for only $29.95 per year total.

www.ipowerweb.com

Integrated web hosting starting at $3.98/ month with no set up fee. They pride themselves on excellent customer support and offer a 30-day money back guarantee. Your special hosting needs are accom-modated through bonus packages of your choice, at no extra cost to you.

www.globat.com

Their basic package is pretty amazing. Starting at $4.44 a month (with no setup fees) you get unlimited web space, unlimited email accounts, free domain registration, and NO pesky ad banners. It's hard to find a more competitively priced paid hosting plan.

www.netfirms.com

Basically a solid hosting service, you can pick up 300 GB of webspace, and 5 free domain names for $9.95 per month.

3. After You Create Your Web Pages, you must upload or transfer all files, folders, and subfolder files to your chosen Internet site. They will probably suggest a *Website Upload Program* or they may already have one built into their website. In any case, they will provide instructions on how to set up the parameters and procedures that provide access to your website. The following Website Upload Programs are FREE. Once the transfer (upload) is complete your website is ready to use, but you should access it and determine that everything is working properly.

www.freedownloadscenter.com
www.nchsoftware.com
http://search.download3000.com/
web-site-upload-tool

Planting Your Family Tree Online: How to Create Your Own Family History Web Site - www.amazon.com

This book is written by Cyndi Howells, owner and webmaster of Cyndi's List, and it's loaded with

You may want to consider NOT using a free web host for several reasons. Read this interesting article.

http://web-hosting-services.top choicereviews.com/why-not-free-web-hosting.htm

Some of the considerations include: Required ads, lack of support, unreliable, lack of storage space, content restriction, poor security, spam.

When sharing or submitting your family history records on the internet, *never include information on living people without their permission.* Please respect the privacy of individuals who may be living.

Privacy and Security

Some people may get upset at finding their names published online without their permission. Make sure to get permission from any living relatives to print their information. You may want to publish data only on deceased people, or publish only enough data to encourage people to write you. Do not share information that may be used to embarrass or harm people who may still be living (such as home addresses and telephone numbers, social security numbers, and mothers' maiden names).

For instance, in the PAF software program, you can mark the *Hide Details for the Living* option. When you mark this option, the program checks each individual that you select. If he or she may still be alive, it includes only a limited amount of information. If you also mark the *Include GEDCOM file* option, the GEDCOM file will contain only deceased individuals. When you need to update your web pages, just create a new set of pages and send them to your ISP, with instructions to replace your existing information with the new information.

Most host sites already have a security system. Usually, as part of the registration process you must select a password and a username. Only those with a valid username and password have access to your site. Initially, the family site administrator (creator) will invite new members and assign a temporary username and password. As family members register, they may change their passwords to ensure complete security and privacy. It is then the responsibility of site members to help keep the site secure by offering password access only to appropriate relatives and friends — those they want to have access to the site.

URLs to Web sites that will give you everything you need to create a beautiful family tree online. It's designed to take you step-by-step through the process of creating a genealogy Web site.

For instance, in the PAF software program, you can mark the Hide Details for the Living option. When you mark this option, the program checks each individual that you select. If he or she may still be alive, it includes only a limited amount of information. If you also mark the Include GEDCOM file option, the GEDCOM file will contain only deceased individuals. When you need to update your web pages, just create a new set of pages and send them to your ISP, with instructions to replace your existing information with the new information.

Most host sites already have a security system. Usually, as part of the registration process you must select a password and a username. Only those with a valid username and password have access to your site. Initially, the family site administrator (creator) will invite new members and assign a temporary username and password. As family members register, they may change their passwords to ensure complete security and privacy. It is then the responsibility of site members to help keep the site secure by offering password access only to appropriate relatives and friends – those they want to have access to the site.

Standards For Sharing Information With Others - www.ngsgenealogy.org/cs/standards_for_sharing_information

Offered by The National Genealogical Society.

Creating Your Own Family Blog

A blog (or web log) is a website consisting of entries appearing in reverse chronological order with the most recent entry appearing

Sample Family Blog

first. Blogs typically include comments, news, photos, and web links. You may want to consider creating your own family blog because it's a great way to connect with your extended family and others who may share your interests. Many people start a blog simply for fun. Blogs are easy to create and update, and rich, useful content will encourage your family to keep in touch. And you don't have to possess any special technical knowledge, or plan for months or be constrained by any deadlines – publish as much as you want, any time you want. *(See Chapter 1 for a list of family history blogs from noted experts and companies.)*

Blogs are very popular today as there are over 100 million blogs on the Web and growing everyday. Anyone can start a blog thanks to the simple tools readily available online. To start a blog, you have to select a blog "host" and blogging software so you can write and upload your blog to the Internet. Here are some popular blogger software and blog hosting sites to help you.

Sample Family History Blog –
http://thechartchick.blogspot.com

Janet Hovorka's blog from Generation Maps.com contains news, views and tips on family history and genealogy charts.

Popular Blogger Software

Blogger.com - www.blogger.com

Many novice bloggers choose to start their first blogs here because it's free and very easy to use.

WordPress.com - http://wordpress.com

A place where you can start a blog in seconds without any technical knowledge. It provides free blogging software with a limited amount of customization with templates you can download for your blog. It is very easy to learn and provides some good features.

Wordpress.org - www.wordpress.org $$$

Offers free blogging software, but users have to pay to host their blogs through a third-party website host such as www.GatorHost.com or www.1and1.com. For bloggers with some technical skills who need advanced customization, Wordpress.org is a great choice. The software, itself, is the same as Wordpress.com, but the customization options make it very popular among power bloggers.

TypePad.com - www.typepad.com $$$

Provides great features and a high level of cus-tomization without the technical knowledge of some other customizable blogging software options. Basic option $49.50/year.

Popular Blog Hosts

BlueHost - www.bluehost.com $$$

A popular blog host that consistently gets positive reviews for its up-time and support services. It offers comprehensive shared hosting packages that are suitable for most bloggers at an affordable price.

Host Gator.com - www.hostgator.com $$$

Offers blog hosting packages that suit beginner bloggers' needs as well as the needs of the most popular blogs and websites. Host Gator has a reputation for reliability and excellent support.

GoDaddy.com - www.godaddy.com $$$

A great reputation of providing blog hosting services suitable for any size blog or website. Negative reviews are typically related to domain name registration searches that yield results showing a domain name is available, but when the potential buyer returns even one day later to purchase that domain name, it displays as no longer available. Aside from that complaint, reviews are typically positive.

1and1.com - www.1and1.com $$$

A popular blog host with competitive pricing. 1&1 is both the world's biggest web host, and the fastest growing. Their global community is 7.83 million customer contracts strong.

Continued on the next page...

Continued from the previous page...

HostMonster.com -
www.hostmonster.com $$$

A reliable blog host with competitive features and affordable pricing; rated the top choice of Top Choice Reviews at http://web-hosting-services.topchoicereviews.com.

Creating Your Own Online Photo Album

Here's some popular websites dedicated to offering image hosting services, as well as web hosting for a photo gallery of your family. Some photo hosting sites sell you prints of your photos and gifts with your photos on them. Others let you create pages to go with your photos. But they are great for creating and hosting your photo albums and videos so friends and family can share them online. It's a great way to backup your precious images off-site from your computer hard drive.

Picasa Web Albums -
http://picasa.google.com > Share

Fast and easy photo sharing from Google; free software for organizing, editing and printing your photos.

You can upload entire albums of high quality photos, and combine your photos, videos, and music into a movie. Each account gets 1GB of free storage - that's enough to post and share around 4,000 standard resolution photos. And you and your friends can download your photos at the same high quality to print and enjoy.

DotPhoto.com - www.dotphoto.com

A popular photo hosting site that allows you to handle all your imaging in one place for free: store, edit, share, organize, and print your photos, create gifts, tell a story, build a photo web site, sell photos, host pictures, print books, store videos and more. You can upload photos from your camera or your camera phone, and create gifts with your photos on them and have them mailed to you or your friends and family.

MyPhotoAlbum.com -
www.myphotoalbum.com

A photo and video sharing service offering extensive features for creating highly-unique, personalized online photo albums and photo keepsakes. Easily add and safely store all your photos and videos. Upload your memories via the web, downloadable software, email, and your camera or cell phone. Unlimited online photo sharing and albums; free video storage and sharing.

Flickr.com - www.flickr.com

A popular photo storage and sharing site to store, sort, search, organize and share your photos online. You can also tell stories about them. You can make all or just some photos private or only viewable by friends and family. Basic version is free. ProAccount $24.95/year.

Shutterfly.com - www.shutterfly.com

Offers a full range of products and services that make it easy, convenient and fun for you to upload (unlimited storage), edit, enhance, organize, find, share, create, print and preserve your digital photos. You can stay connected to your friends and family, organize your memories in a single location, tell stories, and preserve your memories. They make memory-keeping and gift-giving easy with their personalized photo books, greeting cards, and various photo gifts suitable for any occasion.

Kodak Gallery.com - www.kodakgallery.com

A free online digital photo developing service providing you with a secure and easy way to view, store and share their photos with friends and family and get prints of your pictures. The site also provides free editing and creative tools and specialty photo products.

PhotoBucket.com - http://photobucket.com

Upload all your photos, videos, and images for free. Make photo slide shows to share pics with friends.

SnapFish.com - www.snapfish.com

Online photo sharing, storage, and editing tools and software are free, and you can create private group rooms for event sharing with friends and family.

SmugMug.com - www.smugmug.com $$$

A popular, secure, easy-to-use photo hosting site with no spam or ads, and unlimited storage. Free 14-day trial. Standard (unlimited photos) $39.95, Power (+ videos) $59.95.

Organizing Your Family

A family association is an organization formed around a deceased common ancestor to accomplish specific goals. Some of the benefits of organizing your family this way include: Grow closer as a family, develop bonds of love and kindred affection, make family history work easier and faster, and avoid duplication of time and money.

Publishing a Family Newsletter -
www.absolutelyfamily.homestead.com $$$

A book by Jeanne Rundquist Nelson, *A Guide to Editing and Publishing A Family Newsletter*, is for family-focused people who want to keep their far-flung families in touch. $12.00

Holding a Family Reunion
Preserving Special Memories

A family reunion is one of the most special events in life, but planning it can be a little overwhelming. Whether you want to have a small get-together of your closest relatives or a huge gathering of everyone you can find in your family tree, you need to know where to start and how to keep it organized. Check out these great resources to make your reunion fun and exciting.

Your Family Reunion: How to Plan It, Organize It, and Enjoy It -
http://ahaseminars.com/ $$$

A complete guidebook to planning a successful reunion by George G. Morgan incorporates how-to advice, samples of helpful forms, and a wealth of great Web sites filled with invaluable reference material to help you succeed. You will learn all

Family Association Goals

Some of the goals to consider for a family association might include:

Determine and prioritize association goals, such as:

- Create a list of all the descendants of the ancestral couple

- Organize a family records center, and preserve irreplaceable family records and heirlooms.

- Guide, encourage and assist in doing systematic family history research for your common ancestors. Set up a research fund to continue research on the family lines and hold family reunions.

- Publish a family history of your ancestors, and a history of descendants which would be kept current throughout all succeeding generations.

- Create an extended family web site or blog.

Decide how to implement goals

Decide on the organizational requirements necessary to meet the goals; choose officers and committee members, and make assignments.

Identify all living descendants and get them involved in some way

Start an address / telephone / email file.

Create a periodic blog, newsletter, or website to establish communication, maintain interest, report family history research results, account for money received and spent, relate human interest stories about ancestors and living descendants, share family photos, promote and publicize family reunions, etc.

Hold family reunions

about compiling the family address book, developing a realistic budget, choosing a great venue, working with hotels, caterers and other vendors, keeping records, and sending invitations to planning activities to get people communicating, ideas for sharing and gathering genealogical information, setting up the site, managing details on-site, and evaluating the event. $24.95

Family Reunion Organizer - www.family-reunion.com

A free family reunion planning site with organizing tips, activities, finances, food, places to hold family reunions, links to resources, and lots of ideas to make it successful. They also offer software – *Family Reunion Organizer* – that helps you plan the perfect family reunion or a family or neighborhood event as well. A checklist leads users through the steps involved in family reunion planning, including tracking a budget and expenses, creating a schedule, managing assignments, and even keeping a family address book. The program includes tools to create a family Web page. It also allows users to print most of its forms for planning purposes. Users receive a free newsletter and access to a message board to post improvement suggestions related to the product. Free demo. $29.95

FamilyReunion.com - www.familyreunion.com

A website that provides relevant ideas, resources, information, products and services in a safe and friendly online social network environment all designed to help millions of repeat visitors and members make their next gathering of family the best ever.

Basic membership is free. Platinum membership gives you full access to all the services. $15/3 months, $39/year.

EasyFamilyReunion.com -
www.easyfamilyreunion.com

A free checklist for putting together a family reunion. Some of the items on the checklist are basic; you need to do them for every reunion. The others are optional but can make the reunion more memorable and enjoyable. Print out the checklist and use it to guide your efforts to bring your family together.

Planning the Perfect Family Reunion -
http://genealogy.about.com/od/family_reunions

Kimberly Powell at About.com provides free, really helpful things to consider, such as: Steps to a successful family reunion, choosing a location, fun activities, tips, ideas, etc.

Better Homes Magazine -
www.bhg.com/health-family/reunions

The magazines free website provides aids for holding a successful reunion: planning tips, checklists, menu ideas, ice breakers and entertaining activities.

Disney's Family Fun Reunion Center -
http://familyfun.go.com > (search "family reunion") -or- <http://familyfun.go.com/parenting/learn/activities/specialfeature/famreunion_sf/>

Disney's Family Fun Magazine offers great helps with an ultimate, step-by-step family reunion guide, and more.

Family Reunion - www.amazon.com $$$

A recommended book by Jennifer Crichton. Everything you need to know to plan unforgettable get-togethers. A comprehensive, step-by-step guide to planning and staging a gathering to remember. Topics include record keeping, choosing a site, entertaining kids

of all ages, and etiquette, as well as the dynamics and logistics necessary when herding a large group of people. $13.95

Family Reunion Handbook -
www.amazon.com $$$

This handbook by Tom Ninkovich covers how to organize a reunion including selecting a date, getting the word out, creating a budget, and delegating responsibilities. A Complete Guide for Reunion Planners.

Reunions Magazine -
www.reunionsmag.com $$$

The only publication written for all types of reunion planners – family, class, military and others. This is a comprehensive source of tips, ideas, advice and resources to help you plan your reunion. You'll find

articles about resources like facilities, suppliers, tools, equipment, games, activities and services to enhance your reunion. Some of the best reunion solutions are in the stories reunion planners share; published 5x per year. $9.99/year

Family Reunion - www.famware.com $$$

An easy to use system that helps you organize and document your family's history. $79.95

To comment, or communicate with the author:
paul@easyfamilyhistory.com

Here's a nice *glossary* for you.

Family History Glossary

Ahnentafel chart - An ancestor table that lists the name, date, and place of birth, marriage, and death for an individual and specified number of his or her ancestors; an alternative to a pedigree chart. The first individual on the list is number one, the father is number two, the mother is number three, the paternal grandfather is number four, and so forth. Ahnentafel is a German word that means ancestor chart or ancestor table.

Ancestral File - A computer database file located at www.familysearch.org containing names and often other vital information (such as date and place of birth, marriage, or death) of millions of individuals who have lived throughout the world. Names are organized into family groups and pedigrees. To allow you to coordinate research, the file also lists names and addresses of those who contributed to the file.

Ancestral File Number (AFN) - A number used to identify each record in Ancestral File on FamilySearch.

Ancestry chart - A pedigree chart that contains only names and limited information about the people on it.

Archive - A place in which public records or historical documents are preserved and researched. Unlike a Library, archived records cannot be checked out but can be used in the building.

Blog (or web log) - A website consisting of entries appearing in reverse chronological order with the most recent entry appearing first. They typically are free-style, interactive web sites containing news, commentary, photos, web links, etc.

Bookmark - A saved link to a Web site that has been added to a list of saved links so that you can simply click on it rather than having to retype the address when visiting the site again.

Browser - An Internet tool for viewing the World Wide Web. Some of the Web browsers currently available for personal computers include Internet Explorer, Opera, Mozilla Firefox, Safari, Google Chrome, and AOL Explorer.

Bulletin Board - Refers to online message systems to read and post messages.

Call number - The number used to identify a book, microfilm, microfiche, or other source in a library or archive. Library materials are stored and retrieved by call number.

Cascading family group record - An option that allows you to print family group records for a specified number of generations in a family. If you printed a cascading pedigree you could select the same starting person and number of generations to print a family group record for each couple in the pedigree charts.

Cascading pedigree - An option that allows you to print pedigree charts for a specified number of generations. Each page is numbered, which allows you to keep the pages in order.

Census - Official enumeration, listing or counting of citizens.

CD-ROM (Compact Disk Read Only Memory) - A computer disk that can store large amounts of information and is generally used on computers with CD-ROM drives.

Chat Room - A location on an online service that allows users to communicate with each other about an agreed-upon topic in "real time" (or "live"), as opposed to delayed time as with email.

Chat - When people type live messages to each other using a network.

Collateral line - A family that is not in your direct ancestral line but in the same genealogical line.

Compiled Record - A record (usually in book form) consisting of information that has been gathered from original records, other compiled records and verbal testimony.

Database - Information for computer search, storage, and retrieval.

Date calculator - A feature in family history programs that allows you to determine the days, months, and years elapsed between two dates or to determine a date based on the amount of time elapsed before or after a date. For example, this is useful to approximate a birth date for a person who appears in a census.

Default - A computer term for "normal" settings of a program.

Descendency chart - A report that lists an individual and his or her children and their spouses and children.

Domain name - The Internet's way to find unique addresses on the World Wide Web.

Download - The process of retrieving information from another computer to yours.

E-mail - Short for electronic mail messages that are sent from one person to another.

End of line - The last known person in a line of ancestry. An end-of-line person has no parents listed in the database file.

Export - A feature in many family history programs that allows you to save or send information to use in another genealogical program. Information is usually saved in GEDCOM format.

Family group record - A printed form that lists a family—parents and children—and gives information about dates and places of birth, marriage, and death. This is also called a family group sheet.

Family History Center (FHC) - Local branches of the Family History Library in Salt Lake City, Utah. There are currently more than 4,500 around the world.

Family History Computer Software Program - A computer family history program for home use. Users enter family history information electronically, thus allowing information to be printed as a pedigree chart, family group record, descendency chart, or many other formats. Information can also be given to others as a GEDCOM file for instant transfer of family history data.

Family History Library - The main family history library in Salt Lake City, Utah used by genealogical researchers worldwide. It has the world's largest collection of genealogical holdings and has both printed sources and microfilmed records.

FamilySearch - A web site and a term that refers to computer products that help people learn about their ancestors.

Freenet - A community network that provides free online access, usually to local residents, and often includes its own forums and news.

Forum - A set of messages on a subject, usually with a corresponding set of files.

FTP (File Transfer Protocol) - Enables an Internet user to transfer files electronically between computers.

GEDCOM - The acronym for "GEnealogical Data COMmunications." GEDCOM is a computer data format for storing genealogical information so that many computer programs can use it. It is the standard file format worldwide for exchanging

Family History **Glossary**

family information between genealogical databases. If you choose, your family history software program can save your family information as a GEDCOM file.

Genealogy - The study of how individuals and their families are descended from their ancestors. It often includes learning about family histories and traditions.

Given name - A person's first name(s).

Gregorian calendar - The calendar commonly used in Western and Westernized countries. It corrected the Julian calendar, which, because of miscalculated leap years, fell behind the solar year by several days.

Hardware - A term for the nuts, bolts, and wires of computer equipment and the actual computer and related machines.

Home page - A web page that serves as the table of contents or title page of a web site.

Home person - A feature in family history programs that allows you to return to the individual record that is designated to be the home person. The term "home" can also refer to the first person in a file.

HTML - Acronym for HyperText Markup Language, the coding language of the World Wide Web.

Hyperlink Link - Highlighted text that allows you to jump to other information in a file or to another web page or web site.

Hypertext Transfer Protocol - A standard used by World Wide Web servers to provide rules for moving text, images, sound, video, and other multimedia files across the Internet.

ICON - A small picture on a Web page that represents the topic or information category of another Web page. Frequently, the icon is a hypertext link to that page.

IGI (The International Genealogical Index) - A database of names located at www.FamilySearch.org.

IM (Instant Message) - A type of chat program that allows users to send and receive text messages instantly and requires users to register with a server. Users build "buddy lists" of others using the same program and are notified when people on their list are available for messages.

Import - A feature on the menu in family history programs that allows you to add information that is stored in a GEDCOM file into your database.

Immigrant - One moving into a country from another.

Internet - A system of computers joined together by high-speed data lines. It is a repository for vast amounts of data, including family history data, that is accessed by computer through an Internet Service Provider and Web Browser. It includes data in various formats (or protocols) such as HTML, e-mail (SMTP), File Transfer Protocol (FTP), and Telnet.

ISP (Internet Service Provider) - A company that has a continuous, fast and reliable connection to the Internet and sells subscriptions to use that connection.

Julian calendar - A calendar introduced in Rome in 46 B.C. This calendar was the basis for the Gregorian calendar, which is in common use today. The Julian calendar specified that the year began on 25 March (Lady's Day) and had 365 days. Each fourth year had a leap day, so it had 366 days. The year was divided into months. Each month had 30 or 31 days, except February, which had 28 days in normal years and 29 days in leap years. This calendar was used for several centuries (until the mid 1500s) but was eventually replaced by the Gregorian calendar because leap years had been miscalculated.

LDS - An abbreviation for the Church of Jesus Christ of Latter-day Saints, also known as the Mormons.

Link - To define family relationships between individual records or to attach a source or multimedia file to an individual or marriage record.

Living - A person who is still alive. Some family history programs define a living person as someone who was born within the last 110 years whose individual record contains no death or burial information.

Maiden name - A female's surname at birth.

Match/Merge - A feature on the Tools menu in some family history programs that allows you to find duplicate records in a file and combine them into one record.

Maternal Line - The line of descent on a mother's side.

Modem - A device that allows computers to communicate with each other over telephone lines or other delivery systems by changing digital signals to telephone signals for transmission and then back to digital signals. Modems come in different speeds: the higher the speed, the faster the data is transmitted.

Modified register - A report that lists an individual and his or her descendants in a narrative form. The first paragraph identifies the individual and explains birth and other event information in complete sentences. The next paragraph describes the person's first spouse. Children and spouses are listed next. If the person had more than one spouse, those spouses and any children appear after that.

Mouse - A small device attached to the computer by a cord which lets you give commands to the computer. The mouse controls an arrow on the computer screen and allows you to point and click to make selections.

MRIN - An abbreviation that stands for "Marriage Record Identification Number." PAF software assigns each marriage record a unique MRIN and uses it to distinguish one marriage record from another.

Multimedia - A term used to refer to electronic pictures, sound clips, and video clips for use in your family history program or website. To create video and sound clips, you must already have the required computer hardware and software. Multimedia features may include: *Video Clips* - portions of digitized video images that can be displayed through various programs via the Internet. *Sound Clips* - portions of digitized sound clips that can be heard through various programs via the Internet. *Digital Images* - picture (images) that can be displayed on computers or via the Internet. These images can be displayed using various image formats, such as JPEG, GIFF, BITMAP, etc.

Multiple parent indicator - A symbol used on reports that indicate that a person is linked to more than one set of parents.

Navigation bar - Words or images on website pages with links to other sections or pages of the same website

Netiquette - Rules or manners for interacting courteously with others online (such as not typing a message in all capital letters, which is equivalent to shouting).

NGS - National Genealogical Society.

Notes - Information about an individual, marriage, or set of parents that does not fit in the individual record, the marriage record, or sources. Notes can contain additional information, research notes, or other narrative information. Also a feature on the Edit menu that allows you to add or edit the notes associated with the selected individual or marriage.

Offline - Not being connected to an Internet host or service provider.

Online - Refers to computer connection to the Internet. Made possible through the use of an internet service provider and web browser.

Original Record - A record created at or close to the time of an event by an eyewitness to the event. (e.g., a birth record by the doctor who delivered the baby.)

PAF (Personal Ancestral File) - A free family history program available from www.familysearch.org.

Family History **Glossary**

Parent Link - The type of relationship selected for an individual and his or her parents. The options are biological, adopted, guardian, sealing, challenged, and disproved. If a person is linked to only one set of parents, the relationship is assumed to be biological unless you change it. On the Family screen, the parent link appears only if it is something other than biological.

Password - A set of characters that you can use to prevent another individual from inadvertently changing information.

Paternal Line - The line of descent on a father's side.

PDF (Portable Document Format) - A file format that allows a document to be saved in a certain way, no matter what kind of computer is used to display it. The machine must have Adobe's Acrobat Reader (a free program available at www.adobe.com) to display the file.

Pedigree - An ancestral line or line of descent.

Pedigree chart - A chart that shows an individual's direct ancestors—parents, grandparents, great-grandparents, and so forth. This is the traditional way to display a genealogy or 'family tree'. A pedigree chart may contain birth, marriage, and death information.

Pedigree Resource File (PRF) - A computer file containing names and often other vital information (such as date and place of birth, marriage, or death) of individuals who have lived throughout the world. Names are organized into family groups and pedigrees. The information will appear as it was originally submitted and will not be merged with information submitted by others. Available at www.familysearch.org.

Query - An online request for family history information which usually includes a name, date, location and your contact information.

RAM (Random Access Memory) - The working memory of a computer used for storing data temporarily while working on it, or running application programs, etc.

Relationship calculator - A feature on menu in family history programs that allows you to determine how two individuals are related.

Repository - The place where records are stored, such as an archive or library.

Restore - A feature on the menu of some family history programs that allows you to use a backup copy to return a certain file to its state when the backup copy was made.

RIN - An abbreviation that stands for "Record Identification Number" in the PAF program. PAF assigns a unique RIN to each individual record. This number is used to distinguish that individual record from others in a .paf file.

RSS (Really Simple Syndication) - A Web feed format used to publish frequently updated works—such as blog entries, news headlines, audio, and video—in a standardized format. They benefit readers who want to subscribe to timely updates from favored websites or to aggregate feeds from many sites into one place.

Search Engine - A tool designed to search for information on the World Wide Web. The search results are usually presented in a list and are commonly called *hits*. The information may consist of web pages, images, information and other types of files. Some search engines also mine data available in newsbooks, databases, or open directories. Unlike Web directories, which are maintained by human editors, search engines operate algorithmically or are a mixture of algorithmic and human input. Some of the major search engines are Google, Yahoo, Dogpile, Live, Ask, etc. (Note that Yahoo is a directory, not a search engine.) A web directory does not display lists of web pages based on keywords; instead, it lists web sites by category and subcategory.

Server - A computer that allows other computers to log on and use its resources.

Shareware - The try-before-you-buy concept in computer software where the author expects to receive compensation after a trial period. For example, *Brother's Keeper* is shareware.

Slide Show - A presentation that displays all of the multimedia that is attached to an individual. It displays each item for a specific amount of time, in a sequential fashion.

Software - A computer program or set of instructions. System software operates on the machine itself and is invisible to you. Application software allows you to carry out certain activities, such as word processing, family history, spreadsheets, etc.

Soundex - A type of index that groups surnames that sound similar but are spelled differently. Each surname is assigned a code that consists of the first letter of the name. The next three consonants are assigned a number. Vowels are ignored. Soundex has been used to index the 1880, 1900, 1910, and 1920 United States censuses and some other types of records, such as naturalization records and passenger lists.

Sources & Notes - This is a feature in a family history program that displays: The sources used to obtain genealogical data for a specific individual and the notes of those who entered the information to give additional helpful information. This will increase your ability to collaborate and verify your genealogical information with others doing work on your same line.

Surname - A person's last name or family name.

Tag - A word or phrase used to classify the information in a note. Tags should be typed in all uppercase letters at the beginning of the note and be followed by a colon.

Tagged notes - A type of note that uses a keyword to identify the type of information contained in a note in PAF. The keyword is typed in all uppercase letters at the beginning of a paragraph and followed by a colon. For example, in the following note, "NAME:" is the tag: "NAME: This person changed her name."

Twitter - A social networking and micro-blogging service for friends, family, and co-workers to stay connected through the exchange of quick, frequent answers (known as tweets) to one simple question: What are you doing? Answers must be under 140 characters in length and can be sent via mobile texting, instant message, or the web.

Upload - The process of sending a file or message from your computer to another.

URL (Uniform Resource Locator) - The World Wide Web address of a site on the Internet. For example, the URL for the White House is http://www.whitehouse.gov.

Usenet Newsgroups - A system of thousands of special interest groups to which readers can send or "post" messages; these messages are then distributed to other computers on the network. Usenet registers newsgroups, which are available through Internet Service Providers.

Virus - A program that installs itself secretly on your computer by attaching itself to another program or e-mail. It duplicates itself when the e-mail is opened and is usually intended to erase important files in your system

Vital Records - The official records of birth, death, marriage, and other events of a persons life.

Web browser - A software program that lets you find, see, and hear material on the World Wide Web, including text, graphics, sound, and video. Popular browsers are Explorer, Netscape, and AltaVista. Most online services have their own browsers.

Web page - A multimedia document that is created and viewable on the internet with the use of a world wide web browser.

Web site - Refers to one or more World Wide Web pages on the internet.

Worm - A computer program that makes copies of itself and spreads through connected systems, using up resources or causing other damage.

www (World Wide Web) - The portion of the Internet that is written in HTML. A hypertext-based system that allows you to browse through a variety of linked Internet resources organized by colorful, graphics-oriented home pages.

Family History **Glossary**

Index